AND DELIVER US FROM EVIL

A TRILOGY OF MURDER, MINISTERS, AND MILLIONAIRES

AND DELIVER US FROM EVIL

BY MIKE COCHRAN

★
TexasMonthlyPress

Texas Monthly Press
P.O. Box 1569
Austin, Texas 78767

A B C D E F G H

Library of Congress Cataloging-in-Publication Data

Cochran, Mike,
   And deliver us from evil : a triology of millionaires, ministers, and murder / by Mike Cochran.
     p.   cm.
   ISBN 0-87719-159-X : $17.95
   1. Murder—Texas—Case studies.   I. Title.
HV6533.T4C63   1989
364.1'523'09764—dc19
                                                                  89-4363
                                                                  CIP

To
Beowulf and his Mimi

To
Eileen, John, and Robin

. . . and everywhere
The ceremony of innocence is drowned.

—W. B. Yeats

CONTENTS

ACKNOWLEDGMENTS

"Indisputable Evidence" and "Fugitives" are based on stories that were first transmitted in 1987 and 1988 by the Associated Press and the material is used by permission of the AP.

"Unreasonable Doubt" is, in part, an adaptation from *Texas vs. Davis,* copyright 1980 by Michael Cochran.

The column by Laura Miller about Walker Railey is used with the permission of the *Dallas Times Herald,* copyright 1988.

PREFACE

It has been said that journalism is history's first draft. If that is true, then journalism can also be literature's first paragraph.

This book, *And Deliver Us from Evil*, is just that. For Mike Cochran first wrote about the mystery of the Reverend Walker Railey, the Texas fugitive, and the man in black as an Associated Press correspondent. Mike has put more than half a million miles into his AP reporting, which includes stories about the Kennedy assassination, space shots, political scandals, his home state's strangest people, and its darkest crimes.

Some newspaper editors think Mike is at his best reporting on crime, but that's only half of it. It's also the people. Mike once explained that the characters in the Cullen Davis saga, not the crime, led him to write his first book, *Texas* vs. *Davis*.

That's what makes the stories in the trilogy you are about to read so compelling—the people. There is great compassion, great sadness, great strength, and real terror of maddening proportion. There is great inhumanity and no small measure of wickedness. There is wit. And there is also innocence.

Mike and I, as his editor, acknowledge the permission of the AP to pursue a literary forum for his stories, but we also acknowledge the corporate environment at the AP that permits writing to complement reporting. In particular, we appreciate the encouragement and cooperation of Dan Perkes, director of APNewsfeatures in New York.

We also acknowledge the aggressive reporting of the *Dallas Morning News* and the *Dallas Times Herald*, which first made possible the public's understanding of the Walker Railey case. In addition, there are all the other AP newspaper subscribers in Texas and across the country who open their pages for Mike's work.

"Mike is something of a legend around Texas newspaper offices," says Glenn Dromgoole, editor of the *Abilene Reporter-News* in West Texas where Mike grew up. "He is one of the best journalists in Texas today. I would go so far as to say he is among the best in the nation."

Joe Murray, publisher of the *Lufkin Daily News*, puts it differently: "He's journalism's John Belushi. He really is."

So it's not hard to imagine why another colleague said Mike had nine lives and had already used up eight of them. An aftershock of the 1985 Mexico City earthquake left him trapped in the penthouse of a crippled apartment building. He's survived more car wrecks on assignment than a Hollywood stunt man.

"He defecates in your bonnet," said attorney Racehorse Haynes, "and you want to give him a sock in the soupsucker, and then the next time you see him, he has such an effervescent nature, you forget about it."

Mike had to be dragged kicking and screaming back into the book business almost a decade after the publication of *Texas* vs. *Davis*. But newspapers do have a short shelf life and this book will, we hope, provide another forum for Mike's storytelling.

Thanks to Texas Monthly Press, Mike has used the award-winning stories on falsely accused fugitive Kenneth Miller as the inspiration for one part of his trilogy. He also has composed the first complete account of the chilling case of the Reverend Railey, the nationally known Methodist minister whose double life crashed down when his wife was brutally attacked. And we are introducing a new audience to the Cullen Davis cases, updating the lives of those most closely tied to the murders at the Davis mansion in August 1976.

Is it a coincidence that all three of the stories occurred in Texas? You decide.

"Blame it on Hollywood, but there remains a fascination

with Texas-flavored treachery," Mike writes at the end of this book. "After nearly three decades of chronicling the murders and mischief of the Texas rich and not-so-rich, I can only conclude that whatever the appeal, it's very real and it's not going away anytime soon."

Our families and friends have been patient while we collaborated on Mike's new book. But, believe me, you don't "edit" Mike Cochran. You cinch your hands firmly and you hold on. This bronc will take you where it wants to go. And you will be in for one hell of a ride.

John Lumpkin
Dallas, Texas
January 1, 1989

(Note: John Lumpkin has been bureau chief for The Associated Press in Texas since 1982.)

INDISPUTABLE EVIDENCE

The Mystifying Case of the Reverend Walker Railey

. . . nobody enjoys losing. But one of the most unfortunate moments is for an athletic contest to be lost simply because somebody makes a decision based on seeing partially what really happened.

. . . it is unfortunate for people to make decisions when they can't see everything that's there. And it's worse when it comes to life itself. Some of the most tragic moments on earth come when people act on information or insights that do not offer them all that can be seen in a particular situation."

—The Reverend Walker Railey, from a sermon on "The Instant Replay"

Part 1

Dallas, Texas

"Hi, Babe. I'm calling you from my mobile phone. Peg, it's about, oh, I don't know, I don't have a watch. It's somewhere between 10:30 and 10:45, somewhere along in there."

There was no response.

But the gentle voice of Walker Railey continued to flow that warm spring night into an answering machine at the suburban Dallas home where Railey lived with his wife Peggy and their two young children.

"My concern is that you're safe," Railey said into his new car phone.

As he spoke, Peggy Railey, 38, lay critically injured on the garage floor of the couple's custom-built Lake Highlands home, her face horribly swollen and her neck covered with ugly red streaks and bruises.

Seizures racked her body. Her legs twitched and she frothed at the mouth like a dying animal, gasping for air.

She had been savagely choked and left for dead.

The date was April 22, 1987, but the time was not 10:30 or 10:45 P.M. as Walker Railey suggested on the answering machine. A mobile phone computer would later pinpoint the Methodist minister's call at 12:03 A.M.

The implications would be shattering. For nothing was what it appeared to be.

The attack on Margaret "Peggy" Railey devastated three families, split a church, and outraged a city. She survived, but only barely so. Comatose, she could tell no one about her brutal assailant, crippling law enforcement efforts. The assault was labeled the city's most haunting and sensational mystery in a decade. One unrestrained commentator called it Dallas' most extraordinary crime since the Kennedy assassination.

For Peggy Railey was by no means an ordinary homemaker, but the wife of Dallas' most dynamic and socially conscious young minister. At 39, Walker Railey reigned as the senior pastor of the city's 6,000-member First United Methodist Church and loomed as the rising star of his mainstream Protestant denomination. Widely known, locally adored, and deeply respected, Railey seemed destined to ascend to the post of bishop, the pinnacle of the Methodist hierarchy.

The apparent motive for the attempt on Peggy Railey's life was no less disturbing than the crime itself. Police and church officials theorized that the assault could have been a grotesque retaliation for her husband's outspoken stance against prejudice and injustice. A series of typewritten death threats had preceded the attack and the anonymous, abusive letters bore racial overtones.

The last and most ominous letter had been slipped under

the door of a church office just prior to the Easter Sunday services, and the Reverend Howard Grimes, the church's minister of communications, was bewildered.

"How somebody could do it, especially on a busy Easter Sunday, I don't know," he said. "It was very frightening to know that the person or his or her emissary was in the building."

Under the cold scrutiny of security officers, Railey delivered the Easter service wearing a bulletproof vest beneath his robes. "Easter was a terrifying day," he said. "I just don't know what to do. I can't quit living."

With his wife unconscious and in critical condition, Railey stationed himself outside her hospital room, interrupting his grim vigil only long enough for a trip downtown to give investigators an account of his activities the night of April 21.

He said he spent the evening doing research at the Fondren and Bridwell libraries at Southern Methodist University. Returning home about 12:40 A.M., he said, he noticed that a door to the darkened two-car garage was partially open. Driving inside, and with his car lights on, he found Peggy lying on the garage floor, writhing in convulsions. Her face was puffy and discolored. Saliva foamed around her mouth.

Railey said the children — Ryan, 5, and Megan, 2 — were inside and unharmed. He telephoned police and then a church friend. After help arrived, he accompanied Peggy to Presbyterian Hospital, where he appeared at her side in the emergency room.

Following the interview with Railey the next morning, Police Capt. John Holt, the tall, sandy-haired supervisor of crimes against persons, told reporters the questioning of Railey was merely routine. "We don't have any indicators that would point to him as a suspect," he said. While the early investigation focused on the threatening letters, Holt said investigators were not excluding other possible motives. "We're keeping an open mind. We're pursuing some other leads that have come in."

After leaving police headquarters, Railey returned to the hospital to arrange for a suite near his wife. He spent the day greeting the parade of visitors who showed up to express their shock, sorrow, and support. "He's grateful for all the love people have shown him," said Ralph Shannon, a longtime member of First Methodist and chairman of the church's steering committee on policy and personnel. "There have been hundreds of people."

Among those who came to share their grief that day was a striking frosted blonde who carried a single red rose and disappeared into Walker Railey's hospital suite.

Driving to work that morning, a Dallas resident named Norm Kinne heard a sketchy account of the assault on his car radio. As the top assistant in the district attorney's office, Kinne was on a first-name basis with crimes of violence, but he thought it was unlikely he would become involved in the Railey matter. His specialties were cases in which the law allowed the state to seek the death penalty. That did not include attempted murder, whoever the victim was.

Kinne chose to be a prosecutor in 1971 after almost a decade in private practice. That made him unusual. His peers often joined the DA's office first, only to be lured away by the fat fees a crafty defense attorney can command. "For a young lawyer, it was very exciting and challenging and everything, but boy, I got tired of representing criminals," Norm Kinne once said. "When you're over there representing a guy and doing everything you can to get him off when you know he's guilty, it just rubs me the wrong way."

Norm Kinne was little impressed by money and not at all by the social status of a victim or a defendant. But, as he would one day demonstrate, he could be moved by the obscenity of a crime. Kinne had never heard of Walker Railey, although his sermons were televised each week and he was often in the news. But as the veteran prosecutor guided his car through rush-hour traffic, he realized he could become involved if Peggy Railey died, upgrading the offense to homicide.

Then he dismissed the unpleasantness from his mind.

That same morning, Dallas' two large daily newspapers were assembling their initial stories about the nightmare on Trail Hill Drive. But a scrappy blonde journalist named Olive Talley was not among the reporters digging for details.

Talley's assignment at the *Dallas Morning News* that day was a package of stories on health care for the poor. As a recent addition to the *Morning News* staff, her title was general assignments reporter, but she was partial to projects that took advantage of her investigative skills. At 31, she already had helped expose a nasty scandal in Houston that tarnished the city's power structure and changed forever one of its largest charitable foundations. While instinctively as aggressive as a pit bull, she could work a phone as delicately as a doctor performing brain surgery.

She would not become involved in the Railey story or the secrets of its main characters for nearly six weeks. But in time she would put her stamp on the case every bit as much as the affable, pipe-smoking prosecutor Norm Kinne.

Camouflaging chicanery or keeping the sleaziest of secrets was a perilous affair in Dallas because of a vigorous competition among the city's news media, principally its two daily newspapers. Between them, the *Dallas Morning News* and the *Dallas Times Herald* claimed upward of two million readers on Sunday. The *Morning News* won a Pulitzer Prize for uncovering discrimination in federal housing, and the *Times Herald* unraveled a scheme of illicit payoffs to college football players that led to the governor's office.

With ratings at stake, the television stations paid millions for high-tech equipment and six-figure salaries to their on-camera news personalities. Their news departments were not without talented investigative journalists, nor was the city's slick-covered monthly journal, called simply *D*. Another metropolitan daily, the *Star-Telegram* in Fort Worth, and more than a dozen suburban publications added to the media swirl, not to mention the wire services, Austin-based *Texas Monthly* magazine, and nearly forty local radio stations.

Even teenagers who didn't read newspapers got a dose of the Railey story. Between jokes and heavy metal rock, a disc jockey named Kidd Kraddick offered his own indignant commentary in late April, based on the official theory that Walker Railey's outspoken opposition to prejudice might have inspired the attack on his wife.

There were journalists in Dallas, however, who privately were skeptical of the Reverend Walker Railey even before the attack. Mostly, they were uncomfortable with his grand-standing. Given the competition, doubts about appearance and reality often spawned major stories. It was the press more than police who freed a black engineer named Lenell Geter, convicted of an armed robbery he didn't commit. For the case of young Geter was not what it originally appeared to be.

Those same red lights were blinking now in the Walker Railey case, however dimly.

With the investigation in full swing and the FBI attempting to identify the source of the death threats, Walker Railey continued his hospital vigil under heavy police protection.

"He's just numb. . . . He's overwhelmed by it," said church member Ralph Shannon. If Railey was silent, his ministerial colleagues were not. An interfaith, interracial group of clergymen met to express contempt at the attack on Peggy Railey. Rabbi Joseph Ofseyer of Congregation Shearith Israel told reporters that Railey had suffered for his message of justice and equality, but that the religious community would not "be cowed in silence" and "permit such a person to stand alone."

Texas Baptists issued a statement condemning white supremacy as "incompatible with the Gospel of Christ" and declared, "The fact that a minister's clear stand against racial injustice and bigotry would jeopardize his life is an indicting commentary on our society." The Reverend Bruce Theunissen, a Roman Catholic, praised Railey as "one of Dallas' strongest voices for justice and peace," and the Reverend Dan Griffin, pastor of the Temple Baptist Church in Oak Cliff, said, "It's a despicable, cowardly, and brutal act. There's not a word strong enough to describe it."·

In an editorial expressing the city's widespread sense of indignation, the *Dallas Morning News* said, "It is difficult to comprehend the insanity of it: A Dallas minister and his family have been menaced for weeks, apparently because he has unflinchingly preached a message of compassion and racial tolerance. . . . The idea that someone would threaten to take lives to stifle public viewpoints is twisted, repugnant, chilling." The newspaper pointed out that the campaign of terror was believed to be the work of a single disturbed individual and that the city had responded with support for the Railey

family that "bespeaks the kind of human cooperation and compassion Railey has called for from the pulpit."

Peggy Railey's assailant had left virtually no physical evidence. There were no fingerprints, no weapon, and, strangely,
no skin or hair under her fingernails. Because she survived,
forensic experts could not conduct the exhaustive examination they would on a murder victim.

Police Lt. Ron Waldrop had confirmed that the abusive
letters to Railey appeared to be the work of a lone person
and not the concerted effort of a white supremacist group.
"There's no central theme," he said.

A short time later, the FBI determined that the death
threats had been composed on an office typewriter *at Walker
Railey's First United Methodist Church.*

Part 2

On the Sunday after the attack on his wife, Walker Railey
chose not to deliver the sermon. Gordon Casad, First Methodist's executive minister, replaced him at the pulpit.

Casad told the congregation of an event that no doubt
baffled medical science. He said he spoke to the comatose Peggy Railey, assuring her that her children were safe. *Tears had
rolled down her cheeks*, Casad reported. "That tells me the spirit
of God works in mysterious ways in the depths of the human
soul," the minister said. "Nothing is deeper in a woman's heart
than her children and the care of them. Physiologically nothing has changed. But this brings a sense of hope, a sense of
gratitude."

Casad also brought word to the flock from the absent
Railey, still riveted to his wife's bedside. Railey's message said,
"So many emotions have flooded my soul since Tuesday night,
and there is no way I can communicate to you just exactly
what is there. I do not know why senseless violence continues
to pervade society, nor do I understand why the events of
this last week took place. . . . You have proven to me and
all of Dallas that our church is a family . . . I have been
reminded once again that the breath of life is fragile but the
fabric of life is eternal. Keep praying for us and know we are
praying for you."

In a mood best described as somber, parishioners read the Twenty-third Psalm together: "Yea, though I walk through the valley of the shadow of death, I will fear no evil for Thou art with me. . . ."

At midweek, Dallas police confirmed they had "some leads" in the case. While they refused to elaborate, they intended to question Walker Railey about unspecified "inconsistencies" concerning his whereabouts the night of the attempted murder.

Ralph Shannon visited Railey on Wednesday and noticed that, while he had seemed tired and depressed since the attack, "there seemed to be a little more sparkle than usual, and he seemed to be coming along."

The next day, John Yarrington, the minister of music at First Methodist and Railey's confidant, noticed a difference. When he visited the hospital, he thought Railey looked "extremely tired."

That evening, a Thursday, a little more than a week after the attack, Railey retired to his hospital suite early, telling relatives he needed the rest. Sometime that night, Railey sat down with pen and paper and, in a note addressed to no one, began to write.

> *Bury   me   quietly   at   Sparkman-Hillcrest cemetery. . . . Pray for Peggy, take care of my children, and forgive me for the pain I inflict on so many. I have finally made the decision to take care of myself. I have grown weak. God has remained strong. Therein lies your hope. I have none.*
>
> *Walker L. Railey*

The next morning, May 1, Railey did not respond to knocks or telephone calls and officers found the door locked and chained from the inside. A security guard forced his way in and discovered the young minister sprawled across the bed. He was alive but unconscious and in critical condition. Empty bottles and the long, rambling letter lay nearby.

"There is a demon inside my soul," Railey wrote in words that would not be disclosed for nearly a year. "It has always been there. My demon tries to lead me down paths I do not want to follow. At times that demon has lured me into doing things I do not want to do.

"For almost 40 years God has been struggling with my demon, and eventually God always prevails. My demon is working inside my soul again, filling me with despair and taking away my hope.

"My demon has finally gotten the upper hand.

"All of my life people have seen me as strong. The truth is just the opposite. I am the weakest of the weak. People have seen me as good. The truth is just the opposite. I am the baddest of the bad. People have seen me as virtuous. The truth is just the opposite. I am the lowest of the low."

Police confirmed the existence of the letter, describing it simply as an apparent suicide note. They refused publicly to reveal the contents of what some might have interpreted as a deathbed confession.

Asked if Railey was now a suspect in his wife's attack, Park Stearns, supervisor in the Dallas office of the FBI, said, "This is a big no comment."

At First Methodist, Gordon Casad, Railey's top assistant, said the unexpected turn of events had left the congregation "numb, shocked, hurt, and confused." But whatever their inner thoughts, few if any of Railey's flock speculated openly that the suicide attempt might have been motivated by guilt.

That would come later. For things were not what they appeared to be.

If there was a dark side to Walker Railey, it did not surface publicly until after the tragic events of April and May. Railey's rise to clerical prominence seemed almost preordained from his turbulent childhood days in Owensboro, Kentucky, a blue-collar coal mining town on the southern banks of the Ohio River.

The first of three children born to Chester and Virginia Railey, Walker was a nondrinking, nonsmoking teenager who preached his first sermon at age 17 and graduated from Owensboro High School with honors in 1965. All this was despite a family life most notable for its neglect. "He had a lonely and deprived childhood," said a fellow minister and friend, the Reverend Spurgeon Dunham III. "He had a very difficult home life and upbringing. . . . He was never brought up in the church."

As a history major at Western Kentucky University, young Railey became something of a circuit preacher on Sundays at a small town near Bowling Green, taking a turn at the pulpits of two and occasionally three churches. He graduated with honors in 1969, attended Vanderbilt Divinity School for a year, and then headed to Dallas and the Perkins Theological Seminary at Southern Methodist University.

It was there, in 1970, that he met Margaret Nicolai, an equally talented, intelligent, and religiously dedicated young musician from Wisconsin whom everyone called Peggy. A native of suburban Milwaukee, Peggy was an accomplished organist even as a youngster and would in time become a master of the harpsichord. After graduating at the top of her high school class, she obtained a bachelor of arts degree in organ music from Alverno College, a girls' school near her home. She arrived at SMU in Dallas in 1970 and began two years of work on her master's degree in music.

Acquaintances said Peggy recognized early on that young Railey was a man with great ambition and potential, but that she was not much taken with him romantically. His persistence won her over, they said, and the couple was married in August 1971 at the Trinity Presbyterian Church in Milwaukee.

Back in Dallas, the newlyweds lived in a one-room apartment on campus, and both excelled in their studies. Walker obtained a divinity degree in 1972 and a doctor of ministry degree a year later. With her master's degree, Peggy found a job as choir director and teacher of music and fine arts at Ursuline Academy, a private girls' school in Dallas. She stayed at Ursuline until 1978.

Walker ministered to several rural churches in Oklahoma before his appointment in 1973 as an associate pastor at First Methodist, the Dallas church he later would lead. In 1976, he was named senior minister at Christ Methodist Church in Farmers Branch, a Dallas suburb.

At the urging and with the assistance of several influential Methodist leaders, Walker, at age 33, was named the senior pastor of First Methodist in 1980, a remarkable achievement for one so young. An "astonishment," said Methodist theologian Albert Outler, adding: "He leapfrogged over two dozen of his elders who thought they were his equal."

While not the largest Methodist church in Dallas, First Methodist had the reputation as the mother church of Methodism, in no small part because eight of its ministers had gone on to become bishops. For Walker Railey, the appointment was the most dramatic step in a meteoric rise that thrilled and amazed his friends and followers, who saw no end to the accomplishments of this intense and dynamic young man of God.

At least until the tragic spring of 1987.

Under Walker Railey's leadership, First Methodist prospered and grew, its membership approaching 6,000 and its budget doubling to $2 million annually. While Railey himself was short and balding and physically unimposing, his radiant ministry served as a magnet for the young, energetic, and socially conscious while not alienating older, more conservative parishioners.

He spoke out boldly against those who practiced or condoned racial intolerance and, as president of the Greater Dallas Community of Churches, he clashed publicly with a city council member over what he perceived to be the councilman's racist stance on illegal aliens. He challenged Ronald Reagan to take a "more visible and articulate stand" for peace and criticized the Far Right fundamentalists for their "divisiveness," once zeroing in on Jerry Falwell and his Moral Majority. "I have no battles to fight with Falwell," Railey said, "but I guarantee he doesn't speak for the Kingdom of God, let alone the people in it."

His flashing dark blue eyes enhanced a vigorous and highly personalized delivery, and his reputation as an outspoken and innovative voice on contemporary issues spread across the country. Among his numerous honors and accolades was a "Keeper of the Lamp" award, which a seminary in Ohio presented to those preachers considered to be the best in the United States.

His sermons appeared on one channel in the Dallas–Fort

Worth market and he was host of a weekly show on another. In light of later events, friends and associates would say he was too intense, too absorbed, too dedicated, too driven, and most of all too ambitious. The less charitable would say his ambition was insatiable and completely unchecked. With hindsight, his friends would conclude he reached a breaking point.

Before the attack on Peggy Railey, some members of the church wondered privately if her husband's total devotion to the church, its congregation, and its activities might have a flip side of marital neglect. Railey traveled often and far away, even once to Africa, while Peggy was home with the children. They may not have known their minister had another life away from home, but close associates noticed that in recent months Peggy had withdrawn from most church activities. They speculated that she might have grown weary and resentful of the demands on a minister's wife.

But those who knew her best described her not as cool, distant, or aloof but always as gentle, intelligent, and compassionate. They said she was very much a devoted wife and loving mother to her two young children. Even Railey himself once said that "Peggy had a great love for the church, and the impression that she didn't enjoy being a pastor's spouse and stuff I think is unfair to her."

If there was some dark or dreadful reason for her declining visibility, Peggy apparently told no one.

Immediately after the brutal attack on Peggy Railey, much would be made of a sermon Walker Railey delivered three months earlier on the eve of the national holiday honoring slain civil rights leader Martin Luther King.

"The Ku Klux Klan was out in force at Cummings, Georgia, yesterday," he said, "and word has it they sponsor a training camp somewhere between Dallas and Fort Worth. There is more racial tension and polarization in Dallas, Texas, than many fine, upstanding citizens are willing to admit. It will not get any better until we see it and then do something about it."

According to church officials, Railey received the first abusive letter two months later and dismissed it as the act of "some crackpot." But when the threats continued, Railey turned the

letters over to authorities. Still, neither he nor Peggy demonstrated any great alarm. "She talked like she thought it was
no big deal," said Valerie McMahan, a neighbor. Even when
the FBI encouraged Peggy and the children to leave town for
a few days, she didn't appear to McMahan to be overly concerned.

John Yarrington, the minister of music at First Methodist,
pointed out that Peggy was not one to frighten easily. "Peggy is really straightforward and solid," he said. "Just looking
at her, one might think that she was maybe a frail person,
but she's not. She's very strong and very poised." Yarrington
and his wife Diane probably knew Walker and Peggy Railey
better than anyone. In fact, before his suicide attempt, the
troubled minister wrote, "I love John and Diane Yarrington,
and feel closer to him than any man on this earth. He is the
older brother I never had."

Diane Yarrington, one of Peggy's closest friends, said Peggy
told her she and Walker were taking precautions but refused
to be intimidated. Peggy told Diane she did not want Walker to change his beliefs or his sermons. "She said she would
not be terrorized by this kind of thing," said Diane Yarrington. ". . . her greatest concern was that Walker did not have
enough protection, but she was frightened when the notes
mentioned her children."

Long before the attack on Peggy Railey, the Yarringtons
and Raileys pledged to care for one another's children in the
event of death or tragedy.

That pledge would soon come due.

On Easter Sunday, shortly before the 11 A.M. service, a
letter addressed to Railey was shoved under an office door.
The note said, "EASTER IS WHEN CHRIST AROSE,
BUT YOU ARE GOING DOWN."

Although church officials did not yet know the letters had
been composed on a church typewriter, they now had to consider the possibility that the threats might be coming from
a member of the congregation, possibly even from a member of Railey's staff.

As Railey slipped into the bulletproof vest that morning,
police guards scanned the audience for signs of trouble. They

saw only the processional and a large banner displaying a multicolored butterfly, a symbol of the death and resurrection of Christ. They heard Railey hammer home his theme of death and resurrection that morning.

He pointed to the people in the pews and said, "You're going to die. You're going to die. You're going to die . . . I'm going to die."

No one knew that would be Railey's farewell address. Less than two weeks later, he and his wife lay near death in the same intensive care unit.

Part 3

The news of Walker Railey's suicide attempt swept through Dallas like a monstrous tidal wave, but nowhere was it more devastating than at First Methodist, where the congregation was described as shattered and bewildered. There were prayers for his recovery. From those who commented publicly, a theme emerged: this was not the Walker Railey they knew. They hoped the truth was something other than what it appeared to be.

"He is a very strong person, an excellent leader," said the Reverend Bruce Weaver, a Methodist district superintendent. "I don't see this as something he would do." Another stunned associate, the Reverend David Shawver, pastor of Plymouth Park United Methodist Church, hoped that Railey had acted out of grief and exhaustion. "I'm praying that it is *not what it looks like.* I'm praying that what the police are suggesting could never be true. I'm praying this will all come out some other way."

Two days after the suicide attempt, doctors reported that Railey's condition had improved from critical to serious, and soon it would be upgraded to satisfactory. Friends and followers poured into the hospital lobby over the weekend, arriving in such numbers that they temporarily caused problems.

At the Sunday morning worship service, the Reverend Gordon Casad told the grieving congregation to keep the faith. "In the midst of all the police and media reports that attempt to discern fact from fiction, and truth from sensation, we must strive to maintain the quality of mercy that befits the followers of Jesus Christ," Railey's assistant urged. "We must remember our pastor and the troubling of his mind and spirit and keep him in our prayers. . . . The events and happenings of the past days left us shocked, grieved, pained, and in great anguish. But this church has been here for 141 years and it will continue for generations."

That same Sunday night, the CBS Movie of the Week was entitled *Murder Ordained*, based on a true story of a Lutheran minister in rural Kansas. The minister and his girlfriend in the congregation conspired to kill his wife.

There was one bit of light in that otherwise dark weekend. If anything, it probably was misleading. Peggy's condition was upgraded from critical to serious, an announcement tempered with caution by Ralph Shannon. Like everyone, he knew that doctors feared the attack had left her brain dead. "She is still very, very seriously ill," Shannon said.

A CAT scan revealed that the swelling in her brain had gone down some, but she remained in a coma and on life-support systems. "It's not a quantum leap," Shannon said, "but it's good, and we'll take anything we can get."

There were those, like Diane Yarrington, who would never surrender hope. She would stay in Peggy's room for half an hour or so and talk nonstop. She would hang pictures drawn by the children on the wall in the intensive care unit, telling Peggy that Ryan and Megan were fine and what they were saying and doing in school. And always, they missed her.

"I cannot give up hope," Diane said. "I know she wants to be back. Even when medical science says there is not much hope, I cannot give up. My faith won't let me. She is a fighter, and if there is any way for her to come out of this and be anything, I know God will allow this to happen."

If police had wanted to talk with Walker Railey before the suicide attempt, now they were beside themselves to do so. But there was a new hitch. His name was Doug Mulder, a tough, no-nonsense criminal defense lawyer who earned his legal stripes as first assistant district attorney under the legendary Henry Wade. Unknown to Railey, friends in the church retained Mulder as an adviser of sorts. Explained Ralph Shannon: "We're not hiring someone to defend him. We're hiring someone to protect his rights."

Mulder wasn't much concerned that his presence might indicate something sinister on Railey's part. "If Railey's worried about his public image," he growled, "he should hire a PR guy and not a lawyer. It's my job to keep my client out of jail. That's all that matters."

More than a week passed, and Railey did not talk with police about the events of April 21 and 22. He did, however, speak with a writer named Helen Parmley, who for years covered the city's clergy for the *Dallas Morning News* church pages.

"To be honest with you . . . I just don't know anything," said Railey. He told Parmley he did not know who attacked his wife or wrote the threatening letters, and he could not or would not explain the reason for his suicide attempt. He said he had no sense of control over his life but was preoccupied with Peggy and with the children, who had been staying with the Yarringtons since the night of the attack—Ryan, the 5-year-old, knew "someone hurt Mommy" and asked questions about her.

"It's frightening to think what kind of impact this is going to have on him," Railey said. He said he was convinced that Peggy heard some of what was said to her and that tapes of her music and of the children had been played for her in the hospital. "We are not going to just hold her hand. Everyone talks to each other and to her when we are in her room. I'll never give up hope."

He was aware that he had been placed on a leave of absence from his ministry for health reasons but said he intended to return to the church. "When I come back to the pulpit, the first time is going to be real hard, and I am not coming back until I am really ready." Meanwhile, he said, he was "hoping for the best and praying for strength." At one point, he added, "You know the old adage, 'Where there's life, there's hope.' Well, I would add to that, 'Where there is hope, there is life.' That is my faith."

Three days later, it was learned that doctors had removed Peggy's respirator and she was now breathing on her own.

That same day, Walker Railey checked out of Presbyterian Hospital and into Timberlawn Psychiatric Hospital.

Railey entered Timberlawn for rest and recuperation, church officials said, but he was no stranger to the facility. Railey had received counseling at Timberlawn for several months, reportedly in an effort to cope with the stress of his job.

Gordon Casad said Railey was doing too much—spreading himself too thin and trying to accomplish more than his strength would permit. Another colleague characterized Railey as a bomb with a short fuse. "There are still so many unknowns," said Casad, who had assumed Railey's duties in the senior minister's absence. "The Walker we knew would not be the one to do this. But I don't think any of us ever know what someone might do if everything within them broke down. There's always the haunting wonder whether that could have been or not."

During his convalescence, Railey began privately upbraiding church officials as his stature declined, and he wrote at least one heated letter to a colleague whose published comments displeased him. Railey also complained to the bishop after the church canceled publication of some of his books.

Despite Railey's behavior and any number of disturbing questions, First Methodist and its members remained publicly supportive of their troubled minister, none more so than the Reverend Susan Monts, an associate pastor. "There's frustration not knowing what happened," she said. But, she contended, "It's wrong to focus on the mystery instead of the tragedy. We're dealing with people's lives. . . ."

Church leaders asserted that the membership had grown stronger and closer in the face of adversity and that First Methodist's image had not suffered. "We're not afraid of the truth here," declared one of Walker Railey's flock.

But of course the loyal congregation had no way of knowing just how unexpected and painful the truth would be. For, even then, the circumstances simply were not what they appeared to be.

During Railey's early stay at Timberlawn, attorney Doug Mulder arranged a private polygraph test for his client. The test was administered on May 14 by Bill Parker, a former Dallas homicide detective.

Railey was understandably nervous but cooperative and agreeable. He seemed eager to exonerate himself. As their eyes met, Railey said to Parker, "I'm told some people are suspecting me and I hope this can clear me of any suspicion."

"Well, Rev, it may or it may not," Parker replied.

The two men talked for three hours, but only half a dozen questions dealt specifically with the attack on Peggy Railey. And those six focused on two key issues.

"Were you the person who strangled Peggy Railey on or about April 21, 1987?" Parker asked.

"No," Railey replied.

"Before Peggy Railey was injured on or about April 21, 1987, did you conspire with anyone to harm or attack her?"

"No."

The test indicated Railey did not attempt to kill his wife. Presumably because of those results, Mulder approved a police-administered examination the next day. That exercise was described as inconclusive. "The results showed that he didn't have anything to do with the attack, nor did he conspire with anyone," said Mulder nonetheless. "We had some technical problems with the second test that, I think, can be straightened out. When they are ready to give another test, we are ready to take it. And I am totally convinced that he will be cleared completely."

Polygraph results are inadmissible as evidence in Texas courts, but their publicity value was not lost on Mulder. "Lawyer Says Railey Passed Lie Detector," the *Dallas Times Herald* reported. "Railey Passes Lie Test on Attack, Lawyer Says," the *Dallas Morning News* announced.

Though Railey's followers took new heart, investigators seemed unimpressed. All but ignoring the lie detector issue, Deputy Police Chief Martin Price restated the ongoing request to interview Railey about the mysterious "inconsistencies" of April 21 and 22.

Mulder denied the request, telling reporters that "you will find inconsistencies any time you have an alibi that is not premeditated. Everything would fit perfectly if it was orchestrated. Walker is a bright man." Besides, he maintained that "the only issue that we see as needing to be resolved is whether he had anything to do with the attack. That can be settled with a polygraph."

Snapped Price: "We are not accustomed to allowing defense attorneys to run our investigations."

Each side accused the other of being uncooperative, one of the early signs that police were losing patience with Railey's reluctance to talk with them. "We've attempted several times to interview Reverend Railey to clear up some issues related with this investigation," said Police Sgt. Pat Herring. "Obviously, he's been advised by his attorney not to cooperate."

Disagreeing, Mulder said, "I would like to get this thing resolved. But I insist that he be given another polygraph before he is questioned further." He said he wanted investigators satisfied that his client was telling the truth.

Although Mulder said he had no idea who might have harmed Railey's wife, he added, "I know who didn't do it and who didn't hire it done."

The next day, May 22, Capt. John Holt, the supervisor of crimes against persons, accused Mulder of misrepresenting the outcome of the police-administered polygraph examination. Holt suggested that some of Walker Railey's responses were untruthful. "We don't want to investigate this case through the media," he said. "It was not our choice to publicize the facts that came out today, but when that happened, we felt an obligation to respond."

Holt refused to specify what he considered untruthful, but published reports indicated it was Railey's response to questions about the threatening letters. It was the more serious questions about the attack on Peggy Railey that were labeled "inconclusive."

Holt said police and Mulder were at an impasse over who might administer a third polygraph test to Railey, but he indicated that a more pressing issue was Railey's refusal to discuss the case with investigators. "This is certainly within his rights and should not be interpreted as any indication of guilt or complicity . . . ," he said. But the police captain was quick to add, "There are several critical details that only Dr. Railey can resolve."

All but overlooked in the flap over the polygraphs was an unattributed police statement that Railey's account of his activities the night of April 21 was "in direct conflict with indisputable evidence."

The key word: *indisputable.*

In late May, Peggy Railey's hospital routine was interrupted by a bout with pneumonia. While her body resisted that infection, her condition remained serious and her future in doubt. She was, in fact, not comatose as such but in what doctors described as a "vegetative state."

While someone in a coma appears to be asleep, a person in a vegetative state has sleep-and-wake cycles, responds to sound and pain, and does not require artificial life support. Such patients appear to be awake, and they even might stare at visitors. But they do not speak or respond to commands or requests. In fact, they are oblivious to their surroundings. Only after a year in a vegetative state is the condition classified as "persistent." At that point, said a neurosurgeon, "the chances of recovery are nil."

While Peggy lay immobilized at Presbyterian Hospital, Walker Railey spent his days at Timberlawn pacing the floor, weeping, praying, occasionally phoning friends and writing letters. On June 10, he interrupted his self-imposed exile to accompany his lawyer on a flight to Salt Lake City for another polygraph test, this time given by David C. Raskin, a psychology professor at the University of Utah and a nationally recognized expert in his field.

Mulder and Railey never revealed the results of the third test, which some found puzzling and others bewildering and suspicious. In any case, Captain Holt and his detectives showed little concern. "A polygraph exam is an investigative tool," he said. "Regardless of who gives it or the outcome, there are still discrepancies that need to be cleared up." Sounding like a worn-out record, he repeated that the police wanted only to sit down with Railey and discuss his activities the night his wife was attacked. "A polygraph exam—regardless of the outcome—will not affect that," Holt added.

The polygraph debate gave way to a more startling development the next day. Officials at First Methodist announced that a church board wanted a new minister appointed to replace Railey. Unknown to all but a few, church member

Ralph Shannon had met with Railey at Timberlawn on June 5 and the two men had discussed the subject for four hours. It was an emotional meeting with anger and tears on both sides. While his departure from the church was perhaps inevitable, Railey was profoundly disappointed. But he said he understood the need for the church to move forward.

"Dr. Walker Railey agrees with this action," said a statement by Shannon's pastor-parish committee. "In no way should it be considered an indication of guilt or innocence, but it is apparent that any further delay in filling our pulpit will seriously impair the church in its mission." The committee praised Railey for his "dynamic leadership" and expressed its love and support for him and his family. It was a nice, neat, laudatory, and perhaps even compassionate solution to the problem, but the dismissal of Walker Railey from the pulpit at First Methodist would not be that simple.

Within hours, a group of angry church members vowed to fight to keep the pulpit open for Railey's return.

Part 4

The response to Railey's proposed ouster was quick, angry, impassioned, and not at all unexpected. "There are a lot of people unhappy about this," said Ken Menges, a three-year member of First Methodist who served on its administrative board. "I expect an independent petition to be presented to the bishop to protest this move."

Menges, 39, a Dallas lawyer, told an impromptu press conference that Railey had been "forced" to agree with the pastor-parish committee's decision. Menges also disclosed that Railey wrote him about returning to the pulpit. It was a letter filled with baseball jargon, according to Menges. "He said he was looking forward to getting back on the mound and hoped he would not be sent to the minor leagues."

Menges said he had talked with no one who agreed with the recommendation of Shannon's committee. "I don't understand why the church did not call an open meeting or a meeting of the administrative board prior to pulling the plug on Walker Railey. I think this action effectively cuts him off at the knees at a time when he needs our support."

Ralph Shannon assured Menges no one wanted Railey out. "But," said Shannon, "in view of all the circumstances, we asked if he can come back to this pulpit and be an effective pastor. The consensus, including that of Railey, is that he cannot."

That argument fell on some deaf ears. City Councilman Craig Holcomb, a First Methodist member and longtime friend and ally of Railey, said the action of Shannon's committee appeared to be part of a continuing effort by the church bureaucracy to distance itself from a "potentially embarrassing situation."

Though there was fear the committee decision would split the church between young and old, Shannon volunteered that membership, contributions, and attendance at First Methodist had remained steady since Railey's departure. And he said the request for a new minister had nothing to do with whether Railey was involved in the attack on his wife or his refusal to talk with police.

Interestingly, not all found fault with Railey for his cat-and-mouse maneuvers with police. A number of his supporters had grown critical of investigators for their continuing campaign to question the minister about the attack. "I think he's not talking to police because police have decided that Walker Railey is their man," said Menges. "If they had evidence, he ought to be charged," he maintained. "If they don't have the evidence, they should remove the cloud. I don't blame his attorney for doing his best to defend his client against a one-track rabid police department."

Replied Captain Holt: "We are not one-track and rabid, but we are relentless. We'll do everything in our power to find the person who attacked Peggy Railey and bring that person to justice. We do not have a closed mind as to any possibilities in this case. The lack of cooperation by Walker Railey has proved to be a serious impediment to the progress of our investigation."

At the very least, Holt said, Railey "is a key witness in this case. Without his help, it makes it very difficult to find the person who attacked his wife."

The next day, a Saturday, Craig Holcomb, Ken Menges, and other members of the church met to discuss how to save their embattled minister. A petition was drafted amid phone calls of support for their effort. Still, Menges and Holcomb delayed distribution of the petition until they gauged the depth of pro-Railey sentiment on Sunday.

Shannon, meanwhile, took a dim view of the petition, saying it would not make his committee change its mind. "The committee is elected by the congregation to deal with things like this, and we feel like we have made the best decision," he said. "The committee is not in the mood to reconsider, and I don't plan to ask them to change their decision." Sunday evening, about 100 members met to question the church staff and Shannon's committee members about the issue. The session was cordial but not without emotion, and the impasse between Shannon's committee and Menges' faction was not resolved.

Then something totally unexpected happened to defuse the issue. In an appearance on a nationally syndicated television program, Ralph Shannon alluded to a letter from Railey in which he said the minister had asked to be reassigned from First Methodist because circumstances had turned him into "more of a liability than an asset."

When pressed by Olive Talley of the *News*, Shannon said the letter had been written in mid-May and addressed to Bishop John Russell, with Shannon marked in for a copy. No one seemed more surprised than Ken Menges, who wondered why Shannon had waited so long to disclose the existence of the letter and its contents. "I was surprised, first of all, that there was a letter that had not been discussed previously," Menges said. "And secondly, if the letter was confidential at the time, I don't know why he has not kept it confidential."

Whatever the reason, Menges and City Councilman Holcomb dropped their campaign. "We don't want to divide the church," said Holcomb, convinced that Shannon and his committee would not relent. He and Menges focused on a new objective. "We want . . . a public show of support for Walker Railey," Holcomb said. "We want to make certain that Peggy Railey's medical expenses are covered for the rest of her life and we want there to be a living wage for Walker for the next two years so that he has ample opportunity to get his life back in order."

Relieved, Shannon said of the group's new request, "It's certainly not out of the question, but it's something several areas of the church will have to look at."

Church officials said they had no idea how much money would be needed to care for the Railey family. No doubt it was already in the six-figure range and growing.

On June 20, Railey left Timberlawn for his home in Lake Highlands and a reunion with close friends. He once again found an attentive listener in religion editor Helen Parmley, but he cast no new light on the events of April 21 and 22.

"I am deeply grieving," he said. "A tragedy that occurred seems to be forgotten. The tragedy is Peggy, lying in a coma at Presbyterian Hospital. . . . There is some deranged mind out there that did something to Peggy. That worries me."

Railey said he intended to stay elsewhere because the Lake Highlands house held too many reminders of what had occurred. "It's hard to be here. I'm going to find a place to be alone. I haven't been alone since April 21. My spirit is strong. There is a peace within."

He said his plans for the future were uncertain except that he would spend Sunday, Father's Day, with the children, Ryan and Megan, who were still staying with John and Diane Yarrington. "I want some space to sleep, read, and play with my kids," he said. "I'm anxiously waiting, waiting to get on with my life and see what happens."

Remembering that he would turn 40 in less than a week, Railey said he was "at a new crossroads" in his life and ready to meet the challenge. "I feel there's still a sermon in me somewhere," he added, conceding at the same time that he supported the board decision to replace him at First Methodist. He spoke at least twice of "so many unanswered questions" but said he did not want to discuss the tragedy. And yet, in the next few days, he did just that.

In a series of remarkable interviews with print and broadcast reporters, Walker Railey seized the offensive. It was not his pulpit. But it *was* his show.

"I didn't attack my wife," he said. "I didn't plan to have someone attack my wife. I didn't orchestrate a plan to attack my wife. And if I had written the letters, I wouldn't have written them on a typewriter in the church. But I didn't write them."

He called such speculation "ridiculous and absurd" and said that, while he was innocent and unafraid, he was not unoffended by the innuendo. "There are people who are playing 'Murder, She Wrote' with my life and the lives of my family," he said, unaware of how hollow such parental concern would someday sound.

"Everyone on the street corner seems to have some speculation on what happened and who did it. I didn't do it, but there are times when I feel I'm the only one in the world who thinks that." He could not explain his suicide attempt, but tried. "My theology does not hold open the option of suicide. My understanding of life is that it is a gift from God. Suicide is like murder. When I take my life, I am taking a part of God's life."

He said his burden became too heavy to bear in the week after the attack on his wife, and his despair led in turn to the suicide attempt. "Somehow I grew oblivious to the fact that I didn't have to bear it by myself," he said. "Had it not been for some act of grace, we would not be sitting here today. I think I let God down, but God picked me back up."

The attempt on his life, he explained, was the result of many nights without sleep and the desperate situation he found himself in. "It was a suicide attempt. I'm not denying that, but it was not a premeditated attempt." On the advice of friends, he said, he began keeping a journal about the turmoil in his life and was writing in the journal when it suddenly turned into a suicide note. "I was putting my feelings on paper when I looked around and saw nothing but despair." Concluding that everything seemed hopeless, he took the overdose of tranquilizers.

The complete contents of Railey's suicide note still had not been disclosed, but he felt compelled to deal with a publicized reference to "demons" in his soul. "I don't believe in witchcraft. I don't believe the devil runs around with a pitchfork trying to undo our lives. But sometimes there is a battle going on inside us . . . and the battle is the demon. I don't understand why I did it, any more than I understand why

I lived beyond it. I don't think I lost control. I think I gained control."

During his hospitalization, he said, he turned to the scriptures of Romans and Psalms. There he "found a holy presence in my life." In fact, he said, "When everything else was taken away, the one thing I have left is my faith in God. I have never doubted that faith, but I felt I had lost touch with the power that goes with that faith."

Railey said he knew there were those who construed the suicide attempt as an admission of guilt. "I do think I'm being tried in public, and that doesn't make me feel particularly good. It hasn't been easy to see my credibility chipped away by rampant speculation and unfounded accusations by the general public. I didn't assault my wife and I didn't plan for it to happen."

Railey said his refusal to talk with police was a decision made by his lawyer, but that personally he was "more than desirous" to tell his story to investigators. And he saw no paradox in his freewheeling interviews with the media. "I'm not trying to take my case to the public. I've never refused to talk to reporters, and this is the first time I've been out of the hospital and able to do so. If this interview or others clear up some misconceptions, that will be good."

He said he had no ironclad alibi to cover all his activities and whereabouts the night Peggy was attacked, but that should not be held against him. "When you don't have a need for an alibi, you don't go out and create one," he said, never realizing how dazzling that declaration would be in the turbulent months ahead.

Railey shrugged off reports that police had "indisputable evidence" of inconsistencies in his account of that terrible night on Trail Hill Drive. Almost cavalierly, he said his lawyer was in "constant contact" with authorities. Mulder, he promised, would clear up any misunderstandings.

He was wrong.

Homicide investigator Rick Silva had tried for weeks to talk with Mulder, but the lawyer was not returning phone calls. More importantly, no one, including Mulder, could explain away the mysterious "indisputable evidence."

And if Walker Railey believed his accommodating interviews discouraged the darker questions of the case, he would be wrong once again.

It would not be surprising for someone in Walker Railey's circumstances to read the reassuring passages of the Psalms. They speak of strength in adversity, yet their words both soothe and nourish.

The Apostle Paul's letter to the Romans is another matter, for it is filled with admonitions that everyone is under the power of sin. There are several verses in chapter 7 that would have a familiar ring to Railey's torment: "I do not understand what I do," Paul said. "For what I want to do, I do not do."

My demon, wrote Walker Railey in despair, *tries to lead me down paths I do not want to follow. At times that demon has lured me into doing things I do not want to do.*

"I know that nothing good lives in me, that is, in my sinful nature," said Paul to his followers. "For I have the desire to do what is good, but I cannot carry it out."

All of my life people have seen me as strong. The truth is just the opposite. I am the weakest of the weak, said Railey.

Paul: "For what I do is not the good I want to do; no, the evil I do not want to do—this I keep on doing."

Railey: *I am the baddest of the bad.*

Paul had a rationale for his thoughts. "Now if I do what I do not want to do," he said, "it is no longer I who do it but it is sin living in me that does it."

Wrote Walker Railey: *My demon has finally gotten the upper hand.*

Part 5

This is an outstanding home! Completely updated! Light, bright den overlooks gorgeous pool! Bedroom & bath on one side, 3 bedrooms on other. Side yard for kids to play off kitchen! Master has 11x11 sitting room.

As June gave way to July and the fierce midsummer Texas heat, the Walker Railey case languished in what could be characterized as the calm before the storm. While no sign

was posted, the Lake Highlands residence was put on the market for $269,000. The real estate listing was almost cheerful
in its description of what had once been Walker and Peggy
Railey's dream home.

For practical reasons, Peggy's family decided to transfer
her from Presbyterian Hospital to a nursing home in East
Texas where she could be near her parents, Bill and Billie
Jo Nicolai. Though the Nicolais lived near Tyler, they had
spent almost every day in Dallas attending to Peggy's needs
and, as Ralph Shannon pointed out, "It's been very difficult
for them."

Doctors rarely discussed Peggy's condition at length, but
she remained in a vegetative state from which they feared
she would never mentally awaken. Her chronic condition was
such that regular and more expensive hospitalization was no
longer necessary. As much as $1 million for Peggy's care
reportedly would be paid from an insurance policy provided
by the regional conference of the United Methodist Church,
and church leaders thought the sum would be adequate for
quite some time.

Meanwhile, police received an anonymous but tantalizing
letter that indicated the author, apparently a woman, might
have information useful to the Railey investigation. "We would
like very much to talk to this source to see if, in fact, this
person does know something that could be relevant to the
case," said Capt. John Holt.

The woman's note provided no usable information, but said
she had something that might be helpful. If police wanted
to talk to her, they should make a public statement saying
so. Investigators conveyed their interest through the
newspapers, but there was no immediate response.

There was, however, an ominous rumbling from within
the district attorney's office about convening a grand jury to
pursue the investigation. The restiveness could be traced
largely to Railey's penchant for discussing the case with reporters while spurning invitations to talk with authorities. The
rumbling and the restiveness even had a name: Norm Kinne.

Norm Kinne, Dallas' first assistant district attorney, once
thought Peggy Railey would have to die before he became

involved in the case. But he was no longer on the sidelines. He was now talking to detectives about launching a grand jury probe.

"If they have witnesses who are reluctant, who they're having difficulty talking to, including Mr. Railey, we can call them before the grand jury and question them under oath," Kinne said. "Unless you have some kind of Fifth Amendment claim against self-incrimination, you can be compelled to testify."

Suddenly things started to heat up.

Both daily newspapers were committed to the Railey story, and the *Dallas Morning News* had assigned a young reporter named Olive Talley to pursue it. Once a member of First Methodist, she quit the church in disillusionment as the Railey case grew increasingly sinister. Her first major assignment was a background piece on the Railey family, based on a whirlwind trip to Kentucky and the East Coast. But for some time, Talley had been looking into rumors about an attractive blonde psychologist named Lucy Papillon, the daughter of a former Methodist bishop. Then, on July 8, she told readers of the *News* for the first time that Papillon was a potential "reluctant witness" in the Railey case.

Identifying Papillon by name, the story said mobile telephone records revealed that Railey called her twice on the night of April 21, first at her office and later at her home near the SMU campus. The initial call was at 5:58 P.M. and the second at 7:32 P.M. Although the contents of those calls were not known, each call lasted one minute.

Railey had neglected to mention those calls during his lengthy interview with police the morning after his wife was attacked. Phone records also showed that Railey placed two calls to his own home between midnight and 12:30 A.M., the last one about ten minutes before he reported finding Peggy near death on the garage floor. The first call home was at 12:03 A.M. and lasted two and one-half minutes. The second, at 12:29 A.M., lasted ninety seconds.

There were three other calls made that evening from the car phone, the first to the family's private line at 5:55, lasting under three minutes. Railey, who did not wear a watch, made a 6:38 P.M. call to an automated recording that gives the time. Just before 7:30 P.M., he telephoned a babysitter who frequently kept the Railey children.

Investigators refused to discuss the significance of the mobile phone records. Nor did readers learn immediately of the contents of the two late calls the minister made to his home's answering machine. But it seemed safe to assume the records somehow represented the "indisputable evidence" of inconsistencies in the story Walker Railey told police on April 22.

For the moment, however, the most obvious questions raised by Talley's revelations centered on Lucy Papillon and her relationship with the senior minister of the First United Methodist Church of Dallas.

The frosted blonde with the sparkling eyes and colorful past was no stranger to the congregation at First Methodist. In fact, Lucy grew up in the magnificent old downtown sanctuary, the daughter of the Reverend Robert E. Goodrich, Jr., a former senior pastor at First Methodist and later a Methodist bishop. A portrait of Goodrich, who died in 1985, hangs in the foyer at First Methodist.

"Despite the mascara and frosted hair, one look at Lucy and you could see she was Bob Goodrich's daughter," observed journalist Larry Wright, a childhood acquaintance. "She had that knotted Goodrich chin, his thin, drawn smile, and the dark eyes that were his most distinctive feature — eyes that seemed remote but also searching and intelligent. It was a strong face, like her father's, and if in some lights it appeared hard, in others you could detect a vulnerable and even wounded soul who had lived past the point where life surprised her."

Although born in Houston, Lucy and her three siblings grew up in Dallas. Her sister also became a psychologist, one brother entered the ministry, and another became a television sports producer.

As a youngster, Lucy played the piano in Sunday School and later attended the exclusive Hockaday School in Dallas, where she was a cheerleader and member of the Latin and French honor societies and the Glee Club. After graduating from Hockaday in 1959, she entered SMU to pursue a bachelor's degree in music education. Lucy married the

Reverend James E. Caswell, an ordained Methodist minister, in 1963 and taught school in suburban Oak Cliff to support his postgraduate studies.

She resigned in 1965 because of pregnancy and gave birth to the first of the couple's two sons in 1966. She returned to SMU to obtain a master's degree in liberal arts, graduating in 1971. She and Caswell divorced in 1973.

Friends said she worked at a variety of jobs, including a stint as a part-time model for an exclusive women's store. Somewhere along the way she became enamored with psychology and appeared one day in 1973 at a workshop conducted by Irwin Gadol, a psychotherapist. When Gadol separated from his wife two years later, they began dating. Gadol and Lucy married in 1977, a union that ended four years later in divorce.

The following year, 1982, Lucy received her doctorate at North Texas State University in Denton and moved to California to complete her professional training. She worked as a consulting psychologist at a counseling center for eating disorders at the University of California at Irvine and later as a psychology associate at the Humanistic Therapy Institute, also at Irvine.

While in California, she served as a consultant at the Capistrano by the Sea Hospital in Dana Point. According to *D* magazine, there was a "growing restlessness on the part of Lucy to explore different pathways in life." Suggested *D*: "This desire may have inspired her to visit Esalen, a sort of commune for free spirits and free thinkers of various persuasions who gather at Big Sur, California. Esalen disciples hope to undergo a spiritual and intellectual makeover. The goal is to elevate oneself to a higher plane via nutrition, nude bathing, and massage."

It was at Esalen that Lucy decided to take on her identity as "Papillon," French for butterfly.

Returning to Dallas, she brought with her a letter of recommendation from Joseph L. White, a professor of psychology and psychiatry at the Irvine counseling center. "In my opinion, Lucy has the potential to become an outstanding teacher," White wrote. "She is lively, super-talented, well-versed in psychological theory, and has a clear, organized delivery style."

The state granted Lucy a Texas license in 1986, and she opened a private practice in North Dallas. She also joined Green Oaks Hospital as a consultant on eating disorders.

In June 1986, Lucy Caswell-Gadol emerged from the Dallas County courthouse a new woman of sorts. She had legally changed her name to Papillon.

Two years later, after the attack on Peggy Railey, an Associated Press reporter asked a onetime friend and associate of Lucy why it was that Lucy had chosen the French word for butterfly.

"Because," the young woman purred, "she didn't know the French word for fruitcake."

On July 14, Norm Kinne, Dallas County's chief criminal prosecutor, sat down with police and the FBI and heard for the first time all the facts of the Railey case. They brought Kinne their "book," a collection of reports, witness statements, and other evidence from their files. They also brought pictures taken of Peggy Railey after the attack.

His face flushed with anger and his thick moustache almost bristling, Kinne stormed from the meeting room into a cluster of reporters and challenged Walker Railey, as the *Times Herald* headline would later proclaim, to "talk or walk."

Eyes flashing and his finger jabbing at the nearest of four television cameras, Kinne declared, "I'm tired of this man fooling with the justice system and the life of his wife . . . I'm going to tell you, Walker Railey, I'm tired of you messing with the Dallas Police Department, and you're going to come before the Dallas County grand jury and you're going to clear up these discrepancies, or you're going to leave the country!"

Kinne could subpoena Railey to appear before grand jurors, but there was no legal way to compel him to answer questions if he invoked the constitutional protection of the Fifth Amendment against self-incrimination. Nor, of course, was it within the fiery prosecutor's domain to order a reticent Railey out of the country.

But nobody was foolhardy enough to argue the issue at that moment with Norm Kinne.

Later that evening, a vaguely contrite Kinne said it was the photographs of Peggy Railey that so outraged him and triggered the subsequent outburst. "I got irritated because we have a lady here who is a loving wife and mother and who is lying in a hospital more dead than alive," he said. "And we have an alleged pillar of the community who will not talk to us about this."

Dallas County's No. 1 prosecutor vowed then and there to bring Walker Railey before the grand jury. And he left not a shadow of doubt that Lucy Papillon would be summoned right along with him.

Part 6

When Norm Kinne arrived at his office the next morning, his secretary handed him a message saying Railey had called on the chief felony prosecutor's private line just minutes earlier.

"Yeah, sure he did." Kinne laughed, thinking "someone's pulling my chain."

But a few minutes later, Railey's attorney called. "Walker tried to call you a little while ago," Doug Mulder told him.

"He did?"

"Yeah."

"I got this message, but I didn't believe it was him."

"It was him."

"Well," said Kinne, "I'll be glad to talk with him."

"Yeah, I bet you would." Mulder laughed. "You're not going to get to talk to him now."

However, Mulder did assure Kinne that Railey would honor the subpoena and appear before the grand jury. Railey was but one of several people that Kinne intended to call before the panel for what he labeled a fact-finding session. The prosecutor conceded that using a grand jury as an investigative tool was extraordinary but, he sighed, "This is an unusual case."

And it was quickly becoming more unusual. On the eve of the grand jury session, reporter Olive Talley was in print again, revealing that Railey had visited Lucy Papillon the night his wife was attacked. Although reporters did not know for certain, they suspected that the visit, like the two phone calls, had been purposely overlooked by Railey when first recounting for police his activities on the night of April 21.

Some three dozen reporters, photographers, and television cameramen converged on the Dallas County Courthouse that Wednesday morning to greet Railey and attorney Doug Mulder. Outside the jury room, Mulder charged that police had Railey "zeroed in and targeted as the suspect" in his wife's assault. "I don't think they have another suspect," he complained.

Inside the jury room, Norm Kinne was eager to confront Railey. He believed the embattled minister would be instructed to invoke his Fifth Amendment right against self-incrimination, but Kinne had a plan. He knew it was one thing to stonewall the police, but it was something else to sit in the witness chair and say, "I refuse to answer on the grounds that it may tend to incriminate me." Kinne felt it was against Railey's nature to avoid responding to questions. "He's not the kind of guy who's going to let somebody else speak for him," Kinne suggested. "I think he possibly feels he's smarter than all the rest of us and . . . that he might disregard his attorney's advice and say something."

Kinne's strategy was to be harsh and insulting, perhaps even cruel, in his interrogation and force Railey to speak out. It was a good plan, but it didn't work. Walker Railey did indeed plead the Fifth —*forty-three times.*

Kinne sensed Railey's animosity mounting during the intense questioning. "If looks could kill, I'd be dead," he thought. The confrontation left Kinne wondering what made Railey tick. The minister's actions were inconsistent with the upstanding citizen, devoted husband, and loving father people perceived him to be.

People have seen me as good, Walker Railey once said. *The truth is just the opposite. I am the baddest of the bad.*

"I have followed the advice of my lawyer consistently and will consistently do that," Walker Railey explained brusquely when he emerged from the closed-door session of the grand jury. He looked weary and nervous as he left the courthouse. His blue eyes flashed no longer. "I'm tired," he said. ". . . this has been a long ordeal. My church is tired. We're hoping to get this thing finished."

Reporters wondered aloud how the investigation could be finished without Railey's cooperation. Mulder volunteered that his own independent investigation had convinced him Railey was not responsible for the attack on his wife. But the lawyer said he wouldn't produce evidence to support the claim because premature release of the details of his private probe would "dilute the effect."

More realistically, Mulder conceded that Railey's refusal to talk with police or answer questions before grand jurors could be construed as a sign of guilt. "That's just a cross he has to bear. . . . There is absolutely no way on earth to remove the cloud," Mulder said. "He has made it absolutely clear to the press and to the police that he didn't do it. Why say it again? I'm not prepared at this time to let him talk to the police, the grand jury, or anyone else."

On the other hand, Lucy Papillon spent an hour before the panel. She, too, had a high-profile lawyer, Phil Burleson, Sr., whose previous clients included Kennedy assassination figure Jack Ruby and millionaire murder suspect Cullen Davis of Fort Worth.

"She testified fully," said Burleson. He said Lucy knew nothing about the attack on Peggy Railey and so testified. Burleson cautioned reporters against drawing conclusions that his client was romantically linked with Walker Railey. He was in fact quoted by the *Times Herald* as saying that any such characterization was "totally incorrect."

In the dazzling light of later events, Burleson would claim he was misquoted. But it made no difference. The whispered rumors were true. Lucy Papillon was Walker Railey's mistress.

While grand jury testimony is by law secret, "leaks" are not all that uncommon in major cases. After the Railey proceedings, the leak was more like a gusher.

"Railey, Friend Talked Marriage," blared the *Times Herald* headline across the top of page 1 the day after Lucy's grand jury appearance. The story focused on Railey's affair with Lucy Papillon and pulled no punches. "Railey Didn't Tell Police He Visited Psychologist," said the *News*, likewise in a front-page headline. That story emphasized Railey's failure to inform investigators of his meeting with Lucy the night his wife was attacked. Both accounts quoted liberally from unidentified sources, since no one could own up by name to revealing what had transpired behind the closed doors of the grand jury room.

"I don't know who leaked it," fumed Phil Burleson. "We got burned by the grand jury. Somebody violated their oath of secrecy."

According to those present, Lucy told grand jurors she first met Railey on a religious television show and that they became romantically involved in June 1986. She said she had accompanied Railey on several of his church trips and had vacationed with him in a number of cities in California. Nor were their liaisons confined to this country. Lucy disclosed that Railey had stopped over for a prearranged encounter in London while returning from a World Methodist Council meeting in Nairobi, Kenya, in July 1986.

Worse yet, from Railey's standpoint, she said she and her lover had discussed marriage but, as one source said, "there were no concrete plans." In one particularly chilling disclosure, Lucy said they had embraced and kissed in Railey's hospital suite while Peggy Railey lay near death in a nearby intensive care unit. A friend of Railey told the *Times Herald*: "She was there when I left about 10 P.M. on two nights. She was there and went alone to his room."

If police wanted a motive for attempted murder, Lucy had given them one. Yet, despite the sensational revelations, the grand jury testimony raised almost as many questions as it answered. Railey still had not responded to the haunting "inconsistencies" that hung over the case from the start, and the police department's "indisputable evidence" remained obscure.

"We still have a lot of discrepancies, but we're not going to discuss them," said Police Lt. Ron Waldrop, who had been working the case since the day Peggy Railey was hospitalized. He said he was frustrated but hardly about to give up. "There is no statute of limitations on attempted murder, and that's how long we'll be working on it," Waldrop vowed. "I have fourteen more years before I retire, and I'm sure I won't quit working on it as long as I'm here. Our concern is with finding the person who strangled Peggy Railey. We intend to do that, and we're going to commit all the manpower and resources we need to do that. We don't plan to stop."

At First Methodist Church, the disclosures about Lucy Papillon eroded Railey's support, but neither the congregation nor the hierarchy openly turned on him at once. Typical was the reaction of Ken Menges, who had led the earlier fight to prevent Railey's removal as senior pastor. "I don't want to talk about it anymore," he said. He was not alone.

It appeared that concern for Walker Railey had given way to muted disappointment and smoldering outrage. Some might live with vague suspicions of attempted murder, but unchallenged reports of an adulterous love affair were something totally different. A minister found guilty of adultery could be stripped of his credentials under Methodist law.

Within days of the grand jury appearances, Ralph Shannon confirmed that Railey was being dropped from the church payroll at the end of August. But he did not attribute the action to the Papillon affair. "It's just impossible to go on paying him, especially if we're looking for a new minister," Shannon told reporters. He would not divulge Railey's salary, but church records indicated it was $60,500 annually. Travel and housing allowances hiked his total compensation to roughly $90,000.

The undercurrent of sentiment against Walker Railey surfaced publicly on August 6. More than a dozen Methodist ministers, maintaining that the "moral authority of the Methodist Church is at stake," petitioned Bishop John Russell to investigate allegations of immorality against Railey. The ministers specifically asked for a committee to follow up on the published reports about Railey's extramarital affair with Lucy Papillon. "Failure to clear the air on these allegations would be very injurious to the United Methodist Church," the ministers said in their letter. Bishop Russell subsequently rejected the request, citing a lack of evidence. Under the circumstances, he said, such an investigation would be a "violation of church law."

But it was Railey himself who rendered the issue moot on September 2 when he voluntarily surrendered his credentials as a minister in the United Methodist Church. "Since April 22, 1987," he said in his letter of resignation, "I have lived with an increasing amount of stress. Over the last four months the burdens upon me have been tremendous, as have the complexity and confusion of the situation surrounding my life." He said his decision was based on those factors and his concern for North Texas Methodists. "I will cherish forever my twenty-two years under appointment of a bishop and look forward to serving God, however that may be."

Friends, colleagues, and church members expressed genuine dismay that a career once so bright and promising and meteoric could fall so far so fast. "The mood at the church is sad, very sad," said Ralph Shannon. "We were all shocked by it. It's a great loss of talent. I feel sad for him, for the family, and for the church."

Anyone surprised by Railey's resignation was astonished by his next moves. He first surrendered control of his wife's legal affairs to her parents and then granted temporary custody of his children to the friends who had kept them since April 22.

Peggy's mother, Billie Jo Nicolai, had requested that the court grant her guardianship of her daughter, and Railey did not object. One expert in probate matters called Railey's decision "bizarre," unaware of a legal precedent for a husband doing such a thing. And then, on October 30, a state judge signed an order temporarily assigning custody of Ryan and Megan Railey to John and Diane Yarrington "in the best interests of the children." Yarrington, a father of four, emphasized that the key word was "temporary," explaining: "Walker is still trying to decide where to relocate, and he, the grandparents, and everyone else involved thought it was in the best interest to place them with us to give them a sense of stability."

What Yarrington did not say was that he and Diane confronted Railey after the grand jury fiasco and demanded to know about his affair with Lucy.

"It's true," said Railey.

"I'm really sorry to hear you say that," Diane replied. She asked whether Railey was still seeing Lucy. When Railey tried to evade her question, she said she never wanted the children in Lucy's presence again.

"I understand." Railey shrugged, but Diane Yarrington was

not through. She told him she would fight for the children if necessary. Quite possibly, she began to sense even then what others could hardly imagine. She and her husband would one day petition for permanent custody of Walker and Peggy Railey's children.

At First Methodist, the search for Railey's successor focused on a Georgia native named Hal Brady III, pastor at Glenn Memorial United Methodist Church on the campus of Emory University in Atlanta. When Brady's selection was announced, a reporter for the *Dallas Times Herald* named Diane Winston found Railey cleaning out his study in the family home in Lake Highlands. It reportedly sold for $235,000, or $34,000 off the asking price.

Railey didn't want to comment on his successor but said his own future was somewhat bleak. "I have no job and no prospects of one, but I'm still looking. Financially, I'm hanging on by a thread right now."

Railey's friend John Yarrington described the situation even more bluntly: "He has no job and very little standing in the community, and a lot of people in town think he's guilty as hell. That's a hard thing to live with. There's no way I can be objective, but I'm also not naive. We all suffer the consequences of our actions. There are certain things when they get in motion, you can't bring them back."

At that time, Railey was little more than a week away from seeing his name once again in the bold black headlines of the Dallas newspapers. Olive Talley had been at work on a copyrighted article about his activities of April 21 and 22. Despite police secrecy, she had rooted out the "indisputable evidence" of inconsistencies in the story Railey told investigators the morning after the attack on his wife.

And the police were furious.

"Railey Gave Wrong Time in Call on Night of Attack," read the *Dallas News* headline the morning of November 15. Although it took a certain knowledge of the case fully to grasp the significance of her new information, Talley plunged straight to the heart of the matter.

"Forty minutes before Walker Railey reported finding his wife unconscious on the floor of their garage, he left a mes-

sage on his home answering machine that cited an errone-
ous time and suggested that his wife lock the garage door for
her safety," the article said. "Although Railey says on the tape
that the time of the call from his mobile phone was '10:30
to 10:45' P.M., phone records pinpoint the actual time at
12:03 A.M., three sources close to the investigation said."

If the time noted by Railey had been correct, it could have
distanced him from the attack on his wife. Under the circumstances, it did just the opposite. One inescapable inference
was that Railey had laid the groundwork for a nearly perfect
alibi but had been tripped up by phone records he never knew
existed.

Part 7

On the evening of April 21, 1987, Walker Railey called his
wife Peggy on his car phone and told her he was on his way
home from the office. The mobile phone had been installed
at church expense only hours earlier as one of several security measures taken because of the threats regarding Railey's
stance against racial prejudice. Others included a home alarm
system and a private phone line.

A phone company computer recorded the time of that first
call as 5:55 P.M. Moments later, at 5:58 P.M., he telephoned
his mistress Lucy Papillon and talked for one minute. Arriving home shortly before 6:30, Railey said he found his wife
working on a faulty garage door lock with a bar of soap. Investigators later found no trace of soap on the lock, which
was working satisfactorily when they examined it.

Railey said he sat on the hood of Peggy's Chrysler and
talked with her for several minutes. He wasn't hungry, he
said, and the two shared a glass of wine in lieu of dinner.
Railey told Peggy he intended to spend the evening on a book
research project at the libraries at Southern Methodist University. He did not change from his business suit and left the
house a little after 6:30 P.M. At 6:38, Railey, who never wore
a watch, called on the car phone for the time. Presumably,
he got it. Railey said he spent half an hour or so at SMU's
Bridwell Library and was back in his car by 7:26 P.M. At
that time he phoned the family babysitter and discussed plans

for a trip to San Antonio that he and Peggy planned later in the week.

At 7:32 P.M., he phoned Lucy at her home on Daniel Avenue near the SMU campus. He told her he was "real stressed out" and wanted to see her. This was the second call that he failed to mention to the police. He drove directly to Lucy's house, where he spent the next forty minutes or so. After the visit with Lucy was revealed, Railey told a friend he went there to get some relaxation tapes to help relieve his stress. Lucy said Railey lay down for a short time. When he left, his clothes were wrinkled and his hair was mussed.

Between 8:00 and 8:30, Railey was back at Bridwell, where he asked a librarian what time the library closed. At 8:30 P.M., Railey, using a pay phone, called Peggy on their private line. She told him she was putting the children to bed. Peggy then called her parents long distance in Tyler and talked from 8:49 P.M. until 9:14 P.M.

Meanwhile, Railey was pulling into a gas station and convenience store on Greenville Avenue along a popular entertainment strip in North Dallas. He purchased gas at 8:53 P.M., evidence showed. He said he drank a wine cooler and returned to his research at the Fondren Library. But no one saw him there until after 11 P.M.

At 9:30 P.M., a jogger in the Lake Highlands area spotted a man in a business suit and street shoes running through a yard south of the Railey home. Between 10:15 and 10:30, a neighbor heard suspicious rustling sounds in the alley behind the Raileys.

At approximately 11 P.M., Railey telephoned Lucy again to say he was at the Fondren Library and wanted to come over. She said it was too late. They spoke again by phone at 11:35. Upon leaving SMU's library at midnight, Railey attempted to give his business card to a Nigerian student at the checkout desk. On the back of the card was a message requesting help in finding research information. Railey also noted the time, 10:30 P.M., when in fact it was midnight, the student told police.

Minutes later, at 12:03 A.M., Railey called home on the car phone, but this time he used the public line instead of the private line. According to friends, the family seldom answered the public line, which was connected to an answering machine.

"Hi, Babe," he said. "I'm calling you from my mobile phone. Peg, it's about, oh, I don't know, I don't have a watch. It's somewhere between 10:30 and 10:45, somewhere along in there. I worked at Bridwell until they closed and now I'm going to Fondren." This was a lie. He had in fact just left Fondren, according to the police scenario.

"There are three footnotes that I've just absolutely got to get tonight so I can give it to Karen tomorrow morning," Railey continued, apparently referring to his secretary. "Fondren's open until about 2 o'clock, so I'm going to go on up there and I should be finished about 12:30 or so. I'll be in about 1:00. If you want to, go ahead and lock the garage door and I'll park out front. It really doesn't matter to me at this point. My concern is that you're safe. . . ."

If indeed Railey had plotted murder and concocted a counterfeit alibi, this portion of the tape might explain why Peggy would leave the security of her home to enter the garage that night. Even so, Railey would still have to explain why, if he really intended to speak with Peggy at the time, he had called on the public line and left a message.

The taped call continued: "I don't have to go into the office until 9:30 for staff tomorrow so what I'm suggesting is go ahead and put the lock on the door if you wish. I'll park out front and come on in the front door. And then we'll go from there. Love you, dear. Bye-bye."

Twenty-three minutes later, Railey phoned the answering machine again and on this occasion gave the correct time: 12:29 A.M. One might wonder how Railey, who did not wear a watch, now knew the correct time. Just twenty-three minutes earlier, he put the time at no later than *10:45 P.M.*

"Hi, Babe," he began. "It's 12:29 and I'm on the way home from SMU. I am down to absolutely one footnote and that's Ellen Goodman with the *Boston Globe* and I'm gonna call her personally tomorrow morning. Everything really went well. I got a lot accomplished. I had to leave my card with the reference librarian because there was one deal that I couldn't quite work out. I'm not calling on the private line because I know you're already asleep, but in case you get up with the kids,

I just wanted you to know that I'm on my way home. It's 12:30. I'll be home about 12:45. Love you. Bye-bye."

Just past 12:40 A.M., Railey drove into his driveway. He said the garage door was partially open and, strangely, the garage was dark. The bulbs had mysteriously disappeared from the overhead light of the automatic door opener.

With his car lights on, he told police, he climbed from his car and found Peggy lying in front of her Chrysler. She was writhing and frothing at the mouth, her face blue and swollen. Yet her glasses were in place and her hair was still neatly combed. There was no sign of a struggle. There was no skin under her fingernails to indicate she had either fought her assailant or scratched herself when grasping at the wire or cord wrapped around her throat.

Railey said he determined that the children were safe and then notified the police. It was 12:43 A.M. when he spoke with the dispatcher.

"Dallas Emergency, Ms. . . . ." the dispatcher answered.

"This is Walker Railey," he interrupted. He gave his street address.

"What's the problem, sir?"

"Uh, I just came into the house and my wife is in the garage. . . . Somebody has done something to her and my children are on the floor."

The dispatcher repeated the street address back to Railey, who then pleaded, "Send the paramedics and police, please."

"Stay on the line with me," the dispatcher said. ". . . what street crosses Trail Hill on the corner?"

"Uh, it's, it's, it's between Audelia and, uh, White Rock Trail."

"Is it a house or an apartment?"

"It's a house. It's about four blocks north of Lake Highlands High School."

"Okay. What's your name, sir?"

"Walker Railey. R-A-I-L-E-Y."

Railey gave the dispatcher the unlisted phone number and she confirmed it.

"Okay. Has she been beat up or what?"

"I don't know. She's just laying on the floor of the garage. I just got here. She's foaming at the mouth or something."

"Okay. We'll get them out there."

"Please hurry."

"All right."

Diane Yarrington answered the phone at 12:45 A.M. and heard Railey's voice: "Diane, something awful has happened to Peggy. Come quick, come right now."

Railey then ran next door to the home of neighbor Charles Massoud. Awakening him, Railey blurted, "They have hurt my family!" When Massoud accompanied Railey back to the house, he found Peggy lying unattended on the concrete floor of the garage. Her face was swollen. She was foaming at the mouth and convulsing. Her legs were twitching.

Oddly, her clothing was not disheveled. Massoud noticed that Railey did not touch his wife when he knelt beside her. He did not caress, hold, or speak to her. Nor did he cover her with a blanket. Even more puzzling were other aspects of Railey's demeanor. Massoud realized the minister appeared only mildly upset and did not even ride in the ambulance with his wife.

Inside the house, the Railey children were in the living room, the 2-year-old watching a silent television screen and Ryan staring blankly ahead. By the time John and Diane Yarrington arrived, the ambulance was already there. Railey was holding his daughter. Ryan was sitting on the couch.

Mrs. Yarrington spoke to Railey briefly then said, "I'll take the children."

Railey turned to John Yarrington. "Don't leave me," he begged.

"I'll be here," his friend assured him.

Did either child see anything that night? Months later, Norm Kinne told a reporter he thought it possible that Ryan had witnessed the attack, but he said the youngster gave investigators inconsistent accounts of what might have happened that night.

"Maybe Daddy did it," he said once.

Part 8

After the stunning developments of mid-November, Railey

vanished from sight, though he continued to see Lucy almost daily. The *Times Herald* reported that he was spending Thanksgiving with friends in Houston and then intended to move to California in search of a job. "I know he has some job prospects," said John Yarrington.

His pending departure set off no alarms at the police department. Lt. Ron Waldrop explained, "He's refused to talk to us while he's been here, so his leaving shouldn't have any impact on our investigation."

In early December, Railey spoke again with religion editor Helen Parmley by telephone from California. He fled despair, not speculation, when he left Dallas, he maintained. And he was not abandoning his children. "I am not running away from my kids. Any parent wants, among other things, a stable, loving, and—in my case—Christian environment for their children to be reared in. In this case, while I am relocating, looking for work, financially strapped, not knowing where I'm going to end up or what I'm going to be doing, everybody involved in this drama believes . . . the most stable, loving, Christian environment they can be in is where they are."

As he had in the past when talking to Parmley, Railey refused to discuss the seriously flawed account of his activities on April 21 and 22, but he did elaborate a bit on his suicide attempt. He reasserted that it was not a premeditated act but resulted from a struggle with the "demons" within him. He said as he wrote in his journal that night he became "obsessed" with the struggle—Peggy's medical situation, worry about Ryan and Megan, "and a fear there was still someone out there that did that to Peggy. As the letter wore on, I gave in to those feelings and at the end of the letter, I stopped, took the pills, and laid down on my bed."

He indicated the suicide attempt had been misinterpreted. "It was not an admission of anything," he insisted. "It was only someone putting his soul on the sheet and in the process realizing he gave in to the deepest moment of despair he'd ever known."

Lucy Papillon would one day put the suicide attempt in a totally new light.

Before anybody could get too lathered up over Walker Railey's despair, a columnist named Laura Miller put the case in an entirely new perspective. Miller was hired by David Burgin, the mercurial and combative editor of the *Dallas Times Herald*, as a new weapon in his paper's fight with the larger *News*. Fresh from the *New York Daily News*, she was convinced that the Railey story was substantially more compelling than anything she'd been writing about in the Big Apple. She told her editor she wanted to write her first column on the Peggy Railey family and headed off to Tyler armed only with a lot of gall and a vague idea where the family lived.

Finally, near dark, and with a little luck, she located the family home in a small town outside Tyler. She was met at the door by Peggy's grandmother, Ella Renfro, who told her she did not want to be interviewed. But Miller talked her way inside the house and over tea and cheesecake interviewed not only the grandmother but, when he returned home, Peggy's father, Bill Nicolai.

Miller previously had dealt with the family of comatose heiress Sunny von Bülow and said she was "familiar with the extreme pain that a family goes through" when caring for someone in such a condition. "A family like the Raileys will always think and pray that she's going to open her eyes and recognize them," Miller said. And in their case, maybe hear Peggy say, "Walker did it." Miller said talking with Peggy's father and grandmother was an emotional experience for them all, including her. "I think they were happy to talk to some-one finally who felt as they did and who could express their opinion in the paper."

With barely a hint of journalistic restraint, Miller entered the Dallas newspaper war, telling the Railey story from the exclusive point of view of Peggy's family and punctuating the first column with her own anger and indignation.

> *Most people think Walker Railey did it.*
> *But then, most people aren't on the inside; they don't know the details of the police investigation. They rely on the newspapers. They listen to the gossip.*
> *Ella Renfro and Bill Nicolai don't have to rely on second-hand news. They're family. They're Peggy Railey's 87-year-*

old grandmother and Peggy Railey's soft-spoken father. *They know things most people don't know. They have a direct pipeline to the police. They sit right at Peggy's bedside. They mourn.*

And they think Walker Railey did it.

Until now, Peggy's family members have not discussed their feelings with the press. They have not staged, as Walker Railey has, any please-pity-me personal tours of the infamous garage on Trail Hill Drive. And they've never told a bald-faced lie that Walker told a magazine reporter, just a few months ago — that he and his in-laws are still good friends.

Well, Walker, not quite.

Sitting at Ella Renfro's small kitchen table one night last week, Bill Nicolai and his mother-in-law had no kind words for the man they have known for 18 years.

Sick man. Pathological liar. Egomaniac . . .

He's a real charmer, they said. A fake. Satan himself.

It's not just the obvious that pains them — like the 43 times Walker took the Fifth Amendment in front of the grand jury. Or his total lack of cooperation with the police. Or the now-famous "discrepancies" between what Walker claims and what the police know. Or the motive — the mistress.

Miss Butterfly. The brassy, busty Lucy Papillon.

Yeah, the motive. "A divorced man doesn't get to be bishop," says Ella . . .

But it's more than the obvious that pains her. And pains Bill. There are Walker's actions in the immediate aftermath of the assault, in those first horrible moments when countless tubes were stuck into his wife's nose and mouth and throat and arms. There he was, in the hallways of Presbyterian Hospital, constantly — blatantly, unashamedly — huddling with his girlfriend. Walking around with Papillon always at his side. Whispering to her, pulling her out of his in-laws' earshot.

Miss Butterfly had been no stranger to them. She had always been around the family. Peggy had told them she often accompanied Walker to church functions when Peggy didn't want to go. But they had never suspected she was his girlfriend. Peggy had never said that. To this day, they're not sure she even knew.

They do know she wasn't happy with her husband. The egomaniac. "I don't think he ever walked on water, but he probably tried," says Bill Nicolai. "He had a tremendous ego. But Peg knocked him down to size once in a while."

Bill stirs the cream into his coffee. He keeps looking away. It's hard for him to talk about some things. It's hard for him to admit, for example, that his son-in-law no longer calls to see how Peg is doing. Not since Thanksgiving, when he moved to California . . .

"He's a real SOB . . . ," says Ella. "I wouldn't call him if Peg died. I would not."

. . . the family worries that the police will never close the case. . . . The police tell them that everything that's anything is purely circumstantial at this point. As far as Ella is concerned, though, they should have arrested Walker on the way out of the grand jury room.

If this were a betting family, it is clear they would bet two things at this point: that if Walker Railey did do it, he orchestrated the assault but didn't commit it. He didn't wrap the wire around his wife's neck. He didn't watch her staring at him, wildeyed, knowing, clutching for breath, slipping into permanent senselessness. "He's too much of a coward to do it himself," says Bill.

The other thing they would bet is that whoever did do it is kicking himself for not finishing the job.

There have been no arrests, indictments or convictions. But Peggy Railey's family is taking no chances.

"I've told Billie Jo, 'Don't you ever let Walker go in there alone with Peg,'" says Ella. "Not ever."

Part 9

Laura Miller set the tone for her second column with this opening paragraph: "It's not hard to imagine what Walker Railey is doing out there in breezy, free-wheeling California: Walking on the beach. Making new friends. Necking with his best girl."

The column contrasted that vision of Railey with the painful but loving ritual Peggy's parents performed daily in caring for their daughter as she lay unconscious in the Tyler nursing home, her body alive but her brain dead.

"How do you stop hoping?" wondered Bill Nicolai. "We can't. We will always hope that one day she'll come out of it. She'll just wake up." There were no life-support machines pumping blood or air. If there were, Peggy's grandmother said she would be tempted to pull the plugs. "Peggy wouldn't want to be living like this. I know it," said Ella Renfro. "I'm old enough to know that there are worse things than death, and this is one of them."

Although Peggy shared a room, it was brightened by pictures of Ryan and Megan, by flowers and get-well cards, and by small personal items from the home with the pool on Trail Hill Drive. There were no photographs of Railey, her husband of sixteen years.

The Nicolais, fearing permanent emotional scars, would not permit Peggy Railey's children to visit her. While Megan is too young to comprehend, Ryan understands and remembers, his grandparents told Miller. The columnist wrote of the young boy: "He knows that someone has hurt his mother, and therefore he cannot be with her. But who knows what he has been told about his father. Maybe that 'Daddy's traveling' or perhaps more truthful, 'Daddy's hiding from everybody.' Or 'Daddy's with his girlfriend.' "

Ryan's grandparents said they believe Railey is gone for good and that the only sure way his son would see him again is if his father was brought back to Texas to answer to police. "And unless Walker Railey decides to talk, or, as Ella Renfro puts it, 'he stubs his toe,' " Miller observed, "there may never be an arrest. There may never be a case. And there may never be an ending to this painful story."

As the new year arrived, another extraordinary story on Walker Railey appeared in print. It was the work of Larry Wright, a contributing editor at *Texas Monthly* magazine in Austin. The interview on which Wright's story was based actually took place in late 1987 before Railey departed for the West Coast.

Wright grew up in First Methodist and his childhood pastor was Robert Goodrich, Jr., Lucy Papillon's father. His family and Lucy's family were friends. He left the church once in disenchantment but was drawn back by Railey's personal and socially contemporary ministry.

Wright had seen the devastation at First Methodist in the wake of the Railey disclosures, and he was now less a journalist than a confused and angry member of the congregation. He had lost his objectivity — it was not in the journalistic role that he confronted Railey. Furthermore, he was convinced Railey had gotten off too easily in his previous encounters with Dallas reporters. He wanted to tear away "the many veils of falsity and hypocrisy and get to the truth, whatever that was."

Wright disregarded all the rules Railey had demanded before the interview and intruded into areas where no other reporter had ventured. The interview extended from 9 A.M., through lunch, and long past his scheduled 6 P.M. return flight to Austin.

Wright and Railey were roughly the same age and there was a feeling of identity between a minister who wondered about becoming a writer and a writer who wondered what it would be like to stand in the pulpit.

"I know that you have a couple of layers of subjectivity that are influencing your writing of this story," Railey told Wright, "one having to do with your opinions about me and one having to do with your inner quarrels with the institutional church."

That was accurate. At that same time, Wright realized he and Railey were stalking each other with a growing sense of mission. Railey's mission — "old and habitual" — was to get Wright to believe in the church and in Railey himself.

Railey told Wright about seeing a psychiatrist for depression. He spoke of worry about the future. "For the first time in my life, at age 40, I have no earthly idea what, where, when, how, or anything else," said Railey. "Most of the reporters have written that I was drooling on my tie waiting to become a bishop, but that's not entirely true." Secretly, he said, he wanted to stay at First Methodist another decade and then take early retirement. After going to law school at age 50, Railey would open a practice in South Dallas for the underprivileged. Wright regarded that statement as gratuitous and unlikely.

"I had three books coming out in '88," Railey volunteered. "I was speaking all over the nation. I had been the *Protestant Hour* preacher — I'd just finished taping the sermons." Everything he had worked for was coming to pass.

"And now that's lost to you," said Wright. He asked why Railey thought it happened.

Railey did not respond directly, but said, "If I'm asking any question, it's how I can feel the presence of God's healing power in my life right now, when, for the first time in my life, I can't even tell you where I'll be tomorrow."

Railey offered Wright an abbreviated version of the events leading up to the discovery of his wife and then took the writer to the garage to show him firsthand. "I was actually horrified," said Railey. "I have never seen any such thing. Let alone my wife. Her face was purple and bloated, and her body was heaving from the waist up. Those were reflex actions. Seizures, I later came to realize. I tried to shake her, tried to get some kind of response . . . and I couldn't get anything and ran in and checked on the children." Megan was lying down in front of the television, which was on but muted. ". . . she was on the floor and my first impression was that she was dead," Railey said. "I picked her up and she said, 'Daddy.' " The child may have awakened to look for her mother, but Railey didn't think she had found her.

Wright wondered if Peggy's struggle with her assailant awakened the children, and he would later write: "The awfulness of that scene played unhappily in my mind, along with the dreadful suspicion that the person who caused this tragedy was the same polite preacher who was giving me the tour of his home."

Wright asked Railey about his relationship with his wife of sixteen years.

"Peggy was a lot quieter than me. We had a respect for one another. We were not the kind of couple that held hands and watched television on the sofa. When we went on vacations, before the children came, and went out to the beach, we'd take a book and read and listen to the seagulls and watch the waves." Railey said his wife "had a great love for the church, and the impression that she didn't enjoy being a pastor's spouse and stuff I think is unfair to her. She was a private person and didn't talk a lot about the inner parts of herself. I think her best friend on the face of the earth was her mother. I don't know how else to answer. We didn't have a lot of arguments."

Did Peggy know about the affair? Wright asked.

"We—that never came up."

She didn't know?

"I can only say it never emerged."

Did she suspect?

"I have no way of knowing, regarding that, that she suspected at all, about anything."

Railey reminded Wright he did not intend to discuss Lucy Papillon.

Wright was curious about suggestions that Railey leave Dallas to avoid embarrassment to the church and to the city. Railey said no one had to ask him to go. He would do so voluntarily.

Will Lucy join you?

"I don't care to answer that."

Changing the subject, Railey revealed he had slipped into the First Methodist sanctuary recently during funeral services for a family friend. Some of his former parishioners avoided him, but most embraced him. "They could feel my pain," he said, crying. He said he also felt love.

Did you feel a sense of shame? Wright asked.

Railey looked at him sharply, alert to insinuation. "I felt, probably, every emotion you could feel," he said.

But did you feel ashamed?

"I felt a great need to be forgiven, if that's what you're talking about."

Wright decided that was as much of a concession as he was likely to get. But before departing, Wright told Railey he could not construct an innocent man out of Railey's behavior. The journalist recounted the misleading testimony to the police, his avoidance of the grand jury, and his inexplicable actions on the night of the attack.

"I think you are a guilty person," said Wright.

"I hear what you're saying," Railey replied.

Wright did not know what to think. Railey failed to absorb his blunt accusation, choosing instead to analyze it with detachment. "I'm aware that nobody can sit down with all the facts that are supposedly known . . . and just make it all fit. That's a frustration that everyone has felt, including me," Railey said.

"Confess," Wright urged him. "It will haunt you forever, it will drive you crazy."

"I don't know if that's a word of advice, a backhand comfort, or what," said Railey. "I'm not guilty. I didn't do it. I don't feel tormented by the guilt of what I didn't do."

The night was crisp and not too cold, the best of winter in Dallas. The host and hostess spread tacos, *pico de gallo*, and *chile con queso* for their guests in the dining room, then all adjourned to the den. It was an up-scale but diverse group, none of whom knew Walker Railey personally.

The group kept up with the news, for the most part. If there were gaps in their knowledge of the Walker Railey case, a couple of journalists were present to fill in the blanks. Over drinks and before a crackling fire, the talk turned to the guilt or innocence of the former pastor of First Methodist Church.

Two powerful criminal attorneys, both veterans of sensational cases, argued either side. The question was: should Railey be indicted? The "indisputable evidence" was weighed — the lies, the gaps, the inconsistencies. There was no sign of struggle, meaning Peggy Railey possibly knew her attacker.

Circumstantial, yes, but compelling, the attorney for the state's case argued. "Some cases just need to be tried," he added.

The unanimous vote in the crowded den: indict Railey and bring him to trial.

Part 10

Highlights of the Walker Railey case, so intensely reported in Texas newspapers, were carried nationally from time to time by the wire services. But ABC Network's producers did not feel the story's full impact had been delivered to a national television audience. Its plan was to incorporate all the developments of the bizarre case in one package for a segment on its *20/20* program, to be aired in the spring. To add a new element to its report, ABC News was engaged in a behind-the-scenes effort to obtain tapes of the telephone messages Railey left on his answering machine the night Peggy was attacked.

The working title of the *20/20* segment was "Fall from Grace."

Although the press had quoted liberally from the transcripts, neither the 12:03 A.M. nor 12:29 A.M. recordings of April 22 had been made public — nor had the text of Railey's suicide note written a week after the attack on his wife.

Both the police and the DA's office refused a December request by ABC to release the tapes, maintaining they were evidence in a pending investigation. The network then sued the district attorney's office for access to the tapes and again was rebuffed, this time by a state judge who ruled the recordings were not public information as defined under the Texas Open Records Act. But the judge said in effect that investigators could use their own discretion in releasing such information.

ABC did not abandon its campaign; in early 1988, Norm Kinne, the DA's top assistant, was considering the ramifications of making the tapes public when the case suddenly took another unexpected twist. On February 2, Peggy's mother, Billie Jo Nicolai, filed a legal bombshell, accusing Railey of "maliciously" attempting to kill his wife and orchestrating a "clumsy attempt" to cover his actions with a phony alibi. The civil suit sought damages for "physical and mental pain, disfigurement, anguish, and physical impairment" on behalf of Mrs. Nicolai's ailing daughter. The suit further requested exemplary damages "to punish defendant Walker Railey for the brutal attack and to warn others like him of the economic consequences of such actions."

Mrs. Nicolai was not about to let the "other woman" off the hook, pointing out in the suit that while Peggy "was at home faithfully taking care of her duties as wife and mother, Mr. Railey went to visit his lover, Ms. Lucy Papillon, who lives near the SMU campus." The suit alleged that Railey appeared briefly at SMU's Bridwell Library and then, between 9 P.M. and 11 P.M., returned home.

"It was there that he intentionally, knowingly, and brutally attempted to strangle his wife, Peggy Railey, to death," the suit said. "Thinking Mrs. Railey was dead, he left her on the garage floor of their home. Thinking only of himself and callously leaving his two precious children, Ryan, five years old, and Megan, two years old, in the house alone with a comatose mother, Walker Railey then drove to the Fondren Library at SMU in a clumsy attempt to conceal his actions and to establish a false alibi."

Bill Arnold, Mrs. Nicolai's attorney, did not know if Railey could afford damages that might total millions of dollars, but he intended to find out. "That's something Mr. Railey is going to have to tell me when I talk to him," he said.

Unlike criminal lawsuits, a civil suit does not require proof beyond a reasonable doubt. Only what lawyers call "a preponderance of credible evidence" is needed for a defendant to be held liable for damages. Furthermore, a defendant's refusal to testify in a civil case can be considered as evidence against him.

"If, through discovery, facts come out that could help law enforcement, we're duty-bound to communicate those facts," Arnold said. "But that's not the purpose of the suit." Concern over the cost of Peggy's medical expenses was the overriding reason for the action, but the family's decision was also emotional. "They are bitter," said Arnold. "They are angry."

Ted Nicolai, Peggy's younger brother, told reporters he was convinced that Railey was the assailant and declared, "I don't want him to be able to turn his back on what's happened." Nicolai revealed that Railey had visited Peggy no more than three times since she was moved to Tyler. Railey showed up to see the two children at Christmas, but Nicolai said Ryan suffered severe emotional problems afterward. Ryan had a stuttering disorder even before the attack on his mother, but it had improved until the holiday encounter with his father, the boy's uncle said.

As a result of the setback, Nicolai said Ryan's psychologist told his guardians he did not want Railey to see his son during a trip to Dallas in mid-January. That episode added fuel to a rumor that young Ryan might have witnessed the attack on his mother.

Jack Taylor, the *Dallas Times Herald*'s crack investigative reporter, would later reveal that police had questioned the youngster about what happened that night but had gotten only inconsistent accounts. "Maybe Daddy did it," he said once.

Norm Kinne sent an investigator from the DA's office to question Ryan but she, too, was unsuccessful. The investigator and Ryan hit it off well and the youngster talked freely about almost everything. But whenever she asked about the night of the attack, Ryan would tune her out. He would turn his back and try to leave the room. He simply would not talk about it.

"I'm not discounting the possibility that this boy may have seen something **and** may at some point in time be able to tell someone what he did in fact see," Kinne said.

On the same day the Nicolai lawsuit was making headlines, Jack Taylor was back on the front page with a provocative story out of San Francisco, where Railey and Lucy Papillon were cavorting.

Taylor disclosed that Railey and his mistress had signed a one-year lease on a Victorian flat not far from San Francisco Bay in a neighborhood where apartments commanded monthly rents of up to $2,500. The rent for their new home reportedly was $1,600, and both had signed the lease.

The apartment was still largely empty of furnishings, although Railey had been seen moving in some possessions earlier in the week. Taylor said it appeared Railey was trying to avoid being traced to San Francisco because he had not applied for a telephone number, a California driver's license, or a San Francisco parking permit. Utilities for the apartment were not in his or Lucy's name.

According to the article, much of it substantiated by Norm Kinne, Railey and Lucy had made several trips back and forth between Dallas and San Francisco. On some weekends Railey would fly to Texas, while on others Lucy would travel to California. Whatever remorse they may have felt over Peggy's plight, they concealed it well.

The continuing relationship between Railey and the bishop's daughter raised quite a few eyebrows and no small number of disturbing questions. Assuming Lucy knew nothing about the attack on Peggy Railey, as she told grand jurors, what did she later learn from Railey, if anything?

How did he explain to her the inconsistencies in his story that fateful night and was there some explanation for the critical time conflicts exposed by the car phone records? Did she believe him innocent? Would she continue to see him if she believed him guilty?

"She's a little girl in a woman's body," a former friend of both Lucy and Railey told an Associated Press reporter. "She needs the love and she needs the attention, and I believe she's perfectly capable of convincing herself that Railey is innocent, whether deep down she believes it or not. I think we all want to minimize the pain, the disillusion, the loss of trust. I cannot tell you the incredible amount of pain this has caused, how many hearts have been broken."

Said the friend, a younger woman and no less attractive than Lucy: "I'm sympathetic to her needs, but she could have had any number of men. Why this one? And don't kid yourself for a minute. She initiated this affair."

Part 11

Initial attempts to notify Walker Railey of the civil suit brought by Peggy's relatives were unsuccessful. Investigators watched Railey's San Francisco flat for two days in a futile effort to find him and serve the legal documents.

Though Railey succeeded in dodging investigators, two competing reporters from Dallas were still on his trail. Jack Taylor of the *Times Herald* had identified Railey's whereabouts and told readers back home of his new surroundings. Olive Talley of the *Morning News* was in San Francisco, too, looking for the besieged minister.

It was not widely known outside the church that Talley had been a member of Railey's congregation, and the subject was not something she cared to discuss. But she had abandoned the church in disillusionment a short time after becoming involved in the Railey story. Now she had flown to California to track him down. She wanted comment on the Nicolai lawsuit, and she also wondered how Railey was spending his time. And there was something else. Despite all her reporting coups, she had never gone eyeball to eyeball with Walker Railey—and she was eager to do so.

Staking out the San Francisco apartment, she spotted him as he emerged one day. But instead of confronting him right away, she decided to follow at a distance. She'd heard he had found a job and she wanted to know where he worked. Thus she gambled and failed, losing him in traffic. Though she continued to watch his apartment, Railey did not return. Dejected and feeling guilty that she had blown her opportunity, Olive flew home without the story she wanted.

A week later, she verified a tip that he was staying in a motel near the San Francisco airport, and she hopped the next plane out of Dallas. Early the next morning, she found his car in the motel parking lot and waited. When Railey appeared, she did not hesitate. He recognized her at once. "No comment," he said, frowning.

"How do you know if you don't know what I want to talk about?" Olive shot back.

Finally, she persuaded him to talk, and they returned to the motel lobby for what resulted in a two-hour interview. She also offered him a copy of the lawsuit, but he refused even to look at it. She noted there was little trace of the bounce and vigor that had punctuated his spirited ministry. Bloodshot eyes reflected sleepless nights, and Railey's hands shook from the chill in the morning air.

Again he vowed his innocence. "I regret the lawsuit because it puts all the family—the Nicolai family and me—under an even added amount of pressure," Railey said. "My responses to the allegations in the suit are the same they have been all along: I'm not guilty of anything and don't have anything to fear on that point, but it's just another process we've all got to go through and I'll go through it appropriately and responsibly and totally."

He acknowledged that he had avoided his expensive apartment in favor of hotels and friends' homes since the suit was filed. But he said he did it because of harassment by news reporters and photographers. "I'm not trying to be a fugitive," he insisted. "I've got no reason to run away, but I feel like I'm being hounded by the press. I'm keeping a low profile because people are sitting out in front of my flat and I resent that. I know the press is doing its job and I'm just trying to live my life. At this point, there seems to be difficulty in making both of those things work."

Railey said he was not dodging the process servers but that he first wanted to discuss the suit with his attorney, Doug Mulder. And though Mulder maintained he was not involved in the civil issues, Railey said he continued to depend on his Dallas criminal lawyer for "legal guidance."

Railey declined to respond to Talley about the specific allegations in the suit, but he denied claims by the Nicolai family that he'd turned his back on his wife and children. "I didn't run away from my children. I didn't run away from anything. That's been terribly distorted in the press," he said. ". . . in the last ten months of my life, I've done the best I could do on every level of my life."

Railey spoke of the search for a job, the stress of living under a cloud of suspicion, and the pain of scrutiny into his private life as the media sought answers to the many questions swirling around the case. "I'm in a situation where my silence makes people wonder," he said. "When I talk, the way it's used also makes people wonder," he added, referring to interviews he had granted. "I'm kind of between the devil and the deep blue sea. And in a situation like that, it's hard to know what is the best, most honest and responsible way to respond."

He told Olive Talley he moved to the Bay area in search of a new life, free from inquisitive reporters, jeering neighbors, and what he described as a climate of guilt in Dallas. "I get the impression that most people's minds have been made up a fairly long time," he said. "I give the press credit for that. I was tried and convicted by the public media very early. . . . The climate in the city right now is such, with all the attention given this case, that I found it impossible to find a job, and impossible to go anywhere I didn't receive more attention than I felt comfortable in getting."

Unfortunately, he said, the same situation seemed to be developing in San Francisco, where newspapers also were picking up the story. But he was guardedly optimistic. "I feel like I'm going to make it work out here one way or the other, unless I'm publicized to impotence."

He criticized the *Dallas Times Herald* for listing his San Francisco address. "There's still somebody out there who attacked Peggy and, if that person was going after me, now that person has my address in San Francisco, and I resent that very much." Of course, he still had not talked with police, who could also be described as somewhat resentful.

Railey said he chose his new home because of its diversity and job opportunities: "There are a lot of educational institutions, nine seminaries, and the economy is good in the San Francisco area." He said he spent his time reading and walking. He was looking for a job, but he avoided meeting many people. "Given the last few months, I was looking for some good old, dull nonpublic life."

Yet he missed the pulpit. "When the organ prelude starts on Sunday morning, I miss the whole deal. You don't do that for twenty-two years and walk away from it under the circumstances and not feel like a part of you has been ripped away from you. But it's also teaching me how to listen to sermons instead of analyze them."

Railey said he was living off savings and his share of the equity from the sale of the Dallas house. He refused to reveal the amount of his monthly rent payments, rumored to be in the $1,600 range, but said he had given up golf and cut back on entertainment and food expenses. "But just like anybody else unemployed, when my savings and equity run out, I'll have no money," he said.

He had not lost hope for a brighter future. "If I went on like this for ten years, I couldn't make it. But I've always discovered that if you have a fairly reasonable ending to what you're facing, then you can handle it. I've always believed there is a glimmer of hope beyond the darkness of despair. And I haven't given that up."

If Walker Railey was unhappy to see Olive Talley, he would be mighty distressed to encounter Jack Taylor.

Taylor bore the title of investigative reporter, and he looked and lived the part. At 50, he was a generation older than Talley. He was a hard-nosed, no-nonsense chain smoker who played no favorites, including former employers. Using freedom of information statutes, he blocked the *Times Herald*'s previous owner from dissolving his pension plan and withdrawing the surpluses. He had a scrapbook of journalistic scoops dating back to 1962 when he joined the *Daily Oklahoman* in Oklahoma City.

Taylor's instructions at this point were uncluttered: find Walker Railey. He began by staking out Lucy Papillon's office in Dallas and one day followed her on a lunchtime excursion to a cafe on Greenville Avenue. He thought it odd that she purchased a sandwich and proceeded to eat it outside in the car. Then a nearby pay phone rang and Lucy scurried from her car to answer it. *That's got to be Railey*, Taylor guessed, *and they're probably setting up a rendezvous.*

After Lucy left, he collected the pay phone number and flew to San Francisco for a predawn visit to a motel near the airport where Olive Talley had spotted Railey. Railey had checked out, but Taylor persuaded the night clerk to show him the motel bill. It revealed a number of calls to Lucy at home and at her office and one to the phone booth on Greenville Avenue. Taylor ascertained that Railey had also telephoned three resorts up the California coast. Two of the calls were brief, but the third lasted three to four minutes. The longest call was to the Albion River Inn. Taylor concluded that would be Railey and Lucy's destination.

After contacting a San Francisco process server who also was looking for Railey, Taylor picked up a camera from a friend and headed up the coast. At the Albion River Inn, he and companion Steve Adams spotted Railey and Lucy sitting on a bench outside their bungalow, sipping Coors beer in the sunshine. It was about 2 P.M.

The process server could have jumped out and caught Railey right then, but Taylor talked him out of it. He wanted pictures of the couple on their Valentine's Day weekend retreat. Like Olive Talley before him, Taylor gambled and lost.

Masquerading as tourists and shooting pictures of the ocean, the two men moved in on their quarry. However, Railey and Lucy became suspicious and hurried into their cabin. There they stayed for twenty-two hours in a $140-a-night room. Though equipped with a Jacuzzi, it had no kitchen. They turned on no lights, and they answered only those phone calls screened by the inn's operator. When Adams knocked on the door and identified himself as a process server, there was no response. On Sunday night, Railey arranged for food to be sent in.

On Monday, a resort employee carried the couple's luggage to their car and Lucy got behind the wheel. Taylor said he saw Railey run from the cabin with a coat over his head and slump down in the car seat. As Lucy sped away, Adams attempted, but failed, to reach the car as it pulled from the cabin. Then he cut through a stand of trees and caught up with the car as it slowed to turn onto Highway 1. Running alongside, he identified himself and placed the legal papers under the windshield wipers.

"Mr. Railey," he puffed, "you're served."

Lucy would later maintain Railey was not in the car at the time.

Back in Dallas, assistant district attorney Norm Kinne said he was hardly an expert on civil process, "but I'm sure this constitutes good service."

Bill Arnold, the Nicolais' attorney, expressed delight at the news of Adams' success and said that, if Railey failed to respond to the suit within a month or so, a judge could decide if the notification was proper and grant a judgment by default.

Meanwhile, KXAS-TV in Fort Worth reported that Railey was insisting through attorney Doug Mulder that he was not in the car driven by Lucy Papillon. What appeared to be a person hiding under a coat in the front passenger seat was merely a bundle of clothes. According to Mulder, Railey told him he left the Albion River Inn in a pickup fifteen minutes after Lucy drove away. "Walker Railey is not going to testify in a trial, and no depositions will be given by Walker Railey," the lawyer declared. "I've told him to quit talking to the media and to stay lost."

Jack Taylor was unimpressed. "Fastest bundle of clothes in the West," he sniffed.

Part 12

Doug Mulder's admonitions to his client aside, the Walker Railey saga was about to go national. In New York, ABC's *20/20* program was putting the finishing touches on its presentation of "Fall from Grace."

Janice Tomlin, a *20/20* producer from Dallas, had monitored the story for months through her mother in Texas. Public opinion, she thought, had swung against Railey in Dallas after the grand jury furor. She decided this was indeed a national story even if it was not a national obsession.

"Either here was an innocent man who had lost everything, his wife, his children, his church, his home, and his reputation, or here was a guilty man who had not been prosecuted," she said. "It had to be one or the other. That was the bottom line."

Had the press convicted Railey? She didn't know. She wondered if the authorities were hounding an innocent man who had not been charged. She also thought the story had national potential because of its implications in the religious community. "This is one of the largest Protestant churches in the country," she said, "and with SMU, a major center for Methodism. This was a mainstream minister in a mainstream community who had national credentials and suddenly was being investigated as a suspect in the strangling of his wife."

For its presentation, *20/20* desperately wanted the Railey phone tapes, and Norm Kinne, with investigators' approval, now decided to surrender them. "It appears to me at this point in time the investigation is stymied," Kinne said. "I fail to see that releasing any of this information, whether it be the tapes or the suicide note, is in any way going to impair further investigation. I was concerned about that earlier. I'm not concerned about that at this point. I feel like this may very well be the last anyone is hearing of this and I want to fill in the blanks as much as I can," Kinne continued. "I think . . . everyone is entitled to know what has happened until right now."

The assistant DA worked out a deal to give print and other broadcast media besides ABC an even break on the release. It was an unusual decision, one for which he drew both praise and criticism, the latter from those who contended he once again was trying the Railey case in the press. Kinne expressed mock dismay. When he refused to release information, he was accused of a cover-up, Kinne told reporters. When he provided it, he was accused of using the press to prosecute Railey.

"You guys are never satisfied," he grumbled.

An estimated half-million households in the Dallas–Fort Worth area watched the *20/20* show on WFAA-TV, the local ABC affiliate. That was about double the normal viewing audience for the weekly show. The saga of Walker Railey clearly was a ratings hit.

Railey declined an invitation to appear on the show, but ABC incorporated footage from a WFAA-TV interview that showed him denying involvement in the attack on his wife. While the network presentation contained no real surprises, it was crisp and factual, yet assembled and presented in such a manner as to be entertaining and informative and most definitely provocative.

Media critic Ed Bark of the *Dallas Morning News* called it meticulously fair, thorough, and gripping. He said the Railey segment "wields the formidable power of TV's pictures in weaving a spellbinding tale of crime still awaiting punishment." The TV critic for the *Times Herald*, David Zurawik, described the ABC show as "mainly second-hand journalism crafted into almost first-rate prime-time melodrama."

True, ABC was the catalyst for release of the phone tapes. But the Dallas newspapers had covered the case so thoroughly that any subsequent media accounts *had* to be largely second-hand. And though Zurawik later grumped a bit about other local media being hustled by the ABC publicity machine, he concluded it was "not worth getting that mad about."

The end result of the *20/20* show was that viewers around the country probably went away convinced that something extraordinarily evil occurred in Dallas in April 1987 and that Walker Railey's response was at best disturbing and frustrating.

Sara Ivey, a member of First Methodist, offered a more personal reaction: "To casual viewers, the story may appear

as a great mystery. To us, this story remains a human tragedy, whether we ever find out who committed the crime."

At one point in the show, Norm Kinne was asked bluntly
if Railey tried to murder his wife. His on-camera reply: "God
and Reverend Railey know that, not me."

At another point, Kinne said the only thing he could prove
was that Railey lied when he claimed he was at the SMU
libraries all evening. Said Kinne: "I think without some sort
of explanation I could show that he was not where he says
he was at the time he says he was there; he was not making
phone calls at the time he says he was making phone calls.
This does not necessarily make him a strangler. When it gets
down to, 'Mr. Kinne, where is your evidence that he strangled his wife?'—I just don't have any."

As the *20/20* show ended, narrator Tom Jarriel observed,
"The case has left you, as a prosecutor, a totally frustrated
man."

That's right, Kinne conceded. "But I'm patient." The final
frame caught Kinne's face frozen in a blend of anger and de-
termination. Asked later about his "patience," Kinne frowned
and said, "I don't have a lot of choice."

Kidd Kraddick felt "ripped off."

The Dallas disc jockey had taken to the airways of KEGL
in 1987 after Peggy Railey was attacked. His original commentary was based on authorities' initial theory that she almost
lost her life because of her husband's preachments against
prejudice.

After watching the *20/20* program in the spring of 1988,
Kraddick was inspired to offer his substantial teenage audience
a new point of view. He wrote a satirical lyric he called "The
Railey Scam." Recruiting his fellow deejays and the station's
secretaries as vocalists, he recorded his epic in about fifteen
minutes. It was set to the tune of the theme from TV's *The
Brady Bunch*, a family sitcom in reruns, and it pulled no
punches.

> *Here's a story of a man named Railey*
> *Who screwed up a perfect plan to kill his wife.*
> *He blew his alibi on his car phone;*
> *He's running for his life.*

Here's the story of a lovely lady
Who was seeing Walker Railey on the side,
Then they came up with a great idea,
So she could be his bride.

Till the one day when they watched 20/20,
And he knew that he was really in a jam.
Now the whole world thinks he's guilty,
That's the way it came about — the Railey scam.

The Railey scam,
The Railey scam,
That's the way he screwed it up,
The Railey scam.

The tune got a tremendous response. At its peak, disc jockeys were fielding 200 to 300 requests a day on "the Eagle," as KEGL was known. Kidd Kraddick wanted to go to San Francisco and park the station's van in front of Railey's apartment to do a radio show. The scheme was to take along a couple of listeners as Railey spotters, set up a vigil, and turn the whole affair into a contest.

"He's lucky he picked the time he did to get out of town," said Kraddick.

Precisely one year after the events of April 1987, a state district judge ruled that Walker Railey "intentionally, knowingly, maliciously, and brutally attempted to strangle his wife" and to cover up his actions with a "false alibi."

Judge John Whittington issued a preliminary civil judgment on April 22 holding Railey financially liable for the injuries to his wife. The extent of damages would be determined later by a jury. The ruling, while significant, had no bearing on the criminal investigation and probably drove Railey even deeper into seclusion. Whittington's action came after Railey failed to respond to legal notices of the civil suit filed by his mother-in-law, Billie Jo Nicolai. The judge said Railey, by his default, had admitted all the allegations set forth in that lawsuit.

To the surprise of no one, Railey could not be found for

a response. Under siege by the media in San Francisco, he and Lucy Papillon broke the lease on their so-called love nest and fled. For months afterward, it was said that Railey maintained contact through a post office box in San Francisco and that he appeared in person from time to time to pick up his mail. There were other reports he headed south to Los Angeles.

Bill Arnold, the lawyer representing Peggy's mother, said the judge's ruling provided him authority to call Railey as a witness. However, since he did not know Railey's whereabouts, it was a hollow victory. "The court can issue a subpoena that compels him to come answer my questions," Arnold said. "But today I have less of an idea where he is than at any time since this case started." If Railey refused to respond to a subpoena, Arnold intended to request that a warrant be issued for his arrest. "Then the police have to find him," he said.

Judge Whittington's ruling was the first successful step in Arnold's campaign to make Railey financially accountable for his wife's medical expenses, plus whatever punitive damages a jury might assess. The final step, he said, would be to collect those damages, "if possible." Arnold had no private knowledge of Railey's finances. "All I know is that he has been living a very comfortable lifestyle in one of the nicest areas in San Francisco and traveling back and forth. And the money's gotta be coming from somewhere."

With Railey on the run, Arnold moved in on a less elusive but equally reluctant target, Lucy Papillon, whom he subpoenaed at her Highland Park home. She was ordered to appear in his office on May 18 to give a sworn deposition and produce any and all documents relating to her "relationship with Walker Railey . . . and the attack on Peggy Railey." Said Arnold: "It's my understanding that she communicated with Mr. Railey on several occasions the night Peggy Railey was attacked, and I want to ask her about it."

Through her lawyer, Lucy asked Judge Whittington to quash the subpoena. She contended she had been "subjected to much undue, harsh, and adverse publicity in the past" and that "additional publicity will exacerbate damage already done to her personal and professional reputation and disrupt and inure her ability to earn a living."

In opposing her motion, Arnold insisted that a jury would be entitled to hear all the underlying facts and circumstances of the case. "The way I look at the law is that she's a witness and Peggy Railey has a right to have her cross-examined," he said. "One of the issues for the jury is punitive damages or punishment damages, and to do that, a jury must look at Walker Railey's state of mind." Lucy Papillon, he declared, "is one witness who has knowledge of the underlying facts of the night of the assault, as well as the motives."

On May 18, Whittington heard arguments from opposing lawyers and ruled that Lucy Papillon's sworn testimony was relevant in helping determine the amount of damages Railey should pay for the attack on his wife. In denying the motion to quash the subpoena, the judge said, "It is relevant . . . what the motivation of Walker Railey was when he did the acts he admitted he did." Railey had admitted nothing in person, but the judge was referring to the admission by default for Railey's failure to answer the civil suit. "A relationship with another woman," the judge continued, "would be germane to his motivation, so the inquiry is therefore appropriate." Whittington gave Lucy seven days to produce the records sought by Arnold, who was unmoved by Lucy's problems.

"When you compare Peggy Railey lying in a coma in Tyler, Texas, to a witness being inconvenienced," said Arnold, "I think Ms. Papillon's concern about inconvenience in the judicial system kind of pales to insignificance."

Part 13

In June, doctors detected a slight improvement in Peggy Railey's condition, and she was returned to Dallas and placed in the Baylor Institute for Rehabilitation. Dr. William Parker, the institute's medical director, said she could turn her head and hear, but could not assimilate what she heard. "If we can establish anything that seems to stimulate a response that could be interpreted as functional, then we would continue to try, through repetition, to improve on that," he said.

Parker said he didn't think his team of twelve specialists

and therapists would be able to determine with certainty whether Peggy would ever communicate again. "There's no total way to tell," he said. "I can't say that she will never, no. I think the odds are probably going to be against it, but time is the only thing that's going to tell."

Parker later said Peggy could certainly live another thirty years and estimated that her medical expenses would exceed $4.3 million during that time. From Peggy's share of the equity in the Railey home and a savings account, her parents had received several thousand dollars from Railey, but it was a pittance compared to the money that would be needed when Peggy's insurance expired in September 1989.

"We do not know what we'll do after that," her mother said.

After two months in Dallas, Peggy was quietly returned to the nursing home in Tyler, where her parents resumed their tender, but apparently hopeless, daily care. Doctors had downgraded her condition to a "persistent vegetative state," meaning, as a neurosurgeon explained, that her chances for recovery were "nil."

Peggy was now breathing through a device inserted into her throat. She took nourishment through a tube inserted above her abdomen. Her dark hair was cut short and her face was puffy and lifeless. Although she could hold her head up for short periods, she had a perpetually vacant and haunting look in her eyes. Her jaws made chewing movements and her mouth contorted into a silent scream or soundless howl as therapists performed the painful exercises to prevent her limbs from locking into immobility.

Mysteriously, Peggy seemed to communicate somehow with her sister-in-law, Linda Nicolai. Sometimes Peggy appeared to respond when Ted's wife called her name. One day Linda took Peggy in a wheelchair to the solarium at the Baylor Hospital rehabilitation center. Returning, they passed a man using an exercise cord similar to what police believed Peggy's attacker used to choke her. Linda watched in horrified awe as Peggy became agitated. She even began sweating, hyperventilating, and rubbing her arms together. Her eyes started dilating and a wild look crossed her face. Tearfully recalling the incident, Linda Nicolai said, "She kept looking at me and trying to say something."

After more than a year with John and Diane Yarrington, the Railey children had made a remarkable adjustment to their new environment. They called the Yarringtons "Mommy" and "Daddy" and referred to their real father as "Walker." Sometimes, when his father called, Ryan Railey would ask, "When are you coming to my house?"

Said Diane of Ryan: "This is his house. This is his family. He's perfectly willing for Walker to come and visit, but he doesn't cry when he leaves. He doesn't cry for him to come. He's happy for him to come. He loves him."

In late August, John Yarrington resigned as minister of music at First Methodist and revealed that he had just completed a three-month leave of absence for medical reasons. He told religion editor Helen Parmley that the church had granted him leave to seek professional medical help. Since then, he said, he had been under the care of a psychiatrist for depression, which he had overcome.

Yarrington did not mention the stress of caring for the Railey children, now ages 6 and 3, but he did say that after "a year and a half of our life being so public," he decided to leave the church and pursue another career. He did not say what that career might be, but he insisted that leaving the church was "a good decision for us."

It was not certain Yarrington left his post voluntarily. The church did not comment publicly about his departure, but there were rumors that the problems of Walker Railey's confidant and onetime minister of music ran deeper than depression.

Whatever her judicial inconveniences, Lucy Papillon continued her psychology practice into the fall amid rumors that her romance with Railey had cooled somewhat. News media interest in the Railey affair had also subsided.

Norm Kinne had lost track of the former minister of First Methodist, but he hadn't forgotten him. "This guy's a liar," he said. "He's trying to cover his tracks. He wasn't where he says he was at the time of the attack. Now, the question is, if he wasn't there, where was he?"

Judge Whittington set a trial date for the Nicolai damage suit, but nobody seemed optimistic that it would come off as scheduled. Although Railey's whereabouts were unknown, there was no question Lucy would be the star of the legal show. She was, in fact, a genuine celebrity.

In late summer, she appeared at the Tom Thumb store in the Old Town shopping center. The supermarket was near her home in Highland Park. It enjoyed a reputation as a meeting place for Dallas singles on the prowl. "She came strutting into the store like Queen Elizabeth," reported a housewife named Ellen Cabluck, who was in the store at the time. "You could hear necks snap all over the place. It was like a magic spell had been cast over the place. Everyone recognized her from her two hundred and fifty thousand pictures in the paper."

Lucy had fixed her face and her hair for the afternoon outing and she wore a casual purple day dress with a low scoop neckline that brought work to a halt. Although no one spoke, all eyes followed the shapely blonde as she collected four or five bags of groceries, filling her shopping cart mostly with breakfast items and flowers.

She moved through the store, according to Cabluck, looking "sexy and self-assured" and by no means unaware that her presence was causing a stir.

Lucy would emerge from the shadows again, presenting herself one day at the Dallas bureau of the *Fort Worth Star-Telegram*. She wanted copies of the newspaper containing an elaborate Associated Press serialization of the Railey saga that did not appear in the Dallas dailies. *Star-Telegram* reporter Ashley Cheshire spotted her standing in the doorway, blonde, coiffed, sunglasses in place, looking as if she expected something to happen.

Cheshire offered his hand and introduced himself. She offered hers but said nothing.

"What's your name?" Cheshire asked.

"I'm Lucy," she said.

"Ahhh, *the* Lucy."

"Yes. *The* Lucy," she said.

Cheshire wondered what to ask someone who had made a second career of avoiding answers. "Well, how're things going?"

"I would think you would know that as well as I," she said

coolly.

"You know," Cheshire pressed on, "I've thought a lot about this and I know it's been hard on both of you these past several months, but I can understand, too, how a lot of people in the community are really upset about what happened."

Lucy volunteered nothing except that things wouldn't have been so bad if the media hadn't gone wild. And then she was gone.

As the summer of 1988 ended, Olive Talley was pursuing other assignments, though her interest in the Walker Railey case had never subsided. She was becoming less optimistic the truth would ever be exposed. "If I had a wish, it would be that this case is someday solved," she said. "People think they know what happened, but given the string of bizarre events that make up this case, you can't take anything for granted."

Dark rumors continued to surface about Railey and others linked to the events of 1987, and at least three books about the tragedy were in the works. Yet the case remained a mystery, and any number of questions remained unanswered about Walker Railey's double life.

"Almost every aspect of this case has not turned out to be what it appeared at first," said Talley, who knew as much as anyone about its complexities. "Though circumstantial evidence makes you think you know what happened, I will never take anything at face value again. Ever."

And what of the enigmatic Railey himself?

His former colleague and friend Spurgeon Dunham observed early on, "In Greek tragedy, the actors wore masks so that people far away could see their expressions, and those masks are called 'persona.' If you probe enough people who had a relationship with Walker, it's hard to find anyone who knew Walker Railey without *some kind of mask*, even in those moments where there seemed to be so much intimacy."

Before the tragic spring of 1987, when his career knew no limits, Walker Railey delivered a sermon that began with an anecdote from his childhood.

"It's a lot of fun to play hide and seek, but it really gets scary if you fear you've been lost forever," he said, recalling how a game became frightening when his playmates gave up on finding him. "We are human, and as a result we frequently mess up life. And, because in our weaker moments we tend to fashion God in our image instead of remembering we were fashioned in God's image, we think we are too bad for God to love, or else that we are too far gone for God to want us at all. We let our guilt hide us from God."

But, Railey told his flock, "God's love is a hunting love, and it will track us down regardless of where we go or what we do." He neglected to add that God's vengeance, described by Old Testament prophets, could be a hunting vengeance as well.

"It's been a bad year for preachers," reflected Norm Kinne one summer morning as he scanned the newspaper and puffed on his pipe. He spoke first of a Baptist preacher who had just been arrested for rape, but his attention soon turned to Walker Railey. "The conclusion that everybody's drawn is that he was home choking his wife. But that doesn't necessarily follow. There's no proof he was at the scene at the time she was strangled. There's no evidence that he strangled her or that he knew who strangled her or that he arranged or participated in any way."

And therein lay perhaps the most haunting element of the Railey case. The essential truth might, in fact, be close at hand. But, in the view of the Dallas district attorney's office, there was no way by early 1989 to get to it through the criminal justice system. The case against Walker Railey at that point was circumstantial, at best. Not a shred of hard evidence linked him to the attack on his wife. No fingerprints, no witnesses, no weapon. Nothing.

Under civil law, Railey admitted brutalizing his wife when he ignored the Nicolai damage suit. But the civil rulings could not be used against him in any potential criminal action. Still, Norm Kinne seriously considered bringing the preacher to trial for attempted murder. Texas prosecutors, armed only with circumstantial evidence, win convictions all the time.

Kinne visualized going before a judge and jury in criminal court and presenting the evidence regarding Railey's activities the night Peggy was attacked. He could portray Railey as a liar and a fornicator and, with Lucy Papillon's testimony, establish the most basic of motives for what was almost the perfect crime.

Although prosecutors are not required to prove motive in Texas courts, it would be a critical tactic in the Railey case. The presence of a motive might offset or obscure the absence of physical evidence and could expose a major hole in the Railey defense. It would be doubtful that the defense could point to anyone other than Walker Railey who had a motive to kill his wife.

A crucial point in such a trial would be getting Railey's suicide note before the jury. In Texas, mere flight is evidence of guilt, and the argument could be made that suicide is not only an alternate form of flight, but certainly a permanent one.

Prosecutors would have to explain away the scarcity of evidence tying Railey to the garage on Trail Hill Drive that night. They could argue that the assailant would be expected to strike in the dead of night at a secluded place, one with little likelihood of witnesses. And the intruder would want a weapon that couldn't be traced as easily as a handgun or a knife. After all, it was not a crime of passion, the prosecution would argue, but a well thought out, calculated, cold-blooded attack, planned at least as far back as the first threatening letter.

In closing arguments, the prosecution could hammer away at Railey's own revelations in the suicide note: *The lowest of the low, the baddest of the bad.*

Given the opportunity, state's attorneys would no doubt focus on Walker Railey, the "two-worlder": the shepherd ministering to his flock at First Methodist and the Railey no one knew—the liar, the charlatan, the adulterer. It is the darker side that would be put on trial, the smug, arrogant Railey capable of doing these horrible things. They would paint a graphic picture of how he was spending his spare time away from the pulpit.

Here was a man, they would argue, who abused his wife, his children, his church, his community, and the people who put their trust and faith in him. One could imagine the DA's thundering conclusion: "It is time for the jury to tell Walker Railey that enough is enough!"

But there was at least one serious flaw in all this, which Norm Kinne pointed out in discussing the trial scenario he visualized. Assuming, he said, that all his evidence was admissible, he would get it before the jury and then rest the state's case. The defense would move at once for an instructed verdict of not guilty, arguing that his evidence failed to prove the state's case.

"Mr. Kinne, where is the evidence that he choked his wife?" the judge would ask. "Proving that he is a liar is not proving a criminal offense. That's not what he's charged with. Where's the evidence that he choked his wife?"

Kinne has no response. The motion for an instructed verdict of *not guilty* is granted. Walker Railey strides out of the courtroom, a free man. Furthermore, he would be beyond future prosecution, should new and more incriminating evidence turn up. The legal system's prohibition of double jeopardy would preclude him from being tried again for the same crime.

"Not that a jury wouldn't convict him," Kinne said. "They would. I think they would based on the fact that he's lying about all this stuff. Of course, that's not evidence that he choked his wife." Even if a trial judge was inclined to deny an instructed verdict, a jury could acquit Railey because of the state's fragile case. An acquittal could prevent further prosecution, as could a conviction eventually overturned by a criminal appeals court.

"I think a judge would be right in an instructed verdict of not guilty, and it would never get to a jury," said Kinne. "And if a judge ever did let it get to a jury and the jury did convict, I have no doubt that the court of appeals would reverse it. And they would be right."

Despite some grumbling, no one publicly quarreled with the decision not to prosecute Railey. Of course, no one knows better than a prosecutor that the longer a case goes without a trial, the colder the trail grows. Witnesses die, forget, or lose interest. Evidence vanishes or is destroyed. But despite a lengthy lull in the Railey case, Norm Kinne did not surrender hope for a breakthrough. He knew the possibilities were remote, but at least conceivable.

Lucy Papillon might eventually shed new light on the case, although Kinne said he knew of nothing that would incriminate her "since we don't have adultery laws anymore." Perhaps Ryan Railey did see something and someday would be able to talk about it. Best of all, Peggy Railey could miraculously recover and identify her assailant.

Possibly, someone was hired to commit the crime and the authorities would hear from that person. Railey himself might provide the missing pieces. Even so, experience had taught Kinne that the pangs of conscience come early in the game, and the Railey case was long past that. Railey himself had dropped out of sight, and police were not looking for him.

"The last thing you would expect from a guy like him," said Kinne, "would be to give up his wife and kids and flit off to California. Just say to hell with it and take off. It's just not what you would expect from a man of his stature. It gives every indication of guilt, whether he is guilty or not."

Epilogue

On December 5, 1988, twenty months after the assault on Peggy, the Railey case finally surfaced in open court, if only through her parents' civil lawsuit. And it was only fitting that it did so in a majestic old courtroom across the hall from the room where Jack Ruby was convicted of killing Lee Harvey Oswald twenty-four years before.

The symbolic issue was the extent of Railey's financial liability to Peggy's family, but the more compelling subject was Lucy Papillon's love affair with Railey and what role that romance might have played in the attack. Speaking above the din of downtown traffic and the intermittent wail of police sirens outside the window, attorney Bill Arnold struggled to convince Judge John Whittington that Walker Railey's obsession with Lucy drove him to a bizarre murder scheme that ran amok.

Railey, wherever he was, again chose to spurn the court proceedings. Lucy was less fortunate but hardly intimidated. At mid-afternoon, she showed up wearing an off-white turtleneck knit dress, matching boots, and a look that would ice over a Christmas hearth. If she was nervous about her imminent testimony, she camouflaged it well.

Judge Whittington gazed across the partially filled courtroom and told the hushed audience he would not tolerate any displays of hostility toward the witness. He instructed his bailiff to oust any offenders, but there would be none. Peggy's parents, Bill and Billie Jo Nicolai, glared at their son-in-law's frosted-blonde mistress with silent fury.

Arnold, 36, his anger evident, wasted little time on courtesies and moved swiftly to the origin of Lucy's relationship with Railey. He confronted her with the sworn but previously secret deposition she had given in the case, using its contents like a sledgehammer. He also had in his arsenal a detailed statement she gave Dallas police in July 1987.

Lucy testified she had turned to Railey for solace as her father lay dying in a Dallas hospital. After the bishop's death in October 1985, she continued to visit Railey's office for consultation. In the spring of 1986, they met at a park along Turtle Creek, a lazy little stream that winds through an idyllic patch of greenery near downtown Dallas. Arnold then zeroed in on the conclusion of a June rendezvous.

"Did you and Mr. Railey go to your home?"

"Yes."

"Did you and Mr. Railey have intimate relations at your home?"

"Yes."

". . . is it fair to say that from June of '86 until the attack on Peggy Railey on April 21 of 1987 you met with Walker Railey at your home on an average of three times a week?"

"Yes."

"Did you have intimate relations regularly on these thrice-weekly meetings?"

"Yes."

"Did you and Mr. Railey sometimes drink champagne in the afternoon when he was at your home?"

"Occasionally."

"Did you have intimate relations with Walker Railey one week before the attack on Peggy Railey?"

"Yes."

". . . now did the seriousness of your relationship with Mr.

Railey manifest itself on the trips you took together?"

"We did take some trips."

"In July '86, approximately one month after you say the romantic relationship began with Mr. Railey, did you travel to London to be with him?"

"Yes."

Arnold sought to show such liaisons occurred while Railey was conducting church business and, in this instance, was returning from a church conference in Africa. Lucy was evasive, prompting the lawyer to growl, "He didn't go to Africa on safari, did he?"

The attorney brought out that Lucy and Railey had sexual encounters while Railey was on "spiritual business" in London, San Francisco, and Atlanta and also in Austin, Texas, Wichita, Kansas, and Conway, Arkansas. He also forced Lucy to admit she shared Thanksgiving and Christmas dinner with Railey, Peggy, and the two children, then vacationed with him in California in January.

"Did you have intimate relations during that week?"

"Yes."

In Atlanta, Lucy confirmed, she and Railey shared sex after he taped a sermon to be delivered to a national audience on *The Protestant Hour.*

Interrupting his interrogation at one point, Arnold read from Lucy's statement to the police: "My relationship with Walker Railey is serious. In the past, we have discussed in a hypothetical way what we would like to do someday such as moving to California or New York. I believed that my relationship with Railey would be long-term and believed that eventually Railey also wanted it to be a long-term relationship. Railey has theoretically discussed divorcing his wife and I considered him to be sincere. Railey did not plan to bring his children with him to New York or California in the event that they divorced. . . ."

Then there was this brash and revealing comment by Lucy: "Railey and his wife did not have an intimate relationship and Railey did not long for such a relationship before he had me because he did not know what he did not have."

Lucy said she never gave Railey an ultimatum about divorce and maintained that Peggy never learned of her ongoing affair with Railey.

Arnold next sought to show that Railey could not divorce Peggy and marry Lucy without jeopardizing his chances of advancement in the church. The lawyer offered the witness several scenarios. "One is that Walker Railey stops seeing you. Another is that he might divorce Peggy and you could get married . . . and if that happened, it might conceivably have an adverse effect on his becoming a bishop. Another scenario is that he divorces Peggy and decides to stop seeing you. . . . Another scenario is that Peggy mysteriously dies, killed by a white supremacist because Railey has spoken against racism, leaving him with a sympathetic role, free to marry you without loss of respect and . . . free to become a bishop."

Lucy's reply to Arnold's suggestions was inaudible.

Recounting the occasions when she and Railey traveled together and the intensifying nature of their relationship, Arnold asked, "And then approximately four days before the attack on Peggy Railey, you are with him for three or four nights at the Doubletree Inn here in Dallas while he has sent Peggy and the children away to be with her parents. Is that accurate?"

There was an affirmative mumble from the witness chair.

"In your deposition, you were asked this question: "Ms. Papillon, have you ever considered the fact that your relationship with Mr. Railey was increasing . . . right up until April of '87, the time of Peggy's attack? Have you ever thought somewhere in the back of your mind that there might be some connection? Your answer was, 'No, not once.' "

Arnold paused and then inquired, "Is that still your answer today?"

"Yes, it is."

Lucy testified that Railey telephoned her twice the night Peggy was attacked. "Railey indicated he was real stressed out and wanted to come by my home." Although mobile phone records and a witness at Southern Methodist University indicated her timing was a little off, she thought he arrived at 7:30 P.M. and left at 8:45 P.M. "Railey told me that he had a nine o'clock appointment at the library regarding footnotes for a book he was writing. While at my home, Railey had lain down, which caused his clothes to be wrinkled when he left. Railey's hair was also somewhat askew."

She said Railey called her again at approximately 11 P.M. He said he was at a pay phone in Fondren Library and wanted to return to her house. "However," said Lucy, "I was tired and we decided it was too late." She indicated they spoke again by phone at 11:35 P.M.

"You have no personal knowledge of where Walker Railey was when he allegedly left your house at 8:45 P.M. until you say he called you at approximately 11, do you?" asked Arnold.

"He told me he was at the library."

"I asked you — to your personal knowledge — what you saw with your own eyes."

Lucy said she had no personal knowledge of Railey's whereabouts during that time. "I didn't see him," she said.

After the attack, she said, she visited Railey at Presbyterian Hospital three times while he kept a suite near his ailing wife. Once she brought him a single red rose. They embraced and kissed.

"When I saw Railey in the hospital, there was no change in his feeling toward me," she said. However, she told him she was flying to San Francisco to see another man.

"That wasn't true, but I told him that." Two days later, Railey locked himself in his hospital suite and tried to end his life. After the suicide attempt, Lucy was questioned by FBI agents about her romantic involvement with Railey. At first, she denied it, but later told them the truth.

"And you continued your relationship, is that true?" Arnold asked.

"Yes."

"Sometimes . . . at your house here in Dallas?"

"Yes."

"And there were times when you and he would be together and you would back out your driveway and he would duck down in the car until you were far enough away. . . . Is that true?"

She indicated it was. She also confirmed that Railey sometimes used a fictitious name when they traveled.

Moving on to Lucy and Railey's grand jury appearances in July 1987, Arnold asked, "Did he tell you after this tes-

timony that he took the Fifth Amendment before the grand
jury when asked a question about his whereabouts on the night
of the attack on Peggy Railey?"

"Actually, yes."

"Now, before you and he appeared together before the
grand jury, did you and he take a trip to San Francisco
together? Did you and he spend four days and stay at the
St. Francis Hotel?"

"We went to San Francisco. I don't remember where we
stayed."

Lucy told Arnold she had no clue why the threatening letters preceding the attack on Peggy were written on the typewriter at First Methodist, nor did she seek an explanation
from Railey during any of their many encounters.

Arnold was not satisfied, resurrecting a question he had
posed during Lucy's deposition. "Have you ever said, 'Walker,
can I just ask you something? Isn't it strange to you that these
letters were on a church typewriter in a room to which you
had access?' Have you ever in some moment asked Walker
Railey that? And your answer was, 'No. Never have.' Is that
a fair and accurate statement of your testimony?"

". . . yes," Lucy replied.

Arnold was curious about the apartment Lucy and Railey
leased in San Francisco, the shared costs of furnishing it, the
Christmas they spent together there in 1987, and the Valentine's Day trip to the Albion River Inn in northern California. She insisted Railey was not in her car when the process
server with reporter Jack Taylor slapped a notice of the Nicolai
lawsuit on her windshield.

"Now I've heard reports," began Arnold, "that Mr. Mulder, the current defense attorney for Walker Railey, said there
was a pile of laundry next to you on the front seat of that
red vehicle you were driving out of the Albion River Inn.
Is that correct?"

"I don't know what Mr. Mulder said. It was a suitcase."

"Did that suitcase have a little bald spot on top of it?"

Arnold's reference to Walker Railey's receding hair got the
only laugh of the day from the courtroom audience, but no
response from Lucy.

"In March of '88, did he finally come to Dallas to see you?"

"Yes."

"During that trip, did he ever tell you that he'd gone to see Peggy?"

"He didn't say."

". . . the subject of Peggy and the children never came up in your conversation when you were with him in March of '88?"

"That's true."

As Arnold pressed on with his chronology, Judge Whittington reminded him that his questioning should be confined to a year before and a year after the attack on Peggy. The judge had ruled that anything not within that interval was irrelevant to the civil lawsuit. Arnold took a shot in the dark anyway, asking Lucy if she knew where Railey was currently living.

"I choose not to answer that," she purred.

Returning to the time frame allowed by the judge, Arnold brought out that Railey gave Lucy birthday gifts in September 1987 and the following Christmas.

"In Christmas of 1987, when Peggy Railey was in a nursing home in Tyler, Texas, all the clothes she had was a hospital gown. Was Walker Railey giving you any more gifts . . . ?"

"Yes."

"He gave you a gold chain necklace?"

"Yes."

"He gave you a sweater he bought in San Francisco?"

"Yes."

"He gave you a black skirt he bought in San Francisco . . . and a black sweater?"

"Yes."

"Any more gifts that we haven't talked about?"

"No."

Arnold, Lucy, and the judge then debated the relevance, meaning, and timetable of Lucy's name change to Papillon and the symbolic metamorphosis involved. Finally, Arnold said, "You say it's French for butterfly. And that means a process of change. . . . Is that right?"

"Yes."

Arnold then produced four color photographs mounted on a large white board. Two pictures portrayed Peggy as a happy, smiling mother with her family. Another showed her lying in a hospital bed, her face puffy and her neck discolored by ugly red and purplish scars. The fourth showed her comatose with bandages around her neck and head.

"Here are some photographs of Peggy Railey with her family, her children, and photographs of her after the attack," Arnold said, his voice growing sinister. "Would you say that . . . Peggy Railey has had a metamorphosis in reverse? From something free to something that can't even crawl?"

"I don't want to answer that," Lucy whispered, her mask showing signs of cracking. "I don't choose . . . I don't know how to answer that."

"That's all," Arnold snapped.

Generally overlooked that day were the statements Lucy gave police on July 2, two months after Railey's suicide attempt and about a month before the grand jury furor. Although Arnold did not enter Lucy's deposition into evidence, he did offer the police statements. Afterward, an Associated Press reporter pried them out of Judge Whittington's reluctant staff. The most revealing segments dealt with Railey's fear that his affair with Lucy might one day be exposed and his concern over another man in Lucy's life.

"At one point, early in our relationship, in October or November 1986, Railey stated to me that he would kill himself if people in the church community ever found out about our relationship," Lucy told police. "It was my impression that this statement was made to impress upon me the need to exercise caution in our relationship." She said only a couple in California and her sister knew of her affair with Railey.

Lucy also elaborated on the "other man" in her life and recalled the conversation she had with Railey at the hospital two days before his suicide attempt. "On that morning I told Railey I would be meeting a man during my trip to California. Railey knew I had seen this man on prior occasions. I had a speaking engagement in San Francisco and was due to leave that Thursday. Railey was threatened by this man in my life." She went on to explain that the man actually posed no threat to her relationship with Railey and that she eventually assured him that "he was the man I loved."

Lucy told the police that Railey gave no indication that

he might have written the threatening letters that preceded the attack on Peggy and in fact appeared "very frightened" by them. She did say Railey often confided in her: ". . . he would allow himself to cry and sob in my presence, which he would not do around others." Lucy said Railey seldom spoke to her about his wife, but that while his relationship with Peggy was only "functional," he never mentioned any other romantic involvement.

"The driving force in Railey's life was to speak the Word as best he could, to speak the Word truthfully, and to be one of the top preachers in the church. While he wanted to stay in Dallas, he would have considered pastoring at Riverside Church in New York a very high honor."

Lucy revealed for the first time her telephone calls from Railey on the night of the attack. She learned of the attack the next morning in a phone conversation with her mother, who knew nothing about her daughter's affair.

Although investigators thought Railey had been drinking the night of April 21, Lucy insisted that he consumed nothing alcoholic at her home and was never a heavy drinker.

"He will occasionally drink wine," she said. "The most I have ever seen him consume was three Scotches during the course of an evening in London. I have never seen him intoxicated and have no reason to believe he has or ever had any drinking problems." She also told the police she had never seen Railey angry, but added, "He would get an adrenaline flow when confronted with the small-mindedness of Dallas."

Lucy ended her sworn statement with a ringing declaration of innocence: "Walker Railey did not confide in me that he had any involvement in the creation of the threatening letters he received or the attack on his wife. I have never seen or handled the threatening letters and I have had no involvement in the preparation of those letters."

Her formal signature was attached: "Dr. Lucy Caswell Papillon."

Judge Whittington took only a short time to ponder Lucy's testimony and that of other witnesses on December 5. He had seen a grotesque video of Peggy's ravaged body receiving treatment in a hospital and a happier one of her playing the piano at church a month before the attack. The final witness was Peggy's mother, Billie Jo Nicolai, who said, "Each day, I ask the Lord to give me strength for one more day."

The judge ruled that Walker Railey was indeed liable for his wife's medical expenses and other damages. He said there was no way that money could compensate for Peggy and her family's pain and suffering. But he assessed roughly $9 million in actual damages and a like amount in punitive damages. Depending on certain intangibles, the final figure was expected to approach $18 million.

Arnold said he was pleased by the verdict and Peggy's parents smiled bravely into the glare of television lights. Still, no one could say when or if Railey would pay a dime to anyone or if he would ever surface again in Texas. But the ruling loomed as a symbol of justice and a reminder of what occurred one incredibly tragic night in the spring of 1987.

As a reporter left the historic old courthouse and stepped into the December darkness, he could not shake the haunting comment of Peggy Railey's grandmother almost a year earlier.

"I'm old enough to know that there are worse things than death," she had said, "and this is one of them."

2

FUGITIVES

The Strange Ordeal of
Kenneth Miller

Part 1

Fort Worth, Texas

Shortly before nightfall on June 11, 1974, a neatly dressed young gunman slipped into the garage apartment of a Texas Christian University student named Janelle Kirby and pointed a pistol at her head. He removed a pair of handcuffs from his pocket and ordered the young woman to place her hands on the bed.

She complied. But when the man snapped a handcuff on one wrist, she grabbed for the gun. The two struggled, falling to the floor. The young woman screamed. The man slapped his hand over her mouth and ordered her to keep quiet. She bit him. He pulled away and rose to his feet. With both his hands on the cheap .22-caliber pistol, he began firing at point-blank range. Five shots struck her in the head. He rifled her purse and headed out the door.

"You coward," she mumbled. Unable to walk and aware she might be mortally wounded, Kirby dragged herself down the stairs, where she was found by a neighbor and rushed to a hospital. As she drifted in and out of consciousness, she heard a doctor say, "She's almost gone."

After a week in intensive care, the 20-year-old coed began to recover. Sometime later, she identified her assailant from a police photo. The detectives suggested the man's intentions were to rape, not to rob. They heard her say, "He had funny-looking eyes that I'll never forget."

The man she identified was Kenneth Leslie Miller, 24, a brown-

haired laid-back Vietnam veteran, a bachelor with a fondness for guns, dogs, women, and motorcycles. Miller was also familiar to police by virtue of two raids on his apartment, including one that landed him in jail on a marijuana possession charge.

"I am positive that he is the man who shot me," Miss Kirby insisted.

So began a bizarre drama that would span twelve years and embrace the best and worst in law enforcement. It would shake the nation's sometimes schizoid system of justice and inspire whispers of police irregularities. It would send a young man on a cross-country odyssey to avoid prison and condemn a young woman to the life of a recluse haunted by a phantom killer.

And finally, before running its serpentine course, the ordeal would test the limits of the human spirit.

Six months after the lineup identification, a jury convicted Kenneth Miller of attempted murder. But before the panel could assess a seventy-year prison sentence, he was gone. He slipped from the courtroom and then skipped town, heading first to Michigan and then to Georgia. He moved next to Arizona with his girlfriend and finally settled in Las Vegas, Nevada, under an assumed name.

It was there in the summer of 1986, twelve years after the shooting of Janelle Kirby, that a tireless and unconventional Fort Worth police sergeant named Leonard Schilling tracked Miller down through a Crime Stoppers informant. For Schilling, whom colleagues called "Cowboy," it could have been considered the most notable achievement of his checkered career. He also thought it was the end of a long ordeal.

He was wrong. It was only the beginning.

In the spring of 1974, Janelle Kirby lived alone in an upstairs garage apartment near Texas Christian University, where she was pursuing a language degree. She was a bright, attractive, blue-eyed Florida native who by day studied Russian anthropology and Asian history and by night worked at a Mexican restaurant and a college-flavored club called the Hop. The campus and both jobs were within walking distance of her apartment.

After working late the night of June 10, Janelle left the Hop at 1 A.M. for the short walk home. A man offered her a ride, but she refused. When he started to leave his car, she ran to a drive-in cafe and persuaded the manager to walk her home. She tumbled into bed but slept only fitfully. Arising late, she dressed in cutoffs and a halter top and spent the day holed up in the apartment.

That evening, as she opened the door for her cat, she spotted a nicely dressed stranger standing at a gate behind the apartment. She thought he might be lost when he asked to use the telephone. He climbed the stairs; as she turned away to retrieve the phone, he slipped in and put a gun to her head.

When the intruder attempted to handcuff her, she resisted, fighting for the gun until she fell exhausted to the floor. In a final act of defiance, she bit him. He pulled away and leveled the gun. She remembered the blue fire of the shots coming toward her as she covered her eyes.

The first bullet she felt ricocheted off her head and into her chest, collapsing her lung. She thought it was her heart that was punctured. She would remember blood pouring down her face as she groped for the telephone. Unable to dial and with her right side paralyzed, she dragged herself out the door and down the steps.

Her cat abandoned newly born kittens to stay at her side, meowing as they both slowly tumbled down the steps. Near the bottom, Janelle thought for the first time she might survive. She had made it this far.

A neighbor, attracted first by a barking dog and then by Janelle's cries for help, called an ambulance. She arrived at the hospital unconscious. Later, lying in bed, she sensed that a stranger had slipped past armed guards outside her room and was now at her bedside. She thought he was her assailant in disguise. He was a priest.

Later, she would be unable to recall how and when she gave police a statement on the shooting, but she felt no one seemed to want to listen to her. She wanted to say the gunman resembled her brother-in-law. She had seen him only fleetingly, she admitted to herself, yet it was strange how time passed during the ordeal. It seemed so long.

Kenneth Miller was still a teenager when he returned from

Vietnam in 1969 and told friends of winning Bronze and Silver Stars, a Purple Heart, and other military honors. He also returned with some haunting memories and a self-proclaimed reputation as a coolly efficient killer. He said he specialized in ambush tactics and, by his own count, he had disposed of thirty-two enemy soldiers.

One of his closest friends, Lee Mulholland, concluded that Vietnam had left its scars. Here was someone she knew as warm and lighthearted, like a "great big kid," but he could have been a real life Rambo, too. It was Lee's husband, Sonny Mulholland, who hired Miller as a route salesman in the circulation department of the *Fort Worth Star-Telegram*. Miller also worked part-time at a sporting goods store, and his affection for guns was almost a fetish. The Mulhollands believed it was his attraction to guns that led to his first brush with the law.

A neighbor thought Miller was dealing in automatic weapons and notified police. On July 13, 1974, a handful of officers raided Miller's apartment in a search for drugs and illegal weapons. They found only a small quantity of marijuana, but enough back then to land Miller in city jail. A decade later, the same offense would be a misdemeanor, warranting no more than a slap on the wrist.

Miller would later tell his lawyer that a homicide detective appeared at his cell before his release and held up a composite sketch. "See this?" a puzzled Miller quoted the detective as saying. "This is you and I'm going to prove it." With Miller's consent, the detective snapped a color photograph for police files before he was released.

On August 14, 1974, narcotics officers and federal agents returned to Miller's apartment, again looking for drugs and weapons. He was asleep when the raiders arrived. According to Miller, they broke down the door and someone shoved a gun in his face. Two of the raiders yanked him out of bed and forced him against the wall, face first. They kicked his feet apart when he slumped. One of them, whom Miller later identified as city narcotics officer Ray Armand, banged Miller's head into the wall with such force that he claimed it left a hole in the sheetrock. "They really worked me over," Miller said.

This time, the raiders left frustrated and without even scant evidence of illegal guns or drugs. Miller contended they warned him not to make trouble or "you're dead." That same night, in a hospital emergency ward, doctors removed his spleen. Officers insisted later that Miller damaged his spleen in a motorcycle accident, but Police Chief T. S. Walls disagreed. He ordered Ray Armand and a fellow narcotics officer suspended indefinitely and reprimanded the sergeant who headed the raid.

Two weeks later, Detective C. R. Davis took a collection of photos to the university and showed it to Janelle Kirby. It was then, on August 29, 1974, that police said she first identified Miller as her assailant.

Kirby would later maintain she actually identified a photo of Miller from her hospital bed. "They were continually showing me pictures, mugshots, and I always said that none of them was the man because in my mind I had the picture of my brother-in-law," she said. She realized her mental state was too muddled at the time to know if anyone influenced her identification of Miller. "I just knew what I saw, and I was certain of that." She would also remember that the police were very enthusiastic about her picking the photograph of Miller. She felt they disliked Miller and that, to put it mildly, "he had it coming to him."

Curiously, police did not arrest Miller at once. They waited at least a month, until September 30, a date that coincided with a Civil Service hearing on the appeals of suspended officers Ray Armand and his partner. Miller testified at the hearing that the partner did not hurt him.

Armand was a different matter. But Miller was unable to identify him when asked to do so in the crowded chambers. A newspaper article later solved that mystery, reporting that attorney Jerry Loftin had dramatically altered Armand's appearance for the proceedings. "Whereas Armand, as a narcotics officer, usually had long hair, wore jeans, and freely displayed his distinctive teeth," the newspaper said, "Loftin dressed Armand in a suit, had his hair cut short, and made the officer keep his mouth closed."

Before the hearing ended that night, two homicide detectives arrested Miller for the attempted murder of Janelle Kirby. In a matter of seconds, the accuser became the accused and the brutality case against Armand was dismissed. He and his partner were reinstated to the police force about the time Miller was led off to jail.

The events of September 30, 1974, raised disturbing questions. If investigators believed Miller intended to rape, rob, and kill Janelle Kirby, why would they permit him to run loose for at least a month, possibly to commit another act of violence? Was the timing of Miller's arrest orchestrated to influence the hearing on reinstatement for Armand and his partner? Conversely, did authorities delay the arrest because it might "look bad" if Miller was taken into custody before the Civil Service hearing began?

Whatever the answers, arresting officers marched Miller directly from the hearing to the jail and into a waiting police lineup. There Janelle Kirby identified him again and declared: "I am positive that he is the man who shot me."

Unable to raise bond, Miller remained behind bars fifty-four days until friends collected the money to free him. Four months later, he went on trial for attempted murder.

Part 2

The state's case against Kenneth Leslie Miller focused exclusively on Janelle Kirby's testimony and a single piece of circumstantial evidence — a pair of handcuffs found in Miller's possession. Miller's attorney, Bill Magnussen, sought to show that Miller did not look like the assailant Kirby originally described. That person, Magnussen pointed out, was shorter and younger, clean shaven, and neatly dressed. That person wore casual shoes and a wedding band.

Witnesses testified under Magnussen's questioning that Miller dressed exclusively in jeans and T-shirts and that he was sporting a light beard at the time of the attack. They also testified that the young bachelor wore only boots or sneakers, never loafers. He did not own a wedding band.

The discrepancies between Kirby's original description of the intruder and her subsequent identification of Miller raised some doubts among jurors. They appeared deadlocked twice before finally rendering their guilty verdict. As lawyers debated the issue of bond before sentencing, Miller turned to a friend and said, "I'm going." With $1.25 in his pocket, he fled the courthouse and jumped in Lee Mulholland's car. He sped away—almost into the path of an 18-wheeler.

Miller stopped at a phone booth and called a reporter. After declaring his innocence, he said, "I don't know what I'm going to do. I think I'm leaving town." He took refuge in the home of a friend named Dianna Oppermann over the weekend and it was there, on Monday, that he heard the jury had assessed a seventy-year prison term in absentia.

He remained with Dianna for two weeks, then decided to run. Sonny and Lee Mulholland offered to aid his escape. Forcing a smile, Lee told Miller, "Even if man has failed, God will not. He is the God of the hopeless, and this is a hopeless situation. You've got it made. Yours is the perfect situation for Him to act on."

With Sonny's blessing, Lee drove Miller to Michigan, where she planned to deposit him with some people contacted by Miller's father. But, once there, both sensed something was wrong. Was this a setup? They left quickly. "A hell of a long ways to come for a cup of coffee," Miller quipped as they drove away. From Detroit, Miller called a former girlfriend living in Atlanta and told her he needed a place to stay. "Come on down," she replied, and Miller and Lee drove straight through to Georgia.

"Someday, somehow, the truth will come out," Lee Mulholland assured Miller before boarding an airplane for home. "Please do not lose faith. God's hand is in this." Back in Fort Worth, she and Sonny told anyone who would listen that Miller suffered no shortage of money, guns, or girlfriends in 1974 and had little need to rape, rob, or run around with a cheap .22 revolver in his belt.

No one seemed much impressed, least of all Janelle Kirby. She was out with friends from college at a picnic on Benbrook Lake shortly after Miller staged his getaway. Sitting at a table and looking across the windy lake, she wondered, "What if the person who shot me came and wanted to finish me off? What if a rifle is pointed at me right now?" She thought she never again would feel safe.

She was right.

Not long after Kenneth Miller arrived in Atlanta, he was eager to leave. He had spent his days roaming the woods and his nights cloistered in his friend's apartment. While he had few companions, he did acquire a gun, and it rarely left his side.

One day he ventured out to a store and was startled when a pair of Georgia state troopers pulled him over. He had often wondered if he would use the gun to kill. He knew he did not intend to go back to jail. "What am I going to do?" he asked himself, gun in hand.

He never found out. As suddenly as they had appeared, the troopers sped off, presumably in response to a radio command. Within days, a shaken Miller left Atlanta and sneaked back into Fort Worth, where he rejoined Dianna Oppermann, who provided him refuge when he first fled the courtroom.

By long distance from Georgia, he had rekindled his romance with the spunky legal secretary and now she was prepared to join him on the run. A free-spirited child of the sixties, she hid a natural beauty behind long straight hair and glamourless clothes.

Dianna had several motivations to flee. It *was* a chance to make life more exciting. Certainly, it was a challenge. Mostly, however, she loved Miller and wanted to be with him. "He was like a lost dog," she said.

Aside from the obvious pitfall of aiding and abetting a convicted felon, there was the delicate matter of Diana's boss, Bill Magnussen, who was also Miller's attorney. While Magnussen never questioned his client's innocence, he wanted him to surrender and appeal for a new trial. Since Miller was unwilling to jeopardize his freedom, Magnussen was not told of the pair's unusual alliance. Dianna led her friends and family to believe she was leaving town with a girlfriend. Lee Mulholland drove Miller to a rendezvous point to meet Dianna. Unlike the time she accompanied Miller to Michigan, Lee was now more apprehensive. Just the sight of a police car scared her.

Once reunited, the fugitive couple headed to Arizona simply because they liked the lyrics of a song by a popular rock group, the Eagles, "Take It Easy." One verse told of "standing on the corner in Winslow, Arizona."

Despite how it appeared, Dianna was aware of the seriousness of her flight with Miller. Everything went on the line with this, she knew, and she worried about the reaction of her parents. Although she was convinced of Miller's innocence, she thought it would destroy her mother and father if this escapade turned out to be a mistake. "Would you want your daughter running off with a convicted felon?" she tried to explain.

As it was, she and Miller left Texas with her $1,000 savings account, a few clothes, and very little else. She wondered if it was her love for him or her concern about what Texas justice had done to him. She could not say. She did know she risked everything on him, monetarily and emotionally.

The young lovers lingered only a short time in Winslow before moving on to Flagstaff, where Dianna found a job with a criminal law firm and Miller went to work as an auto mechanic. He knew nothing about repairing cars but hung on by using an instruction manual on the sly. One day, his boss caught him with his nose in the book and fired him — not for poor work but for lying about his mechanical expertise.

Assuming the name of an ex-roommate, Miller soon found a job with the biggest garage in Flagstaff, which ironically serviced cars for state and local police. The cops took a liking to the young mechanic and one officer became an occasional dinner guest at Miller's apartment. The young couple even socialized briefly with a former police chief and Dianna's acquaintances were beguiled by her "y'all"s and her "fixin' to"s.

It was not unusual for Miller and Dianna to ride his motorcycle to Phoenix for dinner. Dianna could reminisce about being "on the back of a motorcycle with 100-plus degrees and heat coming up through your shoes and burning your feet." Such trips were "just for the heck of it." There was no money for more extravagant entertainment.

They did not need anything else, she concluded. They had each other. "We were real happy in Flagstaff," Miller said. Dianna agreed.

In the early 1970s, Leonard Schilling was a brash young Texas cop with a high level of street smarts and a low tolerance for authority. Unconventional even then, with bluster and show biz in his blood, he had a dash of Dirty Harry and surely a touch of McCloud. Most of his Fort Worth colleagues liked him, although some would not have disagreed with the fellow cop who called Schilling "borderline crazy."

"I've been arrested twice, suspended twice, and fired three times in one hour," he bragged.

Schilling was a rookie fresh from the Police Academy when he first saw Kenneth Miller in 1974 and he disliked him at once. This was the creep who shot a TCU coed and tried to put the finger on two of his police colleagues. He thought Kenneth Miller was about to get what he deserved. Justice would be done.

Schilling never dreamed twelve years would pass for true justice to be served. Nor could he guess he would be a leading player in the drama.

Part 3

In the aftermath of the trial and Kenneth Miller's flight from the courtroom, Janelle Kirby's world was crumbling. She returned to her home in Florida but could escape neither the horror nor the handiwork of her Texas assailant. Surgeons believed it was too risky to remove one of the .22-caliber slugs from her brain, and the bullet and her facial scars were painful reminders of the attack.

She also struggled to overcome difficulties in speaking and sudden lapses of memory. She was certain she lost one job because of the impairments. Doctors prescribed an anticonvulsant drug to curb occasional seizures, but the medication contributed to the memory lapses. Under its influence, her speech was slowed and slurred. She worried that her garbled words would cause people to think she was slow-witted. She also worried that the bullet in her brain might somehow shift and cause permanent mental damage. But mostly she worried that the gunman would track her down and kill her. After all, no one else could identify him.

When alone, she would not answer the door. She did not care if that seemed antisocial. She was not going to let someone like Kenneth Miller harm her again.

The constant fear also possessed her mother, who soon left Florida and moved to New Mexico. What Janelle perceived as a rejection by her mother deepened her depression. From the beginning, she said, her mother thought it was Janelle's fault "that this man came in and shot me." This hurt Janelle profoundly. When she was in the hospital, Janelle heard her mother say, "You've ruined yourself." In the end, she put her mother out of her mind. If not, she said, "It would drive me crazy, too, along with everything else."

In early 1976, Janelle Kirby's life took a turn for the better. Though estranged from her mother and still under doctors' care, she began dating a pleasant and protective young man named Jim, who had moved to Florida from Chicago Heights, Illinois. He liked her the moment he met her. Rather than overlooking her problems, he saw beyond them.

Jim and Janelle married that year in mid-March — twice, as it turned out, because of a mix-up in the three-day waiting period. The minister married them first on a Friday night, as scheduled, and then repeated the ceremony on Sunday. Jim worked at a variety of jobs and Janelle stepped up her efforts to solve her memory and speech problems. After persuading doctors to take her off the anticonvulsant medicine, she resumed her college studies with the goal of a nursing degree.

She soon realized she had to study longer and more intensely than other students to achieve the same result. When she made her first A, she cried for hours.

After nearly a year in Flagstaff, Kenneth Miller began to feel his past closing in on him. He and Diana had been smitten with the beauty of Santa Barbara on a trip into California, so he headed there in search of work. He found a job, but he also got stopped by the California Highway Patrol in Van Nuys. He had a pistol in the glove compartment, but something told him not to worry. He thought he had been flagged for an improper lane change. Instead, he was arrested for driving under the influence of alcohol—DUI. Although California authorities did not link him to the Fort Worth shooting, Miller knew the police network could nail him at any moment.

He hocked his watch for bail money, quit his new job, and dashed back to Arizona. With California no longer an option, he decided to move to Las Vegas and Dianna soon followed. When she left her job as a paralegal in Flagstaff, her bosses threw a luncheon for her. The justice court closed down so its officers could attend. A cookbook was her going-away present.

"So we were not a detriment to society or anything like that," Dianna maintained. "Everybody accepted us for what we were, not what we were supposed to be. We weren't Bonnie and Clyde. We weren't bad people. We always worked. That was our main goal, to prove we were valuable to society."

Despite her academic success, Janelle Kirby was afraid school officials might deny her a degree if they learned of her medical history. She thought they would be prejudiced against someone who had been shot or assaulted as she was. She tried to hide her anxiety and insecurity behind a lighthearted, happy-go-lucky facade, but suspected she fooled very few. A classmate was overheard to say, "Janelle has a funny way of expressing herself."

Aside from her husband, there really was no one with whom to discuss her ordeal. She wondered if there were therapy groups whose common bond was being a victim of a crime, but she heard of none. She decided to keep her problems inside. Sometimes she coped and sometimes she did not. Jim thought there were times she wished she was dead. He heard her lament, "It would be better for everybody." He knew of her nightmares. She could not forget her assailant's face, his eyes. He shared her worry that the man would return.

One night, Jim arrived late from work and slipped into the house without turning on the lights so he would not disturb her. Janelle awoke anyway. To his horror, she had an ax and a knife on the bed and she was pointing a speargun at him. When she recognized him, she broke down and cried. Though money was scarce, Jim bought a gun.

Months later, he came home much earlier than expected, rattled around a bit in an anteroom, and then entered the house to find Janelle pointing the pistol at him. He could not recall her being more terrified than at that moment.

"I won't shoot without looking," Janelle explained, "but I'm not going to wait for someone to walk in and try to hurt me. When you don't know, you lie and wait."

Although the California episode might have been an omen, Kenneth Miller and Dianna Oppermann were happy and upbeat when they left Arizona for the bright lights of Las Vegas. They blended quietly into the flip side of the glittery Las Vegas lifestyle. At the outset, he worked at several jobs and Dianna soon was hired by one of the top law firms in town. She also worked for a popular Nevada political figure named Harry Reid, who later became a U.S. congressman and, in 1986, a U.S. senator.

It was second nature now for Dianna to refer to Kenneth by his alias, and the couple had grown increasingly comfortable with one another. "It was like harmony," she told an acquaintance later. "Like perfect timing. We'd open a bottle of wine and cook. We didn't really socialize that much. We didn't need to. We had each other."

They also had three Doberman pinschers—Gimlet, Hog Dawg, and Butch—and two cats, Herman and Bertha. The animals replaced the people they didn't have in their lives. Miller's personal favorite was Gimlet, who followed him like a shadow. And Miller treated Gimlet as his only possession.

Miller and Dianna frequently prepared a picnic and gathered up the animals to head for the desert or the mountains on what they laughingly called "family outings." They didn't discuss it, but Dianna sensed that Kenneth had little opportunity for such outings with his own family, and she worked at filling the void. Dianna never developed the heart for deer hunting, but she did accompany Kenneth on fishing and duck hunting excursions. Back home, he surprised her with gifts and flowers that once included a card that said, "Only because I love you."

In the fall of 1977, more than two years after they left Fort Worth, Miller suggested they marry. Surprised and mildly curious, Dianna was neither displeased nor keen on the idea. Since Miller lived by his alias, she wondered if she would take that name, his real name, or keep her own. She would rather have stayed an Oppermann, but he was insistent.

They were married in a small sanctuary called the "Chapel of the West." They honeymooned at the Landmark Hotel. Miller's friends from Fort Worth, Sonny and Lee Mulholland, didn't make the wedding, but they seldom visited Las Vegas without seeing or talking with Miller. Sonny developed an affection for the Las Vegas casinos and Lee accompanied him on many of his trips.

Dianna knew the visits were helpful. The Mulhollands were like friendly in-laws and were the only ones with whom the fugitive couple could talk openly. Miller and Dianna seldom discussed the dark events of 1974, treating them as part of a hidden past that might go away. They struggled to be "normal," but the obstacles included no credit references and a phony name.

Despite the handicaps, Miller eventually landed a circulation job with the *Las Vegas Review-Journal* and before long was bringing home $1,000 or more a week. His reputation was so good he purchased a $16,000 truck on his counterfeit signature.

Against Dianna's wishes, Miller bought a four-bedroom house that included a swimming pool and an acre of land for their dogs and cats to romp around on. Parked outside, by the motorcycle, were a Ford Bronco, a van, and a minitruck. But such good fortune did not translate into happiness. "Once we began accumulating a few material things," Dianna realized, "then the pressure starting building. That's when things starting going downhill."

Miller suddenly seemed to discover that the more he acquired, the more he stood to lose. He feared the authorities would swoop down to confiscate all his possessions, take him to jail, and arrest his wife as an accessory. "Someday there's a knock on the door and that's the end of your life," Dianna fretted.

Awakening once in the middle of the night, Miller told Dianna, "No matter what we've got, what we achieve, they can catch me any day and take it all away. In a way, this is worse than Vietnam." He told a friend he had participated in scores of firefights and ambushes, but the pressure of his flight from Texas was different. "It wouldn't go away," he said. "I began to resent having what I had, being respected, having a wife I loved. I even started resenting her."

Dianna was convinced neither of them could cope with jail. "It would be so wrong to go to jail for something you didn't do," she said. "I think we would rather die."

Although the DUI arrest in California suggested otherwise, Miller had not been a problem drinker. That soon began to change as new tragedies spilled over into others. First his father died, and he could not risk returning to Fort Worth for the funeral. Correctly, Miller suspected that police would be waiting there for him to appear. Then his mother wrote a wrenching letter asking for money. Miller sent what he could. Alone, she suffered a heart attack and died on the floor of her home. Her body lay undiscovered for hours.

Once again, Miller could not go back for fear of arrest.

That evening, Dianna found her troubled husband sitting in a chair, rocking and staring blankly into space. He did not speak and he would not cry. Dianna wondered if he was approaching his threshold of pain and anguish. "There's got to be a breaking point for everybody," she said.

Miller's drinking did nothing to improve his emotional state and even less to improve his marriage. He and Dianna tried counseling, but it failed because Miller could not or would not discuss the Texas nightmare. She loved him. She hated him. She tried to pamper him. She tried to ignore him. Nothing worked. They even discussed having a child. Dianna believed Kenneth Miller would make a good father, but she had other misgivings.

"Why bring a child into the world when there's a chance you might get picked up and put in jail?" she wondered. "What would happen to the child?" There was no solution. "There is nothing we can do," she thought, "and nothing we can change. That thing in Texas is hopeless."

Part 4

The Christmas holidays were always the most dispiriting times for Miller, perhaps a reminder of what he lost back in Texas. During the Christmas season of 1982, the marital troubles between him and Dianna reached a boiling point. During a shouting match, Miller handed her his pistol and asked, "Why don't you just shoot me and put me out of my misery?"

She threw the gun on the couch and screamed back, "Why don't you just shoot *me* and put me out of my misery?"

One night during a quarrel spiked with liquor and pills, Miller went too far. He grabbed Dianna by her throat and pushed her against a wall. "I could hurt you if I wanted to," he said. Dianna did not stick around to find out if he meant it. She walked out and filed for divorce. She rejected his pleas for reconciliation because he wouldn't quit drinking and the divorce was granted in June 1983, almost eight years to the day after they left Texas.

Miller admitted he had become intolerable and was responsible for her departure, but he swore they loved one another. Dianna felt heartsick and even a little guilty. She thought she was deserting a sinking ship, but she also knew there was nothing more she could do. When she moved out of Miller's dream house, she left him almost everything—the Bronco, the motorcycle, the furniture. She hoped to demonstrate that she was not really abandoning him. She figured the world had given Miller such a raw deal that he at least deserved something. Dianna took only her pet Doberman, Hog Dawg.

If Miller was miserable with Dianna, he was devastated without her. In rapid order, he lost his house, his vehicles, his job, and, most of all, his self-respect. Clutching for straws, he fled Las Vegas with a new girlfriend and spent several months roaming through Utah, California, Colorado, Iowa, Idaho, and South Dakota.

"He needs help," fretted Lee Mulholland to her husband. "He's never gotten over Dianna. She was the glue that held him together. She was his whole world."

Not quite. But fate quickly took what little was left. While playing beside the Snake River in Idaho, his dog Gimlet collapsed and died. Brokenhearted, Miller buried the Doberman there beside the river. Then he cried.

With Kenneth Miller alone and adrift in a sea of Nevada booze, Leonard Schilling, the Texas cop, was back in Fort Worth compiling an unorthodox police résumé and dreaming up schemes to catch Miller. "If you could put my career on a graph," Schilling would laugh sarcastically, "it would be straight up and straight down."

It was a career that included nominations for officer of the year and certificates of merit for courage. Rarely averse to a cold beer and a good fight, he also was intermittently suspended or fired and may have been, as he insisted, the only police sergeant in Fort Worth history ever to have been jailed twice.

He survived an early and unforgettable stint as "fag bait" for vice squad campaigns against cruising gays, and he emerged without serious injury from three shootouts as a patrolman in a high-crime area. He served as a sniper on the SWAT team and a detective in the burglary division. As one of the first mounted patrolmen in Fort Worth, he rode a horse in the rowdy Stockyards area, justifying the nickname "Cowboy."

Schilling blamed police work for the breakup of his marriage to his high school sweetheart, and, like Miller, he had taken to drinking often and heavily. Also like Miller, he was crazy about his dog, which he claimed was part shepherd and part coyote. He called the animal Ol' Reb.

Throughout his career, Schilling could not forget Kenneth Leslie Miller. He was convinced Miller was guilty of shooting Janelle Kirby and he accepted as fact the police scuttlebutt that Miller was a drug dealer and a freak for automatic weapons.

At the time he made sergeant, Schilling was drafted for a job no one wanted, coordinator of Crime Stoppers. It was a program in which cash rewards were dispensed anonymously to citizens for tips on solving crimes. In 1984, Crime Stoppers recorded 16 felony arrests, cleared 23 cases, seized $5,000 in dope, and recovered $30,000 in property—a pitiful performance in a metropolitan area. During his tenure, Schilling was proud to note Crime Stoppers made 195 felony arrests, cleared 259 cases, recovered $2 million in stolen property, and seized $160,000 in drugs. One day an administrator told him, "We knew you couldn't hurt the program. We figured if we could keep you in line, off suspension, and out of jail long enough, you could bring this thing around."

Despite his success, Schilling was bored silly in his new job until he hit on the idea of starting a Crime Stoppers "Ten Most Wanted" program. It would be patterned after the FBI posters he remembered as a kid. The thought of catching Kenneth Miller inspired him. There was no SOB more deserving to be hunted down and thrown behind bars.

Schilling went to Don Moore, the district attorney's chief investigator, and together they scrambled through the dust and cobwebs of twelve years of police records to find the file on the Miller case. Schilling said he wanted someone he could "bribe or blackmail" to blow the whistle. He was told early on not to waste his time with Sonny Mulholland. Besides being loyal to Miller, Sonny did not need the money.

Schilling would have been stunned to know that even as he devised a scheme to capture Miller, the troubled fugitive was flirting with the idea of surrendering. "I'm tired of running," Miller told Lee Mulholland on a covert visit to Fort Worth in late 1985. Lee believed Kenneth was at the lowest point in his life. Miller admitted he could recall little of his activities since Dianna left him. "I tried to forget," he said. "After the marriage broke up, I just didn't care."

With the Most Wanted posters still in the talking stage, Schilling traveled to Las Vegas strictly for fun. While out drinking and gambling with a friend, Schilling thought he saw Miller on a downtown street in the glittery city. "Aw, blow it off, Schilling," said the friend, a lawyer familiar with the case. "You're seeing Miller in your sleep and you're seeing him in your soup. Dammit, we're here to have a good time."

In May 1986, Schilling's Crime Stoppers kicked off Fort Worth's Ten Most Wanted program with Kenneth Miller listed as No. 1. Miller's picture decorated newspaper pages and television screens and hung in convenience stores and other public places. The posters portrayed him as armed and extremely dangerous and offered a $1,000 reward for information leading to his arrest.

The undercover raiders of Miller's apartment thought it hilarious that Schilling chose Miller to head his Most Wanted list. "Ain't nobody gonna catch him," Schilling remembered one of them saying.

"Just humor me," Schilling replied.

Dianna Oppermann was visiting her parents in Fort Worth when Schilling launched his campaign and she saw a copy of the Miller poster in the *Fort Worth Star-Telegram*. It was a horrible experience, compounded because her mother and father knew nothing of her relationship with Miller. Lee Mulholland saw the same newspaper. "Things are coming to an end," she shuddered.

In early summer, Schilling received a series of telephone calls concerning Miller, and one informed him that his quarry had been back in town briefly in late 1985, using the name of his ex-roommate. With a bit of luck and some good police work, Schilling tied Miller to several pawn tickets and a suburban traffic accident.

Then came what Schilling thought was the "blockbuster" call. An informant wanting to claim the $1,000 reward said Miller was in Las Vegas, that he'd worked for a newspaper, and that he'd married a legal secretary named Dianna Oppermann. Schilling telephoned a police detective named Arvis Harding of the Las Vegas Metropolitan Police Department and told him Miller, using an alias, reportedly was living there. Schilling wanted him arrested.

Police records indicated a man with Miller's alias had been arrested three or four times on drinking charges and once for carrying a concealed weapon. Though Schilling was insistent that was his man, no arrest was made. Schilling was beside himself. He momentarily considered flying to Las Vegas, renting a car, and going after Miller himself with his .357 Magnum.

Unknown to Schilling or Detective Harding, Miller had sought solace in the arms of a pretty brunette divorcée named Debbie, who succeeded Dianna as a lieutenant in Miller's battle against the bottle. Still, Arvis Harding assured Schilling he was close to catching Miller.

"Close only counts in hand grenades and horseshoes,"

Schilling grumbled.

On June 9, 1986, time ran out on Kenneth Miller. As he moved through the cashier's line at a Las Vegas wholesale store, a suspicious clerk opened a box he was carrying that supposedly contained an inexpensive turbine fan. Instead, it held two videotape recorders and two electric drills.

Miller claimed he was no less surprised than the clerk, contending a brother of a friend had asked him to pay for the item while he went to get his truck. Unconvinced, the store manager summoned police. A metro officer did a routine check and informed Miller there was a DUI warrant out on him. As they stood beside the police car, the radio crackled back to life.

Miller saw the cop turn white then go for his gun. He ordered Miller against the wall and called for assistance. Schilling's campaign had hit the Las Vegas jackpot.

"I know who you are, you're Kenneth Miller," a detective told him after he was taken into custody.

"No, I'm not," Miller replied, offering the name of his ex-roommate.

Not deterred, the detective said, "We *know* who you are."

"I'm glad somebody does," sighed Miller. "I don't."

A short time later, Arvis Harding called Schilling and told him a man using Miller's alias had been arrested and was being held on a check charge. "He's in jail now," Harding said.

"Don't turn him loose, that's Kenneth Leslie Miller," shouted Schilling into the phone. His patience had long since expired.

That evening, with Miller's name prominent on Texas and Nevada newscasts, Schilling headed for his favorite hangout, the Albatross, and an impromptu party celebrating the developments in Las Vegas. He met Bill Magnussen, owner of the saloon and Miller's lawyer twelve years earlier. Magnussen congratulated Schilling on the arrest of Miller but said, "You caught an innocent man." Schilling laughed off the comment.

Not long afterward, the officer received a phone call from a man who refused to identify himself. "We need to talk. It's important," the man said, giving him a phone number.

"Who do I ask for?"

"Just call. I'll answer," the voice replied.

Slightly perturbed at having to interrupt the party, Schilling left to place the return call. "You've done one hell of a job," the voice said. "You've done what nobody could do. And nobody believed you could do it. But you've got the wrong man."

Schilling thought the anonymous caller meant that the man in Las Vegas with the alias was not Miller. The detective told the caller they had matched fingerprints and signatures.

"You're not hearing what I'm saying," the voice said.

"What are you saying?"

"You need to look at that case. You got the wrong man. Miller didn't shoot Janelle Kirby."

"He was tried and sentenced to seventy years for doing it," Schilling protested.

"He didn't do it. Look at a man named William Ted Wilhoit."

The caller said Wilhoit could be found at the state prison in Huntsville. That is where Wilhoit had been since the late 1970s.

Part 5

Fort Worth, Texas, 1973

On a hot summer morning in 1973, nearly a year before the attack on Janelle Kirby, a neatly dressed young man appeared at the home of another TCU coed named Jenny Dennis. He said he had come to welcome her to his south-side neighborhood. Once inside the house, he pulled a knife and ordered the terrified young woman to undress. When she resisted, he took her forcibly, attempting but failing to commit rape only in the legal sense.

Police arrested a suspect. He was 5 foot 8 and weighed 130 pounds, with light brown hair, a fair complexion, and blue eyes. He was soft-spoken and, at the time of his arrest, neatly dressed. His name was William Ted Wilhoit, a married ministerial student who would remember that date, August 27, 1973, as his 20th birthday.

Wilhoit was acquitted by a sympathetic jury, but he could not avoid other troubles with the Fort Worth police. A detective, John Terrell, arrested him twice on burglary charges. And while Wilhoit received a probated sentence in the first case, prosecutors were preparing to send him to the Texas penitentiary in Huntsville if they could convict him in the second.

Jenny Dennis arose that fateful August morning, dressed, and climbed in her car for the short drive to Texas Christian University. She was about to enroll for her senior year as a student in medical technology. She had just moved into a new residence. The previous night, her sleep was fitful and filled with horrible dreams.

Her car died.

While she struggled with the ignition, a young man started across the street toward the car. As he approached, the car started. She gave him a friendly wave and he waved back.

After returning from the TCU campus, she noticed that the door to her house appeared to have been tampered with. She was concerned but not alarmed. In a while, a young man appeared at her door and said he had come to welcome her to the neighborhood. She realized it was the same person who had wanted to help her that morning with the car.

When the young man entered, her pet bulldog jumped at him, snarling. It was not like the dog to be so demonstrative. "I'm afraid of dogs. Could you do something with her?" he asked. She put the dog out.

They chatted for several minutes. When she turned away momentarily, he grabbed her from behind and put a knife to her throat. Instinctively, she grabbed his hands to prevent him from cutting her. Frozen with fear, her mind was a jumble of thoughts. "Where will he take me? How will they find me? Who's going to find me?" She hoped it would not be her mother.

The intruder bound her hands with panty hose and began to undress her. He left her to draw the blinds and somehow she got one hand free. There was a struggle, and the two of them fell to the floor. Though she landed at least one blow, he retrieved the knife and again stuck it to her throat. She frantically apologized for resisting and begged him not to kill her.

The intruder terrorized her sexually for nearly three hours but was unable to enter her because he could not keep his erection. Without penetration, he did not commit rape according to its legal definition.

Against a backdrop of a television soap opera called *All My Children*, the intruder straightened up the room and removed any signs of a struggle. Jenny Dennis remembered thinking, "What's this guy doing? I know who he is. I know where he lives. He can't possibly let me go." When her assailant casually strolled out the door, she was stunned, incredulous, and thankful. She called police and identified the man as William Ted Wilhoit.

Police arrested Wilhoit and charged him with assault with intent to rape. But they failed to take photographs of the cuts and bruises on the hands, arms, and neck of his victim. The absence of such evidence would be pivotal in March 1974, when a jury acquitted Wilhoit of assault.

The jurors' actions during the 1974 trial were no less a mystery to Jenny Dennis than the absence of photographic evidence. They deliberated a mere thirty minutes before freeing her accused attacker. While she sat in the courtroom, she thought she heard them laughing in the jury room. It sounded like a party. She was dumbfounded.

After the verdict, a reporter for the *Fort Worth Star-Telegram* interviewed several of the female jurors. Said one: "We found him not guilty because her story didn't make sense. He never really did force himself on her. She invited him in." The woman added, "She was a college student. Her boyfriend lived across the street and he had a bad temper. She probably led the man on and then felt her boyfriend would get mad."

A second juror, saying she did not doubt the victim's sincerity, was more concerned that Ms. Dennis had not capitalized on her opportunities to escape. "We didn't want to send him away," the juror said of the defendant. "It would have been on his record forever." Another juror, with no photographs to rely on, said, "She contradicted herself. She said he had a knife and that he had cut her. But she had no bruises or cuts. Sure it was six months later, but there should have been some aftermath. I think they were fooling around."

And still another must have overlooked or ignored testimony that the intruder pulled Ms. Dennis' bra down over her arms to bind her. "She was very chesty and that day she didn't have no bra on." If it had been rape instead of attempted rape, it might have been different, the juror concluded.

Jenny Dennis was electrified by the news of the shooting of Janelle Kirby. Only three months had passed since the jury acquitted William Ted Wilhoit of attempted rape in the Dennis case. The description Janelle Kirby gave police keenly reminded Jenny of Wilhoit. She was swept by a cold chill, accompanied by strong intuitive feelings.

William Ted Wilhoit had never been far from her consciousness since the rape attempt. One day, she was in her carport with her back to the street when she sensed a horrible presence. When she turned around, there was Wilhoit sitting in his car in front of her house. She rushed away, nauseated.

After the Kirby shooting, Ms. Dennis telephoned the Fort Worth Police Department and identified herself as the victim who brought charges against Wilhoit in the earlier attack. She pinpointed the similarities between the Kirby case and her own. She told the officer that Wilhoit often visited the church behind Janelle Kirby's apartment and urged him to investigate Wilhoit in the Kirby shooting. At the officer's request, Jenny Dennis repeated Wilhoit's name.

"Well, isn't that a coincidence," the officer said. "I've got his file and his picture in front of me right now. We are looking at him as a suspect."

There was no record of investigators following up on Jenny Dennis' lead. Wilhoit apparently was not under scrutiny in the Kirby case, despite what the officer told Jenny. When Janelle Kirby recuperated enough to assist police, she was emphatic about the identification of Kenneth Leslie Miller as the man who shot her five times and left her for dead.

Even though William Ted Wilhoit dodged Jenny Dennis' second attempt to nail him, he could not elude Detective Terrell. The second burglary offense resulted in a five-year prison term. In addition, Terrell considered him a prime suspect in several unsolved sex crimes on Fort Worth's south side. Terrell's interest was not diminished when, after the second burglary arrest, officers opened Wilhoit's "burglary bag" and found several pairs of women's panties. "Those belong to my wife," Wilhoit said, unaware that his wife had entered the room and was standing behind him.

"Those aren't mine," his wife said.

Terrell told his colleagues the aspiring minister could have committed at least three other assaults. In two of the cases, the victims were slain. In the third, the surviving victim identified Wilhoit, but the case was irrevocably tainted because she was shown a solitary mugshot of Wilhoit. To pass a court test, Wilhoit's picture should have been scattered among a selection of mugshots of different suspects at the same viewing.

On February 24, 1976, Terrell talked with a witness who identified Wilhoit from a photo spread as a man seen at a south-side bowling alley the night a high school cheerleader named Carla Walker, 17, was abducted, raped, and killed. After meeting with the witness, Terrell drove down to the state prison to observe Wilhoit take a polygraph test. Wilhoit denied involvement in the Walker slaying. He flunked the test.

Afterward, Wilhoit blamed the unfavorable test results in the Carla Walker case on a similar offense for which he contended he could never be prosecuted. Terrell theorized this was the Janelle Kirby case, but Kenneth Miller had been convicted by then and was still on the run. Also, a homicide detective offered him a bit of advice: "Keep this quiet."

John Terrell did not speak out about the Kirby case, but he maintained his interest in Wilhoit. In 1978, he learned that Wilhoit had been released on parole and was living in the West Texas town of Abilene. He was surprised to hear that Wilhoit's wife had stuck with him and was now pregnant. He was even more surprised that Wilhoit had resumed his ministerial studies, this time at Abilene Christian University. Terrell telephoned Lt. Ray Portalatin of the Abilene Police Department and asked if any sex crimes had been committed by a man of Wilhoit's description. He was told there were none.

On a hunch, Terrell bundled up his file on Wilhoit and sent it to Portalatin with a note that read: "He cleared at least twenty or twenty-five cases of burglary for me, one armed robbery, was brought to trial on rape . . . did take ladies' underclothing in at least one burglary. This guy will in my opinion commit some sexual offense if he has not already done so. To my knowledge he did not receive any treatment for such while in the joint. He is a very cool customer and comes on as a very likable type."

Terrell ended the note with a chillingly prophetic comment. "If his wife is pregnant, I'm sure he'll be on the prowl."

Part 6

Abilene, Texas, 1978

While blow-drying her hair in the bedroom of her southwest Abilene home, a 26-year-old woman turned to find a man with what appeared to be a toy gun or an antique pistol pointed at her. He demanded drugs and money. When told she had neither, he ordered her to strip and lie down on the bed. He bound her hands with thumbcuffs. Then he raped her.

She later described her assailant as white, clean shaven, and in his middle 30s with thinning blond hair and blue eyes. He wore a button-down shirt and double-knit slacks. As Janelle Kirby had done four years earlier, the young woman in Abilene spoke of the man's distinctive eyes.

The date was September 20, 1978.

About nine months earlier, Deborah Hankins and her husband Elton, a pharmaceutical salesman, had moved from a suburb of Dallas to Abilene in West Texas oil and ranch country. They brought a son and a daughter, both preschoolers, with them.

Mrs. Hankins' assailant did not threaten to kill her and, once his authority was established, was not abusive. For the briefest of moments, she considered fighting him, but something inside her said, "Don't push this guy." She was afraid the man would harm her if she did not submit. She was also concerned about the safety of her 2-year-old son, the only child at home that day.

"The Lord is my shepherd, I shall not want," she recited as he forced himself on her. The words of the Twenty-third Psalm helped her block out the assault, so much so that she was unaware of her son opening the bedroom door.

Before leaving, the man ordered her into the bathroom with the warning: "Stay in there or you'll be sorry." She assumed he would shoot her if she came out. Her fear heightened momentarily when she guessed he might even fire the gun at her through the bathroom door.

She waited just long enough for him to get past her children's room and out of the house before she ran from the bathroom and locked the outside doors. She had no second thoughts about reporting the rape. As unbearable as the burden and stigma of the attack would be, she forced herself to believe it was preferable to dying. Otherwise, how would her children cope with what happened if she was not there to help them?

What made her bitter in retrospect was that she did not fight back. She considered herself strong, even combative, if her own or her family's safety was at stake. Even though her submissiveness could have saved her life, her bitterness grew. So did her guilt and her anger. She could not talk about the attack without crying.

The same day Deborah Hankins was terrorized, a woman named Carla Aston saw a man running across a vacant lot in front of her home. She watched as he jumped into a small metallic blue car and sped away. Unaware that a rape had occurred, she did not immediately report what she had seen. But she thought she recognized the man in the blue car.

Within hours of the attack, Lt. Ray Portalatin of the Abilene Police Department spoke with investigator Ed Carter about the similarities between Mrs. Hankins' assailant and the ex-convict described to him by Fort Worth detective John Terrell. Carter arranged a photo spread for the victim. With her husband Elton at her side, Deborah pointed to a mugshot of William Ted Wilhoit.

A short time later, Carter received a telephone call. Elton Hankins told him they had driven by Wilhoit's apartment after leaving the police station and saw Wilhoit as he walked from the residence. Hankins said his wife burst into tears. In his report prior to Wilhoit's arrest, Carter said the incident outside Wilhoit's apartment indicated to Mrs. Hankins "there was no doubt in her mind that that was the subject who had raped her."

The case against Wilhoit was bolstered even more when

the district attorney's office located a witness who said she'd seen a man running from the vicinity of the victim's home on September 20. Carla Aston wondered at the time why William Wilhoit, a former employee at her husband's steak house, was scrambling across a vacant lot with a black briefcase under his arm.

Now she knew.

Five years after her own ordeal, Jenny Dennis was scanning the back pages of her Fort Worth newspaper when she spotted an article about the rape of an Abilene housewife. The article did not identify the victim, but it reported that police arrested a 25-year-old convicted burglar and alleged sex offender named William Ted Wilhoit. It also noted that Wilhoit was a ministerial student at Abilene Christian College.

Jenny Dennis was stunned. In her head echoed the laughter of the jurors who had freed Wilhoit after he brutalized her. She was heartbroken and enraged that he was allowed by society to do what he did — again. She was also strangely relieved. For years, she was consumed by her anger at the jurors in the case. In her mind, they had said it was her fault Wilhoit entered her home and sexually abused her. She, the victim, was guilty instead of him. Intellectually, she knew she had done nothing wrong, but the jury did not believe her. So she was tempted to doubt herself and feel guilty, and the anger would return.

It had been another hurdle for Jenny Dennis in her struggle to recover. A marriage to her college boyfriend had failed. She would forever be concerned about her safety, but she was determined not to permit her assailant to ruin her life. She felt Wilhoit's attack on Deborah Hankins restored her own credibility and, in effect, repudiated the jury's decision. She could say with moral certainty, "I told you so."

But in doing so, her guilt returned. How could she somehow feel better because William Ted Wilhoit struck again? How could there be any "good side" to the devastation of another family? She did not know. Driven by her anger, guilt, and sympathy, she learned the identity of Deborah Hankins and contacted her in Abilene. She volunteered her help. Thus, when Wilhoit went on trial in November 1978, Jenny Dennis was seated on the front row of the Abilene courtroom, her eyes focused on the defendant. And there she remained throughout the proceedings.

Largely on the testimony of Mrs. Hankins, a jury convicted Wilhoit of aggravated rape and assessed a forty-year prison sentence.

Deborah Hankins was unable to forgive herself for not resisting Wilhoit's attack. She realized she was courageous enough to report the crime and to testify in open court against him. She believed she might have saved other young women, but she remained deeply troubled. "If I was strong enough to do that, why wasn't I strong enough to fight?" she asked herself.

She developed tendencies toward suicide, according to her counselor, and so did her young son, not yet a teenager. He suffered from both emotional and learning disorders. The daughter was also affected and Mrs. Hankins judged her to be the "silent sufferer," keeping her feelings bottled up. Those feelings surfaced in the daughter's poetry, which Deborah Hankins thought was sad and somewhat morbid.

One day, Mrs. Hankins received a phone call from a clinical psychologist who examined her son. "I know you're going to think I am a quack," the psychologist began, unaware of the family's ordeal. "But I believe your child has witnessed a rape, or possibly has been sexually abused. But I really believe he's witnessed a rape."

Deborah Hankins wanted to scream.

Part 7

Fort Worth, 1986

The anonymous phone call that interrupted Leonard Schilling's celebration at the Albatross also cost the Texas cop a night's sleep. The next morning, he waded into the police files for information on William Ted Wilhoit, the traveling rapist. He found plenty.

Schilling quickly realized that Wilhoit's description matched the one that Janelle Kirby originally gave the police. He also discovered there had been several sexual attacks in Wilhoit's old Fort Worth neighborhood and that Wilhoit lived within blocks of Janelle Kirby's apartment in 1974.

It was not long before Schilling was convinced he had been tracking the wrong man. Kenneth Miller did not shoot Janelle Kirby; Wilhoit did. But Schilling knew that Wilhoit was never a suspect in the Kirby case until now, twelve years later. He was profoundly puzzled and just a little suspicious. It was the worst police investigation in Fort Worth history, he thought, or something even darker.

Meanwhile, with Miller's arrest still a hot news story, the Criminal Investigation Division of the Fort Worth Police Department assigned two detectives to determine if Miller might be linked to the 1984 disappearances or deaths of half a dozen young women on the west and south sides. The investigation was a short one. Miller was quickly cleared, but one of the detectives, Danny LaRue, then joined Schilling in a reassessment of the Kirby case. They were not the likeliest of partners. LaRue's style was conservative and deliberate and he was not altogether comfortable with Schilling's flamboyance and impatience. But LaRue liked his rowdy colleague and thought he was a good street cop.

When word of Kenneth Leslie Miller's arrest in Las Vegas reached Janelle Kirby in Florida, she said, "It makes my heart pound to hear it. I'm glad they caught him. But quite frankly, I'd like to put it out of my mind and forget it ever happened."

She could not forget it, of course. In fact, she was more apprehensive than relieved about Miller's capture. She was convinced that she would be dragged back into that pit in Fort Worth from which she struggled so long to escape. She dreaded a confrontation with Miller, explaining: "I like Fort Worth, but I don't want to be around him. I don't need my life wrecked again."

It had been precisely twelve years since the shooting, and now, at age 32, she was little more than a year away from earning her nursing degree. She still could be frightened to tears by the sound of exploding firecrackers or a television gunfight, and her husband Jim had grown accustomed to investigating the slightest noises, night or day. Jim, she realized, was a quiet but constant source of strength. "If I didn't have him, I would never have gotten this far," she told a friend. "He's encouraged me all along the way."

Janelle Kirby's world in 1986 centered on Jim, her studies, novels, a cat named Morris, and the movies the couple rented and watched on their video recorder. Using an inheritance from the grandmother in Virginia who raised Janelle as a teenager, they built a small but comfortable home and rarely left it. Janelle Kirby often felt no less a fugitive than Kenneth Miller.

Aside from sporadic calls from reporters and a rush of chilling memories, Miller's arrest was on the surface a minimal disruption in her slow but steady climb toward stability. She wanted it to be that way. "I've done my best to go on and try not to think about it," she said. "But you never forget."

She was unaware of Detectives Schilling and LaRue's new investigation or the strange phone call that precipitated it. And she was totally unprepared for the biggest shocker, less than a month away.

Working hard to prove somebody innocent, thought Danny LaRue, was a whole new ball game. Yet he soon joined Schilling in the conclusion that Kenneth Miller did not shoot Janelle Kirby. LaRue was troubled by the 31-day delay between the time Miller's picture was identified by Janelle Kirby and the time of his arrest. The detective told others, "That delay has its own implications." He conferred with his superiors and then entered a new phase of the reopened Miller case. Assuming Miller was innocent, was there a frame? Meanwhile, Schilling had a troubling thought: what if Miller killed himself while attempts were underway to establish his innocence? The detective deviously notified Las Vegas police that their prisoner was "suicidal" and recommended he be kept in isolation.

Guessing that a confession from Wilhoit was a long shot, Schilling and LaRue decided to play some mind games. A meeting was arranged with Wilhoit at the state prison in Huntsville, but neither detective showed up. Then Wilhoit was brought into Fort Worth on a judge's bench warrant and left to cool his heels in a jail cell for several days. The maneuvering continued until a deal was struck with Wilhoit and his attorneys. He would be granted immunity from prosecution in the Kirby case in exchange for a full confession.

Surrounded by detectives, investigators, and lawyers, Wilhoit related for the first time what led to the attack twelve years earlier on Janelle Kirby. He told how he drove around the TCU area, parked by a church, walked down an alley, and entered a gate leading to the Kirby apartment. "Observing no one around, I climbed the stairs and entered the apartment," he said in a written statement. "Once inside, I was surprised by a white female that I later learned was Janelle Kirby." He described the jewelry and blouse she wore and added, "I am certain she did not have on a dress."

As he handcuffed one of her wrists, "she started to fight me." He said he raised his pistol and she grabbed his hand. The pistol, he said, became tangled in her hair and discharged several times. "She then fell to the floor." Wilhoit said he removed the handcuffs from Kirby's wrist and dumped the contents of her purse on the bed. Then he fled the apartment and ran to his car.

Schilling shuddered as Wilhoit recounted the events of 1974 coldly and unemotionally and in a monotone that made the officer's skin crawl. There was no feeling, excitement or otherwise, in Wilhoit's eyes. There was no regret or remorse in his voice.

Danny LaRue marveled at Wilhoit's ability to recall so vividly his victim's apartment, jewelry, and clothing, but it was Schilling who asked the key question, one that only the gunman could have answered. The assailant left behind the ejection rod from his .22-caliber pistol, but crime scene investigators overlooked it. Kirby's boyfriend later found it buried in the carpet and turned it over to the police. An officer tagged the rod and stuck it in the evidence room and there it remained for twelve years until Schilling and LaRue stumbled across it largely by accident. Schilling believed this to be the only piece of evidence not mentioned at the Miller trial or otherwise made public.

With his pulse quickening, Cowboy Schilling asked Wilhoit if, upon returning to his car that evening, he noticed anything strange about his pistol.

"I noticed the cylinder pin had come out of my gun," the inmate replied. The two detectives exchanged glances. They finally had the right man in the Kirby shooting. A subsequent polygraph test supported the Wilhoit confession.

Wilhoit told investigators he learned at one point that a man had been arrested and later convicted in the Kirby shooting. He said the man escaped from the courtroom before sentencing. Of all his misadventures, Wilhoit told the investigators, the Janelle Kirby attack was one he thought he would never have to worry about.

One night in early July, Leonard Schilling, Danny LaRue, and Miller's lawyer, Bill Magnussen, flew to Las Vegas to retrieve Kenneth Miller from jail and return him to Fort Worth. Miller was unaware that someone else had confessed to the shooting of Janelle Kirby. From behind bars, he was still insisting he be called by his longtime alias, even though fingerprint and handwriting samples suggested otherwise.

When the trio from Texas arrived at the Las Vegas jail, Magnussen went into the interview room alone. It had been more than eleven years since the trial and Miller did not recognize him immediately.

"Bill?" he asked.

"Yeah."

"What's going on?"

"It's all over," the lawyer said.

At first, Miller did not believe it when Magnussen told him he had been cleared in Texas of the Kirby shooting. "You'll be loose by Friday night," Magnussen predicted. By the time Schilling and LaRue entered the room, both the lawyer and Kenneth Miller were in tears. "These guys are on your side," Magnussen said, pointing to the investigators. "Tell them anything they want to know."

Schilling was stunned by the appearance of the man he once thought to be an arrogant and cold-blooded gunman. He was nothing like the armed and dangerous fugitive portrayed in the Crime Stoppers poster. Miller was so beaten and frail, like a quivering rabbit.

Although Miller wanted to believe the three men from Fort Worth, the stories they were telling him did not compute.

It reminded Schilling of those movies about POWs who were scared of their liberators. Before leaving, Schilling told Miller, "We've got the guy who did it."

It would be hours into a sleepless night before Miller grasped in full what he had been told. Then, just before dawn, he telephoned Fort Worth. "Your prayers have been answered," he told Lee Mulholland. "They're setting me free."

Lee was delighted but acted as if she was not surprised. "God does not start something that he doesn't finish," she said. "Some great good is going to come from all this. God's not through with you yet. Not by a long shot."

Schilling, LaRue, and Magnussen spent much of the night gambling in the casino at the Sahara Hotel and returned early the next day to take Miller back to Fort Worth. Instead, they became ensnarled in red tape. One of the problems involved the criminal complaints pending against Miller in Nevada, the most serious a hot check charge. An unlikely source solved that problem. Dianna Oppermann used the mortgage on her small home to raise bond money.

Next, Las Vegas authorities pointed out that Schilling had put an official "hold" on Miller via a Texas warrant issued several weeks earlier, and they were not about to surrender Miller without a release order. Miller and his benefactors missed two flights back to Texas before a Texas judge was contacted to cancel the warrant. A third plane broke down before takeoff. A final flight took them to Texas via Denver.

While they drank beer during the layover in Denver, Schilling gazed at Miller. "I'm as amazed at him as he is at me," Schilling thought. The hunter and the hunted discussed the shared trauma of a recent divorce and the grief of losing a dog that was more companion than pet.

"Schilling, I got to ask you something," Miller said at one point. "Why were you obsessed with me? With catching me?"

The detective chose to explain it in terms of fate. "Kenneth, all this happened because it was meant to happen. You ran because you were meant to run. A lot of people said if you hadn't run, you'd have been proved innocent. But that's bullshit. You were meant to run and I was meant to catch you and to prove you innocent."

Miller was not satisfied. "But why did all this happen? Why did you want me arrested so bad?"

"It was just fate," said Schilling, now admitting the answer sounded lame. "If you wouldn't have run, you would have done your time by now. I wouldn't have chased you, but you wouldn't be going back to Fort Worth an innocent man. You had to be caught to be found innocent."

Miller told him it was a good thing he caught him when he did. "If it had been much later, you'd have needed snowbirds. I was going to Alaska."

The two also discussed a much uglier scenario. "As much as I know about you, I always wondered when I found you, who was going to get shot first," said Schilling. "I was afraid I'd have to come get you and you'd point a pistol at me and you'd have been history."

Miller confirmed it would not have been a peaceful surrender. "If I had a gun, and you'd cornered me, I would have pulled it. I'd rather die than go to prison for something I didn't do."

Part 8

Back in Fort Worth, lawyers, judges, prosecutors, and police worked quickly to obtain Miller's freedom. The procedure was complicated because of the legal issues raised by his abrupt departure eleven years earlier.

Defense attorney Bill Magnussen's 1975 motion for a new trial was still pending, and a judge was now persuaded to grant it. District attorney Tim Curry then filed a motion for dismissal, and the judge endorsed that. "At best we have an imperfect system, but it is directed toward justice," Curry said. "In this case it finally worked, even if it did take twelve years."

On July 11, 1986, Kenneth Miller, ex-fugitive, walked out of the courtroom to face a battery of newspaper, radio, and television reporters and an uncertain future. "This is just like the TV fugitive, when a police officer chased David Janssen for all those years," said Lee Mulholland as she stood beside Bill Magnussen. "He was found innocent, just like Kenneth."

"Yes," replied Magnussen. "But their show ran for seven years. Ours ran for twelve."

For Leonard Schilling, the Miller case marked the end of a colorful police career. "This was the biggest thing in my life," he said on the eve of his departure from the Crime Stoppers program. "It really was an obsession. But police work ain't no fun anymore. I think I knew that Miller was my last deal." Opting for a legal career, he applied and was accepted at the South Texas College of Law in Houston. He enrolled for the spring semester. "Miller was the highlight of my career, the first time I ever worked to prove somebody innocent," Schilling said. "I know now that I was meant to do that. I'm just glad it ended up like it did, instead of how it could have."

Cowboy Schilling left the police force convinced of Miller's innocence and Wilhoit's guilt. "Beyond the slightest doubt," he said.

Kenneth Miller returned to Las Vegas for a time, his misfortune now a way of life. He was in and out of jail, mostly on charges related to his drinking. Yet, in the aftermath of his twelve-year flight, he said, "I have no animosity. If Janelle Kirby really thought I did it, what can you say? If she really thought it was me, there is nothing to say." Originally, he thought he was framed by the Fort Worth Police Department and discussed the possibility with Bill Magnussen and others. "I don't know now," said Miller, shaking his head.

Danny LaRue, the straight-arrow detective, concluded there had been no frame-up despite "under-the-carpet" talk around the police department to the contrary. Miller, he said, was a victim of bizarre coincidence. LaRue's investigation did not determine why Wilhoit was not a suspect in 1974. Nor did it explain the unusual 31-day delay between Janelle Kirby's mugshot identification and Miller's arrest at the civil service hearing for Ray Armand and his partner. LaRue refused to speculate on the reason for the delay.

Armand, who rose through the ranks to become director of the department's super-sensitive Internal Affairs Division, said he stayed "within the system" in 1974 and thereby disproved Miller's allegations of brutality. He said he hoped Miller held no lingering animosity. "I certainly don't," he added. Several sources within the department said the Internal Affairs Division was ordered to look into the events of 1974 that led to Miller's arrest but that the investigation fizzled about the time Armand took over the division. "It was really kind of blown off," said one veteran officer. "It was a strange deal."

Chief of Police Thomas Windham, who took the top job in 1985, defended the internal investigation and said it uncovered no evidence of police improprieties, "From my perspective twelve or thirteen years later," he said, "I'm satisfied we have looked into this about as deeply as we can."

Meanwhile, Miller indicated it no longer mattered to him. Las Vegas authorities dropped remaining criminal charges after Miller pleaded guilty to a bad check complaint in exchange for a brief probated sentence. He neither knew nor cared who turned him in to Schilling's Texas Crime Stoppers. "I hope they enjoy the $1,000," he said.

He moved in temporarily with his girlfriend Debbie and her two daughters. Returning to work as a mechanic, he insisted he was trying to rebuild his life. He thought he was on an even keel most of the time, but friends said he remained emotionally erratic and in deep turmoil. "This thing has totally wrecked his life," Debbie said. "He can't get a grip on it. He can't cope with it. For the last twelve years he's had to run so much and lie so much, and now he's drinking as a way to forget." She believed Miller wanted to help himself but did not know how. She was uncertain what she could do. "He's headed for big-time trouble, and it scares me to death."

Accounts of Miller's ordeal were national news, given the legacy of David Janssen's TV series. There were inquiries about a made-for-TV movie. Not much money was involved, but a movie house on the West Coast formally took out an option. Typical of Miller's luck, a writer's strike delayed the project before any money changed hands.

In her Abilene home, Deborah Hankins read about how police now connected her attacker, William Ted Wilhoit, to the Janelle Kirby shooting years ago. It transformed her. She found absolution from the deep guilt of not fighting Wilhoit. She realized she had probably saved her life and maybe her son's. Janelle Kirby fought him and, left for dead, came close to paying the ultimate price.

Her personal burden lifted, Deborah Hankins counseled with her family and decided in 1987 to identify herself publicly as Wilhoit's rape victim. She sought out an Associated Press reporter who wrote extensively about the case. She also joined an effort to pass legislation denying automatic parole for felons like Wilhoit, who could be freed by 1992. Her children, now 13 and 11, and her husband Elton, supported her, as did the Abilene district attorney, Jorge Solis. "I really admire her," said Solis. "She's tough and she's handling this as best she can."

Deborah Hankins encouraged other rape victims to contact her if they needed help. "Some good has got to come out of this evil for me to accept it," she said.

Jenny Dennis, whose attempted rape case in 1973 ended in Wilhoit's acquittal, came forward, too. Allowing her name to be used, she disclosed that she had made a call to Fort Worth police in 1974 pointing to Wilhoit as a possible suspect in the Janelle Kirby shooting. "The police were negligent," she asserted in an Associated Press story. "They were remiss, because they knew. Somebody knew. I know they had that information. I know they were looking at him. I wasn't talking to the janitor. I was talking to the policeman who was on that case. And if they never showed Janelle Kirby his picture after what I told them, explain that to me. Explain that to Kenneth Miller. Explain that to Janelle Kirby."

Jenny Dennis talked of the bonds she felt with Janelle Kirby, Deborah Hankins, and even Kenneth Miller. "We've all been fugitives," she said. She was affected by the new developments in the Wilhoit and Kirby cases. "I'm not reliving what happened to me thirteen years ago in its worst sense, but I'm having trouble sleeping. I've been sick at my stomach. I feel the same anger and frustration at a system that has worked to let him go. They should have had Wilhoit on the Janelle Kirby case."

Her own case was different. "I wasn't a good victim, because Wilhoit got off on my deal. But what would they have given him even if he had been convicted? Two years? A suspended sentence? At some point he would have been turned loose. He would have raped and killed a different group of people. Somebody gets the black marble. You can't question the past."

When Jenny Dennis disclosed that she had pointed police to Wilhoit on the Kirby case in 1974, it made interesting newspaper copy but little more. Detective LaRue, now pursuing other assignments, talked with Jenny but said the department would not reopen its inquiry a second time. He found Dennis sincere, intelligent, and credible, but he would not comment on the new questions raised by her disturbing story.

"This case is closed," he said.

Dianna Oppermann had her own reaction to Miller's release. "Nobody can ever understand why I did what I did," she said of her years with him on the run. "I don't either, really. I loved him, you know. I wanted to help him. But would I do it again? I don't know. Now, at my age, probably not. . . . If I knew that it would come out like this, yeah, maybe. But then if you ended up with a shootout on Interstate 15, forget it. You just don't know until you're there. Then you pick your road and you live with it."

She bore no bitterness. Just hurt. "Who can you be bitter at? Not the state. The state didn't put him away. The jury convicted him. Even that Janelle Kirby, he's never said anything about wanting to get even. Man, if I was her, I'd be scared to death. But wherever she is, he's not after her at all. He could care less."

Close to crying, she said, "I think he just wants to be left alone, to forget the past."

As the news reports on Miller's release flowed across the country, Detective Danny LaRue received a telephone call from Janelle Kirby. From her home in Florida, she demanded to know what was going on. He talked for what seemed to him to be about an hour and gave her as complete an account as he could. She did not interrupt, even to ask a question.

He completed the phone conversation, thinking she wanted to apologize to Miller for what had happened. A time and place for her call was arranged; the next day, Miller sat by the phone in attorney Magnussen's office waiting to talk to the person who had so dramatically altered his life.

The call never came.

Janelle Kirby was stunned and confused by the news from Fort Worth. She could not believe it, nor could she understand why it was happening. She felt she'd been badgered by Detective LaRue into offering an apology she considered premature. Until now, she thought the Fort Worth police had been kind to her and treated her with exceptional courtesy, but she believed Detective LaRue disliked her without knowing her.

Her husband Jim was alarmed at how upset his wife had become. He insisted that she not call Miller.

"What am I going to do?" she asked.

"I don't know," he replied. "But don't call him. We're not sure yet. We haven't seen this Wilhoit guy." They appealed to authorities in Texas for a photograph of William Ted Wilhoit but received nothing. The episode disrupted Janelle's studies, but she was back in class in the fall.

In January, an Associated Press reporter flew to Florida with a 1974 photograph of Wilhoit and the wanted poster bearing Miller's picture at the time of his original arrest. The reporter was uncertain he would see Janelle Kirby, but, after she and Jim held a tearful conference, the three of them met.

"We just try not to think about it," said Jim. "It doesn't matter anymore. Nothing that happened can be changed. We've just got to try to go on."

Jim viewed the pictures before Janelle and noted the similarities. He said he understood how difficult a positive ID might be for a critically wounded survivor of an attack such as the one on Janelle. But he was supportive of his wife and knew better than anyone her terrible ordeal in 1974 and the fear and anxiety of the last twelve years. "She's been in hiding every bit as much as Kenneth Miller," he said.

Brushing back tears, her hands shaking, Janelle compared the photographs for the first time. "That man doesn't look a thing like the person who shot me," she said of the Wilhoit picture. "The nose and the mouth are completely different, and the man's eyes . . ." She said she vividly remembered the eyes.

"Does this look like the person?" the reporter asked, handing her the Miller poster.

After a long pause, she replied, "If I say yes, now that they have declared him to be innocent, isn't that slander?"

"No."

"Then I've just told you what I believe."

3

UNREASONABLE DOUBT

The Bizarre Story of Cullen and Priscilla Davis

Other sins only speak; murder shrieks out.
                                    —John Webster

If there was some way I could do it, I'd like to turn
back your lives to the fall of 1968.
—Judge Clyde Ashworth, upon granting a divorce
                        to Cullen and Priscilla Davis

Part 1

Fort Worth, Texas

*The first person to see the man in black was Andrea Wilborn, young-
est of Priscilla Davis' three children. He shot her once through the chest.
She died on the basement floor of a $6 million mansion. It was August
2, 1976. She was 12 years old.*

*When Priscilla returned to the mansion that night, she was accom-
panied by Stan Farr. He was her live-in lover, the second since her
husband Cullen Davis had moved out in 1974. It was after midnight,
and Stan went directly upstairs to the master bedroom. Priscilla entered the kitchen, switching off lights. She saw the bloody hand print
on the basement door frame, and she screamed. Moments later, the man*

in black stepped from his hiding place. He wore a woman's black wig. His hands were covered with a dark plastic bag. He said, "Hi." Then he fired a bullet through her chest.

When Priscilla fell to the floor, the man in black turned his gun on Stan Farr. The first shot penetrated a door and then tore into his side. The two men struggled. A second shot struck him in the chest, knocking him to the floor. The gunman fired twice more. Priscilla watched Stan die. Outside, a Chevrolet Blazer pulled on the grounds. A young couple was returning from a date.

The man in black intercepted the couple at a courtyard gate. "What's going on? Where is everybody?" asked Bubba Gavrel. "Right this way. Follow me," the man replied. He led them through the darkness and down a walkway. As they rounded a corner, Beverly Bass spoke. The man turned instantly and fired. The bullet hit Bubba. It tore through a rib and into his spine, knocking him backward. Beverly retreated into the darkness. When the man ran after her, Bubba tried to get up. But he could not stand. He was paralyzed.

Beverly could hear the man behind her, running. She screamed at him not to shoot. Out of breath, she stopped and looked back up the hill. She could see him silhouetted against the glowing mansion. Again she begged him not to shoot. The next time she looked, the man in black was gone.

On the night of August 2, Mr. and Mrs. Clifford Jones retired early. It had become their habit to do so, because both were getting on in years and Mr. Jones had not been well. They lived in a subdivision south of the Davis mansion, separated from it by a field several hundred yards long.

They were awakened by the sound of their dog barking; while Jones silently cursed the hound, his wife crawled out of bed to investigate. Approaching the front door, Mrs. Jones spotted a figure moving outside the house. It appeared to be a woman, who began ringing the doorbell frantically. "Please . . . oh, please, help me. I'm Priscilla Davis. I live in the big white house on the hill. I've been shot. Please help me. Please, can I come in?"

Mr. Jones, hearing the commotion, was now at his wife's side. They stared at one another as if transfixed.

"It's Priscilla Davis," the woman on the porch continued. "You must call the police. *Cullen is up there shooting everybody.*

He is killing everybody, and I'm wounded very badly."

As a child, Cullen Davis collected stamps and raised purebred chows, never acquiring an interest in participation sports. He customarily wore suits and ties to public schools. That may not sound too unusual, but in Texas, and particularly Fort Worth, it suggested a lifestyle on a par with the Court of St. James. Had it not been for his formal attire, Cullen might have made it through high school unnoticed by his classmates.

Cullen said he always knew of the family's great wealth, but his father insisted there should be no boasting about it. He had a rebellious streak, but defiance of his father was not easy. He both loved and feared the old man. He developed a stutter in his father's presence that irritated others in the family. When he overcame the impediment, it was never mentioned again.

At 14, Cullen went to work for one of his father's many businesses. "That was fine with me; it was just what I wanted to do," Cullen said, but it was not quite what he expected. Using a rubber stamp, he affixed the date to every page of every document that arrived at the office. Years later, Cullen personally put a stop to the whole process, saving countless hours of labor.

Cullen was shy and reticent and his fondness for girls was not artfully expressed or frequently productive in his early days at Arlington Heights High School. Despite his money, or maybe even because of it, Cullen did not make a splash, but his Power Glide Chevy did, and he charged his classmates a nickel a trip to the ice cream parlor.

One of Cullen's most notorious escapades occurred in 1960. The occasion was a stag party signaling the end of bachelorhood for one of the city's young lions. Among those present that night in a rented motel cabana was Tim Curry, who later would become district attorney. Cullen arrived late and apparently recognized one of the nude dancers about the time she recognized him. She stopped in mid-shimmy. She was overheard to say "I'm sorry" before Cullen dragged her from the party, shoved her into his car, and sped away in a cloud of rubber and smoke.

Fog, drizzle, and cold rode a Texas norther into Dallas on January 2, 1968, slashing nighttime visibility at Love Field Airport to an eighth of a mile. Holiday travelers mingled with a noisy football crowd, remnants of the New Year's Day Cotton Bowl Classic. Cullen Davis' alma mater, Texas A & M University, had just upset the Crimson Tide of Alabama, 20–16, but he had not been among his school's maroon-clad revelers.

Neither the Texas Aggies nor the Alabamans noticed the man at the window. He stood alone and unsmiling, watching the passengers emerge from the big jet. His gaze fixed on a young woman. She was short and shapely, her hair long and blonde. She wore a white miniskirt and lugged a big teddy bear. The man at her side was lean and darkly handsome, of average height, in his mid-30s. As the couple passed through the gate, the sentry scurried away to join three companions. When the couple's Pontiac swept out the entrance to the airport, a sedan slipped in behind. A third car followed at a discreet distance.

The caravan turned west as it left the airport, traveling away from Dallas. About 10 P.M., the Pontiac rolled into the parking lot of the Green Oaks Inn, the finest of Fort Worth's modest hostelries. The man secured a key from the desk clerk, then crossed the deserted lobby and rejoined the young woman. She laughed softly as she took her companion's arm and accompanied him around a corner and up the flight of stairs.

The couple entered their room and undressed for bed. Minutes later, a raiding party led by a man named Jack Wilborn kicked in the door of the darkened love nest. They sprayed Mace, popped flashbulbs, snapped photographs, and upset an otherwise perfectly good evening.

"You can't do this!" protested the man, leaping from the bed in his shorts. Jack Wilborn pinned him against the wall, their eyes only inches apart. The young woman, nude, fled into the bathroom, locking the door and screaming, "Wilborn, you son of a bitch, if you don't get out of here, I'll call the police!"

"Open the door," Wilborn told his wife Priscilla, "and I'll hand you the phone."

Outside the door, watching and listening with poorly concealed fury, was a woman named Sandra Davis. Finally, she marched through the fumes to confront her husband, whose back was against the wall. She waved a finger in his face. "Cullen Davis, you dirty son of a bitch," she declared before storming out.

The Green Oaks Episode, as it came to be called, accelerated two pending divorce suits and furnished a provocative new item for Fort Worth gossip.

It was not Cullen and Priscilla's finest moment, but they recovered handily. Eight months later, they were married in a sedate and stately downtown church. Their wedding date would also be remembered as the day Cullen's father died.

Sandra Davis had never actually caught Cullen Davis with another woman until Jack Wilborn's raiders broke down the door at the Green Oaks Inn. Even so, she was present when Priscilla and Cullen first met. It was on the tennis courts of Ridglea Country Club on the eve of the 1967 Colonial National Invitational golf tournament.

Cullen perceived Priscilla to be an attractive young woman, even without the breast job he would one day insist upon. Her hair was not yet the ice-blonde it would become in later years, but it was long and light, and he liked it. There was a piquant air about her and also a sly sauciness that would become almost a trademark. Her eyes were big and brown, and though some would describe them as smoldering, they always had a wide and childlike quality.

Priscilla next saw Cullen in the bar at the Colonial Country Club, and this time there was no doubt as to Cullen's intentions. She thought him rather childish and even slightly rude in his flirtation, like a boy tugging a little girl's pigtails.

A short time later, Cullen flew to the Paris Air Show, leaving his wife Sandra behind. Just about the time the plane took off, Sandra filed for divorce. If Cullen was heartbroken, he disguised it well. When he finally returned to Fort Worth, he and Sandra separated, which meant Cullen could devote all his time to pursuing Priscilla. She was not an unwilling quarry.

Priscilla separated from Jack Wilborn on June 9, 1967. Four days later, he sued for a divorce he did not really want.

However, he most definitely wanted custody of his children, Jackie and Andrea—and even Dee, Priscilla's daughter by a previous marriage, if she preferred him to her mother. He had no children from his prior marriage and he would stop at nothing to keep his young son and daughter. Priscilla was not overly concerned at the time. She hired a lawyer to aid her in the custody fight, but for the moment she was just happy to be free again.

The morning after the Green Oaks episode, Cullen arranged a meeting with Wilborn, who brought an investigator with him. Cullen's first comment was, "You're not getting any of my money."

"I'm not interested in your money—the only thing I want is the custody of my children," Wilborn said. He rejected Cullen's proposal to split the Wilborn children up.

At one point, Cullen sat back in his chair and said, "I haven't made up my mind to accept the responsibility of Priscilla yet." But after he and the millionaire parted ways, Wilborn knew the children were his. He mentioned to the investigator that Cullen seemed visibly relieved to learn his money was not the issue.

"Yeah," chuckled the investigator, "he became downright friendly after that."

Part 2

It came as a shock to no one, least of all Cullen and Priscilla, that Cullen's father, Stinky Davis, was less than pleased with his son's choice of a prospective second bride. There were certain unfortunate gaps in her lineage, beginning with her father, whom she never met. The only thing her mother told her about him was, "If you ever met him, you'd like him."

When Priscilla's father forgot to send money, her mother didn't complain. He was a "geologist" by profession and a rodeo bum by preference, and the latter won out in the long haul. Priscilla's family never had to cope with the problems of the wealthy, and Priscilla said she and her brothers were blissfully unaware of money shortages. "We had a sandpile and swings, and all the kids played in our yard."

When Priscilla was 15, she and her mother made a strange

odyssey to California, where they lived with an alcoholic social worker. Priscilla first attended high school in Van Nuys,
which she enjoyed, and later in Hollywood, which she did
not. She preferred drag races to schoolwork and spent many
a pleasurable day with the boys at the Bakersfield speedway.

Her mother quickly tired of California, and together they
returned to Texas, where Priscilla promptly met and married a dashing 21-year-old ex-Marine named Jasper. Most
of their marriage consisted of Priscilla being pregnant, which
Jasper found annoying. He would brood for hours, usually
with a sympathetic barmaid. Their union was doomed from
the start.

The baby came on July 21, 1958. It was a girl named Ange-
la Dee, but called Dee. Soon after, Priscilla packed her bags
and moved in with her mother, spurning Jasper's overtures
for reconciliation. Then she fled to California with her daughter to be with a friend named Gary, but that, too, was a disaster. Deeply discouraged, Priscilla accepted a ride back to
Texas in a pickup truck that was as close to a breakdown as
she was. If someone would have told her she was destined
to marry a multimillionaire, she would have laughed in his
face. She was 17 years old and dead broke.

Back in Texas, Priscilla took a job at a department store,
but it bored her. "I went to lunch with friends one day and
just never went back," she said. One evening, she accompanied a group to a Houston club called the Tidelands and there
she met a car dealer from Fort Worth. She liked the man immediately. For one thing, he was older and different from
any of the men she had known. He was soft-spoken and
charming, prematurely gray with a deep tan and a Europe-
an look that she found distinguished and appealing. When
he asked her if he might call on his next trip to Houston, she
said, "Please do."

Priscilla was 18 and Jack Wilborn was 40 when they became lovers and, subsequently, man and wife. She bore him
a son named Jackie and a daughter named Andrea. He was
not a wealthy man, but they could afford a nice home in Fort
Worth and membership in a country club. Priscilla drove a
big car, hired a maid, and had, by her own assessment, the

best of everything. "To my knowledge, he didn't run around on me," Priscilla said. *"And he didn't beat me."*

Jack and Priscilla were not alike, however. He was an easy-going family man. She tried to be active in the PTA, do volunteer work, and have a Brownie troop, but she became terribly depressed with her life as a middle-class matron. She thought there had to be something wrong with her and started seeing a psychiatrist. She also started thinking about divorce.

Jack opposed a separation because he loved the children too much. As an escape, Priscilla began playing tennis and took to the game like a duck to oil. She was awful. At the same time, she decorated the Ridglea Country Club courts nicely, and it was there that she met a not-so-happily married millionaire named Cullen Davis.

The divorce of Cullen and Sandra Davis was final on August 5, 1968, seven months after Jack Wilborn had shed Priscilla. Three weeks later, Cullen belatedly took Priscilla for his lawfully wedded wife, but not before she was confronted with a prenuptial agreement surrendering any claim to the billion-dollar family businesses. The newlyweds moved into the home of Cullen's father, conveniently vacated earlier the same day by the old man's death.

"I had no intention of remaining there for very long," Cullen explained of the oddly timed move. It was a fact that Cullen was already planning his dream home. It would be a hilltop mansion overlooking the Colonial Country Club. With his father's sudden death, he could almost afford it.

Priscilla settled comfortably and quickly into her new lifestyle and reveled in her good fortune. Overnight, she became a lavish and pretentious spender and Cullen showered her with gifts.

She and Cullen had what Priscilla called their "deal"—out of town she could wear anything, but not in Fort Worth. Consequently, she had her "Acapulco bikini," her Vegas outfit, and even a flesh-colored T-shirt that appeared to show bare breasts.

Cullen and his feisty wife appeared at all the proper social and charitable galas in Fort Worth, but Cullen had his friends and she had hers. "I thought she would be liked, but that turned out to be wrong," Cullen said. "I thought that she was kind of pretty, but I was mistaken about that, too." His disenchantment with Priscilla became evident in the bedroom. "I can't even take my clothes off without you grabbing at me," Cullen once told her. Priscilla thought that excessively strange, because "what he had liked about me was my aggressiveness."

There was a dark side to Cullen that surfaced even before he and Priscilla moved from their first home to the new mansion. On a midsummer night in 1971, shortly before her thirteenth birthday, Dee Davis was awakened by Cullen. She had decided to live with her mother the year before and Cullen had legally adopted her. She could smell liquor on her stepfather's breath as he jerked her out of bed and marched her downstairs.

"What did we forget tonight?" Cullen asked heavily.

"I forgot to lock the back door," Dee answered.

"Why do we lock the doors at night?"

"So nobody will steal your precious junk."

He repeated the question. Again she replied sarcastically. Cullen knocked her into the door, breaking her nose. Hearing the commotion, Priscilla ran into the kitchen carrying a kitten. Cullen grabbed the kitten and slammed it to the floor. As the kitten lay there quivering, he picked it up and threw it down again, killing it. Then he broke two chairs.

By mid-1974, the moody millionaire had compiled what Priscilla claimed was a travelogue of violence. She said he beat her black and blue in Palm Springs, cracked her collarbone at Marina del Rey, and broke her nose in the mansion poolroom. Cullen said Priscilla deliberately contrived several such incidents with Dee and branded them as lies. Even so, child-welfare authorities came away impressed with Cullen's expertise with a belt after he punished Dee for a report card notable only as a forgery.

For himself, Cullen traced the couple's problems to a skiing accident, after which Priscilla "got on painkillers and started staying up late at night." When Cullen would not stay up with her, she invited others over to his mansion. When he put a stop to that, she went out. He said their relationship ended when she started staying out all night "doing hanky-panky." Priscilla denied Cullen's accusations, although lamely.

The marital suspicions and discord prompted Cullen to pack his bags and leave his beloved mansion on July 30, 1974, Priscilla's 33rd birthday. It had been six years of agony and ecstasy, with emphasis on the former. The next day, Priscilla converted a credit card into $1,500 and marched into the office of attorney Ronald Aultman to launch divorce proceedings. He asked her the value of her home and she guessed $6 million. At first, he thought it was foolishness, but it did not take Priscilla long to convince Aultman he had a million-dollar client on his hands.

Despite arguments to the contrary, the mansion Cullen built was never intended as a "dream house" for Priscilla. It is possible she thought so, but more likely such a claim served her divorce suit nicely. Then, too, Cullen may have told her this during happier times. In fact, Cullen built his mansion for himself. "I have proof of this," he said once. "Plans for the house were started five years before I even met Priscilla."

In the summer of 1969, Cullen took a file he had accumulated for years to architect Albert Komatsu, a friend of his father. "It contained specifications and pictures and clippings from magazines depicting what I wanted the house to contain and the type of architecture and materials," Cullen said. "His people laid out the plan connecting it all up in logical fashion, incorporating everything I had given them." When completed, it was both opulent and outlandish, and exactly what Cullen wanted. In some way, it was more than just Cullen's house; it was Cullen himself. "I am extremely pleased," he told Albert Komatsu.

By day, the mansion loomed as a glittering, trapezoidal monument to money and architectural originality. At night, it glowed like a garish ghost ship surrounded by a sea of darkness. Above all, some people felt it was a $6-million symbol of Cullen's position in Fort Worth society. It was not only a very expensive product of *nouveau riche*, it was also remote. From the hilltop, Cullen could look down on everybody else. The house was conspicuous and at the same time inaccessible. Many thought it important to have Cullen and Priscilla at their parties; but once out of earshot, they condemned them to hell and back.

The mansion also became a symbol of the divorce. Priscilla had it and Cullen wanted it. His brother Bill later contended that Cullen was possessed by the mansion and would even kill for it. Some said he did. Like Cullen, the house had a certain cold charm about it, particularly in the lush and shaded courtyards that provided the haunting, mysterious shadows that danced through the night lights. It took on a distinctively different atmosphere after nightfall. As an attorney observed late one evening, it was the perfect place for a murder.

Part 3

On August 2, 1976, Cullen Davis was a man under siege, not only by Priscilla and her attorneys but by brother Bill, whom Cullen and Ken Davis ousted from the family business empire. Bill's lawsuits accused his older brothers of manipulating stock and breaking contract agreements to keep him from cashing in on his holdings.

Bill further charged that "T. Cullen Davis feels compelled to engage in a continuous series of multimillion-dollar expenditures based on his emotional needs rather than any exercise of business judgment." One of those expenditures was the mansion. Bill placed Cullen's personal debt at $16 million and his business debt at $150 million.

Closeted in his attorney's office with Ken, Cullen was plotting a legal counterattack in Bill's suit when notified that the judge in his divorce suit had increased Priscilla's support payments to $5,000 monthly. Judge Joe Eidson also granted her request to postpone the divorce trial. Cullen seemed to take the news in stride, but Priscilla said, "Cullen does not like losing. It's not the money; it's the battle."

Stan Farr, Priscilla's live-in companion, wheeled his black Thunderbird past the "Private Property" signs and up the dusty winding trail toward the mansion at 4200 Mockingbird Lane. The courtroom victory behind her, Priscilla and Stan had gone to dinner with three other couples. Beverly

Bass, a friend of her daughter Dee, would arrive soon to spend the night, even though Dee was at the home of a boyfriend. With Priscilla at dinner, her youngest daughter Andrea was alone in the big dark house.

Farr parked outside the garage and guided Priscilla along the darkened walkway toward a plate-glass window. She saw the bank of lights on the security panel and realized that the double locks had been deactivated. She was startled but not alarmed, since both Andrea and Dee were prone to carelessness. Once inside, Stan ascended the steps to the master bedroom. Priscilla **entered** the kitchen, switching off lights as she approached a door leading to the basement. She noticed the basement light on and reached for the switch. It was then that she spotted the bloody hand print.

"Cullen—Cullen did it!" said Beverly Bass.

She had run from the mansion after the shootings and flagged down a motorist. He drove her to a convenience store and called an ambulance and police. She was waiting impatiently when she spotted a security guard at a nearby service station. She told the guard a man had shot her boyfriend and chased her across the grounds of the Davis residence.

"Are you certain?" said the guard when she identified the gunman.

"Yes," she said, "I saw his ugly fucking face."

Outside the home of a woman named Karen Master, a paramilitary operation was unfolding as Cullen Davis sat on the edge of her bed. Squad cars crept through the darkness, their lights dimmed. Police, armed with pistols, rifles, and automatic weapons, approached the house warily. Trained attack dogs strained at their leashes.

When the phone rang, Karen answered, then handed the phone to her lover. Cullen was told the house was surrounded.

"Is it all right if I get dressed first?" he replied. "Then I'll come out."

When his time was up, Cullen walked through the door and into the glare of what seemed like a hundred spotlights. He could not see the officers with the loudspeakers and the drawn guns and the dogs, or the newsmen and photographers.

At 4:35 A.M., Lt. B. J. Erby stepped from the darkness into those lights and said, "Mr. Davis, you are under arrest."

On August 19, prosecutors decided after spirited debate to file capital murder charges. Cullen had been out on bond since the mansion murders of Andrea Wilborn and Stan Farr and the near-fatal shootings of Priscilla Davis and Bubba Gavrel, Beverly Bass' boyfriend. To seek the death penalty, a novel legal theory would be tested, based on a recent decision by the U. S. Supreme Court that the Texas capital murder law was constitutional. The law provided that murders committed in the course of certain specified crimes like burglary would be subject to the death penalty. Since Priscilla had been awarded possession of the mansion in the divorce proceedings, the state would argue that a man could burglarize his own home and commit a capital murder during that burglary.

The next morning, district attorney Tim Curry was listening to prosecutor Joe Shannon's report on Priscilla's condition when the radio monitor on Curry's desk crackled alive: "Subject vehicle turning westbound on Camp Bowie." Together, they monitored Cullen Davis' trip to Meacham Field, the airport where his jet was waiting in a hangar with its engines running. The DA's investigators watched until Cullen entered the hangar and approached his blue and white Lear. Then they took him into custody with a grand jury attachment.

With Cullen detained, Shannon and investigator Morris Howeth quickly departed Curry's office on another mission — to obtain Priscilla's signature on a formal complaint. In a hospital chair, she signed without hesitation.

"This means he could get the death penalty," said Shannon.

"He shot my little girl," Priscilla replied.

On advice of his lawyers, Cullen refused to appear before the grand jury, which was in session at that moment. Howeth read Cullen his rights and took him downstairs to jail. Cullen said nothing. He did not so much as blink.

Meanwhile, Shannon was called to the telephone. "The grand jury indicted your man eleven to zero in all four cases," he was advised.

"It won't be that easy in front of a trial jury," Shannon predicted.

The first courtroom testimony against Cullen Davis came in a bail hearing three days later. To keep Cullen behind bars, the state would have to convince a judge that a jury was likely to assess the death penalty and that Cullen was likely to commit more violent acts. It meant prosecutors would have to show their evidence and that Priscilla would have to testify.

Amid the popping of flashbulbs, Priscilla swept from the elevator toward the third-floor courtroom in her stainless-steel wheelchair. She was surrounded by DA's investigators, a nurse, a chauffeur, and others who would become known as her entourage.

Priscilla told the packed courtroom she first noticed the bloody prints on the wall when she went to switch off the basement light. "And I turned, and then I saw a bloody hand print on the door frame. So I turned around and started walking back through the kitchen and screaming for Stan. I said 'Stan, come here! Stan, come here!' And then, just as I passed the staircase leading to the bedroom, I screamed, 'Stan, come here!' And Cullen stepped out."

Her husband, she said, "was dressed all in black. And he had on a black wig." She continued, "He had both of his hands together, and it was a black or dark-colored plastic bag around his hands, and I couldn't see his hands.. He stepped out and said, 'Hi.' And — and — and — then he shot me."

The bullet struck Priscilla between the breasts just below the breastbone. "I grabbed where I had been shot, and, of course, I automatically felt a big hole and blood and . . ."

Prosecutor Joe Shannon asked, "What did you do then?"

"I screamed. I said, 'I've been shot!' I said, 'Cullen shot me! Stan, go back!' I could hear Stan coming down the stairs, and I said, 'Go back!' And Cullen ran past me . . . and he was standing . . . There is a door at the bottom of the steps, and Stan had slammed that door and he . . . was holding it and . . ."

Priscilla said Cullen stood before the stairway trying to push the door open. Cullen fired the gun into the closed door. She heard Stan cry out.

"I knew he had been hit. And then, all of a sudden, he didn't try holding the door anymore. And Cullen stood there and then — he opened the door, and it came open, and then Stan came out after him and it was like . . . Stan grabbed him by his — his — hand, wrists, kind of — and they were kind of wrestling around, and they turned to where Stan's back was to me and it was like . . . I was watching Stan. It was like all of a sudden he jerked back . . . Cullen kind of jerked. He just jerked away from him, and I heard a shot. And then Stan turned around and fell down and he — he was looking at me."

Then, testified Priscilla, Cullen pumped two more bullets into Farr and dragged him toward the basement by his ankles. Tears wells up in her eyes as she recalled the scene. Her voice cracked. She struggled to regain her composure.

She told of her attempt to escape to the courtyard, only to have Cullen catch her when she fell. "Cullen, I love you. I didn't — I have never loved anyone else," she pleaded as he dragged her back toward the door. "Please, please, Cullen. You are hurting me. It hurts to move. Please don't make me move." Then, she testified, "he kind of let me down . . . He let go, and he walked right past me into the breakfast room and he went right out of my sight."

Before running across a freshly mowed field to a neighbor's house, she said she heard a voice she thought was her daughter Dee's. She did not know it was Beverly Bass. She also did not know that Andrea was dead by the time she and Stan arrived. As she scrambled away from the mansion, she said she heard another shot and then screams.

At the defense table, Cullen listened to the chilling testimony and stared intently at his wife. She did not return his gaze.

The defense did not make many mistakes, but calling Cullen's brother Ken to the witness stand was one of them. In an attempt to torpedo the state's legal theory that Cullen burglarized his own home, Ken Davis testified he owned one-half interest in the 181-acre estate. Attorney Phil Burleson sought to show through Ken that Cullen had permission to be on the property at any time.

Judge Tom Cave did not buy the defense gambit, and the state chose to ignore it. Instead, prosecutor Shannon questioned Davis about a phone conversation with Cullen several hours after the murders. Ken confirmed he had told Cullen that the police were looking for him and asked Cullen what he was going to do about it.

"And what was his response to that question?" Shannon wanted to know.

" '*Well, I guess I will go back to bed,*' " Ken recalled his brother saying.

The exchange weighed heavily against Cullen in the mind of Judge Cave. He ruled the millionaire defendant would be held without bond until his trial.

Part 4

Richard "Racehorse" Haynes came by his nickname not because of the speed or sleekness associated with a thoroughbred racer but just the opposite. As a high school football player, he often ran toward the sidelines instead of down them, and his coach wondered out loud if he thought he was a racehorse. In reality, Haynes had the physique of a floor safe, but the name stuck and he did little to discourage it.

He was a master storyteller and courtroom spellbinder, inspired as a student by the legendary Percy Foreman. He drank good Scotch, drove fast cars, raced a fleet of motorcycles, and sailed the Texas Gulf in his own forty-foot sloop. In 1976, he was not yet bigger than life, but his ego was and, like the universe, it was ever expanding. He seemed ready-made for a trial involving the richest man ever accused of murder. And so it was that Cullen Davis accepted the recommendation of his defense team to bring Racehorse Haynes into the fray.

To Haynes, Cullen was "the citizen accused." The citizen had agreed to a $225,000 fee plus expenses.

Cullen was no ordinary prisoner. He received hundreds of visitors, and on Christmas Day Karen Master cut through red tape and regulations to visit him in the tenth-floor cell area of the Tarrant County jail.

Possibly, Cullen's lawyers had persuaded Sheriff Lon Evans that the visit was in keeping with the holiday spirit. But more likely the lawman had taken a strange liking to his celebrated prisoner. A big, jovial man, Evans was politically astute and popular with reporters. Once, when a newsman inquired about Cullen, Evans said, "We'd probably a-throwed him a barbecue if he hadn't killed that little girl."

That kind of sentiment led prosecutors to try Cullen first for the shooting of Andrea Wilborn. Whatever jurors would feel about the shooting of Priscilla and her lover, there was no justification for killing a child in cold blood. So the tedious process of jury selection began on Washington's birthday in a capital murder trial in the courtroom of Judge Tom Cave.

By April, with only eight jurors chosen, a crisis arose when an anonymous caller told prosecutor Joe Shannon that a juror had been talking about the case. There was enough evidence for Cave to declare a mistrial, whereupon the defense attempted again to have Cullen freed on bond.

In the second bond hearing, Cullen's attorneys tried to link Priscilla to a "subterranean drug culture." The vehicle was a nine-page affidavit from David McCrory, who had been with Priscilla and Stan the night of the shootings. The signature line of the affidavit, however, was *blank*. Interviewed by the state, McCrory denied the contents of the defense statement. He also claimed that he was plied with liquor by defense lawyers and indicated they held out rewards if he would cooperate. McCrory signed the state's affidavit.

Throwing Cullen's plea out on a technicality, Cave cited defense lawyers Racehorse Haynes and Phil Burleson for contempt in the filing of the McCrory statement. Cave also began shopping around for another city and another judge to try *Texas* vs. *Davis*.

And, in the strangest of twists, the state would hear from David McCrory again, at another time and in another case, before the decade was out.

The Tarrant County prosecutors flew west to Amarillo on June 21 to begin preparations for what would be the longest, costliest, and possibly most bizarre murder trial in Texas history. Cave finally persuaded a bachelor judge named George Dowlen in that Texas Panhandle city to take the case. Cullen's lawyers were not ecstatic about Cave's choice. In conservative West Texas and Amarillo in particular, juries held a legitimate reputation for super-swift justice, and Dowlen himself was a former prosecutor.

If the defense lawyers were apprehensive about Amarillo, Karen Master was not. Her father, before buying a small ranch in Arizona, had lived in the Panhandle and his contacts were solid and extensive. His name was Ray Hudson, and he was the stereotype of a well-heeled Texan who could wheel and deal at the drop of a ten-gallon hat. He joined the defense effort and began feverishly spreading the word that Cullen was framed by a vindictive wife. He spent freely, tipped lavishly, and learned much. Ray Hudson also befriended two local citizens in particular. His two new friends would be the bailiffs assigned to the jury in the Cullen Davis murder trial.

A day after the prosecution arrived, Priscilla and her entourage landed stylishly in a rented baby-blue Lear jet. The local press beat a path to her door, and within hours her picture decorated the front page of the *Amarillo Globe-News*. A cross hung at her neck and a news story told of her carrying a Bible down the halls of the Hilton Inn. Cullen's attorneys said that smacked of hypocrisy, and a substantial number of newspaper readers agreed.

Thus was a campaign waged outside the courtroom for the hearts of Amarillo's citizenry. Despite the legacy of West Texas juries, it was a campaign Cullen could win. The defense hired a local lawyer named Dee Miller who squired Racehorse and Burleson to the finest Amarillo nightspots and country clubs. Miller himself would be on a first-name basis with many prospective jurors.

Haynes brought in a psychologist to assist in jury selection, and the defense commandeered Davis company computers to compile cross-references and personal data on each prospective juror. Tim Curry's prosecutors could recruit no such resources, but a larger concern was their star witness.

In fact, the state was considering not calling Priscilla at all. Joe Shannon confronted her at the mansion with the drug and sex allegations in David McCrory's unsigned defense statement — she branded them all lies. She refused to cooperate with Shannon, and he left angry and dejected. She also relied to an alarming degree on the painkiller Percodan and sometimes preceded responses with a long "uhhhhh," giving the impression of concocted answers. In the end, however, prosecutors felt they had no choice but to call Priscilla. Otherwise, said Shannon, "Racehorse will stick it in our ear." He once watched Haynes win a celebrated case by cross-examining an empty witness chair.

Priscilla took the stand on August 22, two days after the trial began. Jury selection lasted an excruciating eight weeks, but now the tiny courtroom was packed in anticipation of her appearance. She chose for her grand entry a high-necked cream-colored dress with long sleeves and a hemline below her knees. A ribbon decorated her ice-blonde hair. She appeared frail and thin as she walked past the jury box toward the witness stand. Her testimony would last thirteen days.

Under questioning by Tim Curry, she repeated the story she had told at the bond hearing in Fort Worth. Haynes objected repeatedly to her narrative and succeeded in unnerving her. But the prosecution struggled through. Curry suddenly ended his direct examination by asking, "Now, Mrs. Davis, on the evening of August 2, when you left your home with Stan Farr, was your daughter, Andrea Lee Wilborn, alive?"

"Yes, sir," she replied.

"Is that the last time, Mrs. Davis, that you've seen your daughter Andrea alive?"

Her lip quivered, her eyes clouded, and in a voice barely audible she said, "Yes, sir."

When Cullen's defense team arrived in Amarillo in June, one of its number was on his way back to Dallas–Fort Worth Airport. He was Steve Sumner, chosen at age 30 from Phil Burleson's junior staff to direct defense investigation efforts. Sumner's familiarity with Fort Worth was minimal and his dark, vested business suits were not in character with the underbelly of the city he had been examining. But his enthusiasm was boundless.

For ten months, Sumner tried to penetrate the nocturnal "second world" he was convinced Priscilla often visited. His life was threatened twice, his motel room in Fort Worth was burglarized several times, and he was the rumored target of a kidnapping plot. Only when he realized that Cullen kept certain friends and Priscilla kept others did he make progress. Those who associated only with Cullen knew little of Priscilla's "second world" and its unsavory drug characters.

As the jetliner streaked toward DFW Airport, Sumner wondered if his investigation might be missing its mark. What if Stan Farr, not Priscilla, was the killer's prime target? Phil Burleson had advanced such a theory. If the gunman had wanted to kill Priscilla, Sumner reasoned, she would be dead.

Something else disturbed him. More and more, he kept running across the name of Horace Copeland. Sumner knew little about the man. But Copeland was no stranger to Farr's Rhinestone Cowboy saloon. Sumner decided to explore the possibility that Farr was the prime target. And he would check out Horace Copeland.

Part 5

By the time Priscilla Davis took the stand in Amarillo, Horace Copeland was the prime defense vehicle to steer the jury away from Cullen. Copeland was also dead. He awakened an acquaintance and a girlfriend in Fort Worth and, pistol in hand, accused them of stealing drugs. When a roommate arrived from work, there was a struggle and Copeland was shot. He died in a pool of blood on the bedroom floor.

Racehorse Haynes had been waiting to cross-examine Priscilla for months and mounted his attack deftly. He fancied he knew more about Priscilla than she knew about herself, largely through the efforts of Steve Sumner. He laid down a barrage of questions and insinuations about her background, love life, lifestyle, and activities while the prosecution struggled to protect its witness with objection after objection.

Prosecutors knew Judge Dowlen's most critical ruling was at hand. If he permitted Haynes to delve into drugs and sex at the mansion and elsewhere, Priscilla's credibility could be destroyed. They knew Priscilla would deny such activities and they suspected Haynes now had witnesses to contradict her at every turn.

Joe Shannon argued that Priscilla's morals had no bearing on the shootings. Haynes disagreed, saying the defense believed the shootings resulted from "a drug deal that went bad." Shannon branded the theory a "smokescreen" and contended there was no evidence to support such an argument. Haynes asserted such evidence was forthcoming, though, in truth, the trial would end three months later without it.

Dowlen ruled for the defense. He did not force Haynes to produce evidence about the "drug deal" theory before the attorney questioned Priscilla about her escapades. It was a major victory—Haynes charged into one closet after another, extracting the skeletons in Priscilla's life. With no warning, he produced a poster-sized photograph of Priscilla, her surgically enhanced breasts spilling from a halter top. Holding a drink, she was linked arm in arm with an acquaintance named W. T. Rufner. Rufner's only clothing was a red-and-white-striped Christmas stocking indiscreetly covering what Haynes called his private parts.

The state objected vehemently to the manner in which Haynes flourished the photo. Priscilla insisted she did not recognize it. Although the back of the picture was to the jury, the paper was thin and the jurors could see what it depicted. Dowlen refused to admit the photo into evidence, but Haynes accomplished his purpose. Among the defense lawyers, Rufner was henceforth known as the "five-striper."

Haynes also was curious about any relationship Priscilla had with a man named Horace Copeland. She said she saw him only at Farr's saloon and she knew of no trouble between him and Stan. She also said she understood Horace was now "deceased."

Prosecutor Joe Shannon scribbled on a yellow note pad in front of him: "Looks like they are trying to lay it off on a dead man." He was partially right. As Haynes continued to fling other mysterious names about, it gave rise to the A-B-C theory of defense: Anybody But Cullen.

Meanwhile, Cullen had the run of the courtroom. He mingled with friends, spectators, and well-wishers, signing autographs and greeting children during recess. He dined in a third-floor jury room, sometimes on catered meals served by a gold-jacketed waiter. Spectators were asked to join him and Karen and seldom was the offer refused. "Here's a guy on trial for executing a 12-year-old girl in a dark basement," fumed Tim Curry, "and they treat him like a fucking hero."

Outside the courtroom, Priscilla charged, "I'm not saying I'm Miss Goody Twoshoes, but their only defense of Cullen is to destroy me. I realize that while Cullen is the one on trial, it's really me they're after."

Although Haynes failed to shake Priscilla's account of the shootings, he laid a series of traps to undermine her credibility. Her hollow denials about the drug-laced exploits at the mansion raised serious questions with the jury. By the time her grueling testimony concluded, one juror believed she was a liar and another wondered if she was so high on drugs that she did not know what was going on.

Priscilla came unraveled only once. With the jury excused, she was asked to testify about something Dowlen had already ruled was inadmissible. Her first answer was unresponsive and her second was inaudible. Her gaze was fixed, almost trancelike.

"Goddamn, she's seen those body pictures," Joe Shannon whispered to fellow prosecutor Tolly Wilson. The full-color photographs of Andrea Wilborn's blood-spattered body inadvertently were left on the witness stand by a previous witness. Priscilla had never seen her daughter in death.

Realizing too late what had happened, Dowlen ordered a recess. Priscilla broke into tears and was helped out of the room. As always, Cullen watched the proceedings with cool detachment. In fact, he smiled.

A month into testimony, the state sought to shore up the accounts of Priscilla and a second eyewitness, Bubba Gavrel, by producing police officers and crime scene investigators. Bit by bit, these witnesses introduced a mass of physical evidence: bloody clothing, bloodstains, bullets, pieces of plastic, a telephone, a ten-foot door, and hundreds of photographs and fingerprints. Before Gavrel took the stand, the defense won a small victory: the judge agreed the jury should not see the paralyzed young man wobble on his crutches to the witness stand. Gavrel was seated before the jury entered.

The trial was approaching a critical stage. Both the state and defense felt the case could rise and fall on the testimony of Beverly Bass, the only uninjured survivor. Cullen's attorneys intended to establish that a "special relationship" existed between Priscilla and Beverly. Their contention would be that the pair hatched a conspiracy to frame Cullen.

Beverly Bass dressed demurely for her appearance. Led by Curry, she put Cullen behind the gun that shot her boyfriend Bubba. Her eyes met Cullen's at that point and his jaw clenched perceptibly.

During his cross-examination, Racehorse Haynes refrained from using the word "abortion" but he forced Beverly, now 19, to admit she once had a "surgical solution" to a physical problem. Visibly shaken, she confirmed that Priscilla took her to a pregnancy clinic and that she faked her sister's name on the clinic records. When Haynes pointed out that she had lied, Beverly cried, "It was something that I wanted to forget and I *had* forgotten about it!"

The state rested its case on October 24 after twenty-four witnesses and forty-seven days of testimony. As Haynes left the courtroom to prepare for the defense's opening statement, a bearded, bedraggled figure moved toward him carrying a small brown sack.

"Mr. Haynes? I'm W. T. Rufner."

Rufner thrust his hand into the sack and pulled out a T-shirt. He held it up to Haynes' chest, as though he was a tailor measuring a fit. On the shirt was emblazoned a full-color likeness of Rufner in the altogether with the now famous red-and-white Christmas stocking in place. The inscription was "W. T. Rufner Socks It to 'Em."

"I'm selling these for a hundred dollars apiece," Rufner announced. "Since you dragged my name through the dirt and made it a household word, I wanted to give you the first one."

Holding the shirt at arm's length, the lawyer eyed the bright red stocking and sneered, "That looks like trick photography to me."

Two days later, Haynes launched Cullen's defense by informing the jury he would prove Priscilla fabricated her story for one pure and simple motive: greed. Peering over his Ben Franklin glasses, Haynes promised to show Cullen was somewhere else at the time of the shooting. He would demonstrate that murder victim Stan Farr knew and feared the late

Horace Copeland. Then, with Hollywood flair, Haynes finished his opening statement by saying, "There may be, before the conclusion of the defense case, some developments that will surprise even you, that even at this juncture are not foreseen."

One of the defense's opening targets was the shaky identification of Cullen by Bubba Gavrel. The first police officer to question Bev Bass' wounded boyfriend at the scene said Gavrel did not know the identity of the gunman, and a man who said he shared a hospital room with Gavrel testified that Gavrel's father coached Gavrel to accuse Cullen. By now, some of the jurors were discounting Bubba. Thought one, "He's operating through the power of suggestion."

The next target of Cullen's lawyers was the prosecution's time sequence, thereby implying a conspiracy between Beverly and Priscilla. A passerby who was waved down by Beverly Bass after the shootings estimated the time as 12:20 A.M., yet the elderly couple who called the ambulance for Priscilla said they were awakened at 12:45 A.M. If the passerby was correct, then what had Priscilla done for twenty-five minutes? Had she really run across the freshly mowed hay field in three to four minutes, as she claimed?

To establish an alibi for Cullen, Haynes and Burleson decided to use girlfriend Karen Master and avoid putting Cullen on the stand. They did not want to expose their client to vigorous cross-examination.

Cullen, in fact, had offered an alibi, but not one the defense would use in open court. In a chance meeting in Judge Dowlen's office, Glenn Guzzo, a reporter for the *Fort Worth Star-Telegram*, asked Cullen where he was after he left his office on the night of August 2. Cullen stunned Guzzo by saying he went to a restaurant and then to a movie.

"Alone?"

"Yeah."

"What movie did you see?"

Cullen smiled but did not answer. "We got to save something for later," he explained.

The exchange appalled Cullen's lawyers, especially after it appeared on the front pages of the Fort Worth newspaper and then was picked up by the Associated Press and distributed across the country. In private, they dressed down the millionaire like a group of colonels talking to a boot camp private. To the press, Haynes said, "We got an alibi but we just can't prove it."

If Cullen testified, Haynes knew he would be cross-examined about the telephone conversation with his brother. Cullen would be asked what possible explanation he could have for his apparent nonchalance. Racehorse feared the prosecution also would probe into Cullen's purported extramarital affairs and would tarnish the image Haynes sought to project of his client as a successful businessman. Indeed, the prosecution intended to do just that.

Therefore, the defense would rise or fall on the alibi provided by Karen Master. When she entered the courtroom in early November, she smiled at the jurors. In the front row, one of them smiled back. "Aw, bullshit," Joe Shannon whispered to fellow prosecutor Marvin Collins.

Cullen's lover said she went to bed alone between 9:00 P.M. and 9:30 P.M. after Cullen called from the office to say he would not be home for dinner. Although Karen said she did not know what time Cullen returned home, she said she awakened at 12:40 A.M. and he was asleep beside her. "He had on his shorts and did not have anything on his top," she said in response to Racehorse Haynes' questions.

Joe Shannon had waited for six months to cross-examine Karen in open court. He had her previous grand jury testimony at his fingertips and nowhere in it was a claim that Cullen was home at 12:40 A.M. Surely, thought Shannon, the jurors would conclude her latest story was a concoction.

Karen conceded she did not tell the grand jury about Cullen being home at 12:40 A.M., even though she was asked to disclose anything that could shed light on the charges against Cullen. "Well, in my opinion, the twelve-forty, at that particular time, did not prove guilt or innocence either way. It had no relevance," she said, even though that was the time just after the murders occurred.

Shannon's voice was incredulous. "You just didn't think the grand jury ought to hear it that time — is that your testimony today to this jury?"

"*It didn't seem significant,*" Karen replied.

Part 6

William Tasker Rufner was by trade a union electrician but in spirit the carefree captain of a houseboat on Possum Kingdom Lake west of Fort Worth. He was a motorcycle enthusiast, and his affection for strong drink and sensual women was not a well-kept secret. The defense also intended to paint Rufner as violent and perhaps capable of murder.

Until now, the jurors in Cullen's trial had only heard references to the man called "W. T." so there was more than idle curiosity when they watched him swagger to the witness stand. What they saw was a man of medium build and muscular frame with long sandy-brown hair, a beard, and a moustache, wearing a leisure suit and loud print shirt. They were unaware he was permitted to enter the courtroom only after surrendering his "Sock It to 'Em" T-shirt and his pocketknife. He came to Amarillo willingly, because he was ready to match wits with Racehorse Haynes.

Though Haynes wasted no time in inquiring about drug arrests and escapades with Priscilla, Rufner admitted no intimacies prior to her separation from Cullen in 1974. He indicated his stay at the mansion was more extensive than Priscilla remembered, but he did not otherwise damage her credibility. Surviving the first day of grilling, he passed the evening cursing Haynes and frittering away Cullen's money on a bar tab exceeding eighty dollars. Rufner and a group of young ladies agreed it was money well spent.

The next morning, W. T.'s eyes resembled a road map and his hair could have been styled with a Mixmaster. His return engagement with Haynes was a disaster. Though Rufner tried first to take the Fifth Amendment, Haynes eventually drew from him an admission that he and Priscilla had met recently to discuss her testimony about their relationship.

"How long was this meeting?" asked Haynes.

"About a six-pack," said Rufner.

Haynes sensed Rufner's defiance was eroding and, with a few quick questions, established that Rufner and Priscilla had sex on two trips before her separation from her husband. That contradicted Priscilla's sworn testimony and the credibility of the state's first eyewitness to the murders took an immediate nose dive.

Haynes was not as successful in portraying Rufner as a violence-prone candidate for the "man in black," and few thought after his testimony he was capable of murder. Haynes even indicated as much in an exchange at the judge's bench.

"Anybody that keeps time by six-packs, well . . . ," Judge Dowlen observed.

"Can't be all bad," Haynes concluded.

The defense next began what prosecutors called "the parade of lovelies." Through Priscilla's associates, Racehorse wanted to illuminate her lifestyle and the shenanigans at the mansion after Cullen's departure. The trial was at yet another critical stage because prosecutors believed they needed to keep the jury from being inundated with drug testimony. They contended the mere presence of drugs in 1974 had no relevancy to the murders in 1976.

Defense lawyers claimed that the shootings occurred as a result of a "drug deal which went amok." Joe Shannon suggested to Judge Dowlen that it would be improper to permit evidence of sex orgies and drug parties before the defense demonstrated some connection to the night of August 2. It would be putting the cart before the horse.

Haynes' associate, Phil Burleson, countered with a bold statement. "We made representations to the court that we'll carry this right up to the summer of '76, the same type of thing. And we have to do it witness by witness."

Joe Shannon knew the ruling by Dowlen could foretell the outcome of the trial; when Dowlen authorized testimony on the drug and sex escapades to continue, Shannon said, "The big one has gone against us."

One character in the defense's parade of lovelies was Sandy Guthrie Myers, who claimed to be a witch. She told of meeting W. T. Rufner and Priscilla in 1974 and moving to the mansion. While living there, she received a ten-year probated sentence for cocaine possession. Much of her testimony was out of the jury's presence, but the panel was allowed to hear her account of a 1975 discussion with Priscilla about Priscilla's pending divorce.

"She became very intent," Sandy Myers said, "and she told

me that something heavy was coming down and she wanted to talk to me. . . ."

What, asked Haynes, did Priscilla mean by "something heavy"?

"Some trouble."

Joe Shannon wanted to cross-examine his witch, but another prosecutor argued against it. Shannon acquiesced. It was a tactical, perhaps critical, error. Cullen's attorneys believed that Sandy Myers' "something heavy" testimony made an impact on the jury. They were correct.

Toward the rear of Haynes' courtroom parade was a mystery witness to all but the defense. Kimberly Lewis was an innocent-looking 19-year-old who said she and Stan Farr were secret lovers before the murders. Kimberly said she asked Farr why he carried a gun and he told her it was because "people are after me." In a telephone call on the day of his death, she said Farr sounded edgy and did not invite her out. In one final surprise, Hayes asked her how Farr referred to Priscilla.

"His investment."

Grinning, Cullen cornered reporter Glenn Guzzo and told him, "Make sure Priscilla gets a clip of this story."

Before the state and defense could complete their cases, there was one more bizarre episode. With coal-black hair and resplendent in a three-piece suit, Arthur Uewayne Polk had the serpentine look of a riverboat gambler when he entered the courtroom. A landscape specialist, he described how he failed to collect a $677 debt from Priscilla after decorating the mansion with assorted plants. So, on the night of August 2, he set out along the Trinity River near the mansion to repossess them.

Resting, he saw a "kind of chunky" man with a sack over his shoulder coming toward him. The man stopped for a cigarette and went on. Polk said he resumed his furtive mission but froze when he approached the mansion and saw the same man near the swimming pool. Haynes then paused for effect and asked, "Was the man you saw in the swimming pool on the night of August 2 Cullen Davis?"

"Definitely not," said Polk.

The tale was quickly assaulted by the prosecution, which produced Polk's estranged wife overnight from Fort Worth. She said that Uewayne told her about going to the mansion several days *before* the murders. She also cast doubt on Polk knowing the exact time he saw the mysterious man near the river. She said his watch was broken.

As defense attorneys debated whether to call more witnesses, Karen Master's father, Ray Hudson, told them the jury was solidly for acquittal. He did not tell them how he knew this. But he said he expected only one vote for conviction.

So ended testimony in the costliest murder trial in the state's history. Joe Shannon and Racehorse Haynes went to work at once on the most important final arguments of their careers. On November 16, with spectators lining the halls and security at a maximum, Judge Dowlen moved the arguments to a larger Amarillo courtroom to accommodate the overflow crowd. Each side would have three and a half hours to sum up its case.

Prosecutor Tolly Wilson attacked the defense theories first, ridiculing Karen Master's alibi and blasting Polk's claims as ludicrous. He summarized the eyewitness accounts of Priscilla, Bubba, and Beverly and surmised Cullen executed Andrea Wilson "once Cullen was discovered by this child and once his intentions were fully known. . . ."

Defense attorney Mike Gibson summarized the testimony of Cullen's forty-four witnesses thus: Cullen was unbothered by the alimony increase of August 2. He was with Karen Master at the time of the shooting. Priscilla Davis was something other than she would have the jury believe. Bubba Gavrel did not know who shot him. Stan Farr feared Horace Copeland.

Next Phil Burleson attacked Priscilla on all fronts and suggested she framed Cullen as a cover-up for her activities with Stan Farr at the mansion. This was only a warm-up for Haynes, who dismissed the testimony of Beverly Bass and Bubba as he focused on Priscilla Lee Davis. "She has influenced those young persons to tell lies," he said. "She is the Machiavellian influence behind this whole evil thing."

Haynes extricated himself from a promise in opening statements, admitting he did not show Priscilla, Stan Farr, Horace

Copeland, and another underworld figure were linked. Then he switched quickly back to Priscilla, calling her "the queen bee." He reminded the jury of a doctor's testimony that she could be a "two-worlder," a Jekyll and Hyde. He said the jury must try to exclude every legal hypothesis about Cullen's innocence. If it could not, it should render a verdict of "not guilty."

"Boy, I smelled like a turd," Haynes whispered as he finished and slumped into his seat. Inexplicably, he had lost his outline that afternoon.

Joe Shannon had his, having worked on it until 2 A.M., but he abandoned it in the heat of his oratory. Regardless of Priscilla's associates, he told the jury, "It did not give anybody the right to go in there to slay a 12-year-old girl." He insisted the defense did not put "a single dent" in Priscilla's eyewitness account.

After a recess in which he nurtured a fading voice, Shannon turned from evidence to emotion. Gesturing at Cullen, he said, "This man has been accorded a whole lot more rights than he gave Andrea Wilborn. He has had twelve people sitting up here in judgment of him. Andrea Wilborn didn't have anybody sitting in judgment of her, and I wonder what she thought when she looked down the muzzle of that .38 before he snuffed out her life. I wonder if she pleaded with him, begged him. I don't know, and we'll never know. And I submit to you, ladies and gentlemen, the time has come to make a decision. . . ."

The prosecutor collapsed in his chair. He only vaguely remembered leaving the courtroom, the mob outside, and the trip up the stairs.

Part 7

"Ladies and gentlemen," Judge Dowlen warned, "the court will not tolerate outbursts or demonstrations when the verdict is announced."

It had been almost five months since the first juror in Amarillo was chosen. Now the twelve men and women, having notified the judge they had reached their decision, filed into the jury box on November 17, 1977. Cullen Davis rose, his face drained of color. He trembled slightly.

He looked at Dowlen as the judge opened the folded verdict form. Dowlen read aloud: "We the jury find the defendant . . . " He paused and glanced at Cullen.

"*Not guilty.*"

Despite the judge's warning, the defense forces and friends erupted. Cullen sagged back into his chair. Tears trickled down his cheeks. Karen grabbed him and cried, "I love you, I love you."

What followed was unusual, even by Texas standards of jurisprudence. Cullen, his lawyers, and his friends headed for a popular nightspot called Rhett Butler's. They were soon joined by Judge Dowlen and his date, several members of the jury, and courtroom bailiff D'Ann Hill.

The bailiff rushed through the crowd and threw her arms around Cullen, tears streaming down her face. "Isn't this illegal or something?" Cullen asked of her display.

"Not anymore," D'Ann answered. "It's all over now."

Ray Hudson, Karen's father, grew increasingly effusive as the whiskey flowed. "Them prosecutors, they was cold turkeys. They had no charm. They come to town and they didn't say 'howdy,' " he growled. "They didn't have a chance, brother. Those cocksuckers never realized it was put together that way. There wasn't nothing left unturned. It was all covered . . . *I knew when a juror sneezed or farted. I had the finger on the pulse. We had that son of a bitch won before the jury ever sat down.*"

Juror Muskrat Watkins disclosed he and several others did not necessarily believe Cullen innocent. But he said the defense had raised serious doubts about his guilt. According to Watkins, the jury could not find Cullen guilty *beyond a reasonable doubt.* Another juror added, "I just couldn't believe Priscilla. I never will."

With Cullen at his side, Racehorse Haynes appeared before television cameras and opened fire on Priscilla. Flushed with success and a heavy dose of Scotch, he said, "She is the dregs. She's probably shooting up right now. She's the most shameless, brazen hussy in all humanity. She is a charlatan, a harlot, a liar. . . ."

Haynes' associates were alarmed, but he ranted on, "She is a snake, unworthy of belief under oath. She is a dope fiend, a habitué of dope. She is the most sordid human being in the United States, in fact, the whole world. Someone ought to put a barbed-wire fence around her house and not let her out."

A reporter pointed out that Priscilla said Cullen would still "have to answer to God and . . . that's one he can't buy."

"How would she know?" Cullen snapped.

The next day, he and Karen said good-bye to Amarillo by hosting a luncheon party for the jurors.

Cloistered in Cullen's $6-million mansion in Fort Worth, Priscilla heard about the verdict by telephone from an Associated Press reporter. Then she called a friend and said, "Cullen always thought he was invincible. Now he knows he is."

By Christmas 1977, Cullen and Karen reigned as genuine celebrities at home, on the Colorado ski slopes, and elsewhere. It was a heady time for the millionaire and his blonde mistress, and their photographs adorned the front pages of more than a few newspapers.

Cullen, free after fifteen months in jail, talked half-seriously about a movie project, wanting either Al Pacino or James Garner for the leading role and Ann Margret to portray Karen. He liked Phyllis Diller for Priscilla and Mickey Rooney for Racehorse Haynes. Hearing of these choices, Priscilla said, "Ask the son of a bitch who he's going to get to play *Andrea*."

When Cullen crawled out of bed on Sunday morning, August 20, 1978, Karen hardly stirred. The party after the Dallas Cowboy football game included drinks at a hotel near Texas Stadium and she was in no mood for sunrise activities. Cullen slipped on a pair of slacks and a pullover sport shirt and drove directly to his office. There he unlocked the safe and retrieved a plain brown envelope. It contained $25,000 in hundred-dollar bills.

As he climbed back in his Cadillac, an FBI surveillance plane flying overhead radioed his activities to federal, city, and county officers on the ground. The team of lawmen had been assembled after hearing a strange story from David McCrory, Cullen's one-time drinking and pool-shooting buddy. According to McCrory, Cullen wanted to arrange the death of his divorce judge and others. From the aircraft, an agent reported Cullen was "washing his trail" by veering on and off the interstate highway and making U-turns. His destination was a modest chain restaurant named Coco's Famous Hamburgers.

Cullen eased the Cadillac to a stop near a white van in the parking lot, got out, and pounded his fist against the right door. After walking to the rear of the truck, Cullen jumped back in his car and spun away. "I thought he had us," said FBI agent Jerry Hubbell, who was hidden inside with three colleagues. Then he and the others proceeded to photograph and record a very strange meeting between Cullen and McCrory.

In an inside pocket, McCrory was carrying an envelope. It contained Joe Eidson's identification cards and a snapshot of the "slain" judge, compliments of the FBI. Told of Cullen's hit list, Eidson agreed to pose in a ketchup-stained T-shirt as a dead body. McCrory also had a .22-caliber Ruger pistol, hastily fitted with an illegal silencer at Cullen's request.

"Who do you want to get next?" asked McCrory, who had lied to Cullen about hiring an out-of-town hit man. "I never have gotten ahold of him to change my plans. I've got more fuckin' pressure on me right now than you can imagine."

Cullen was unmoved. "Okay. What are you going to do with these?" he said, apparently referring to the contents of McCrory's envelope.

"I'm going to get rid of the motherfuckers."

"That's good. Glad to hear it."

"All right," said McCrory. "Who do you want next?"

"The ones we talked about."

"Bubba . . . ?" McCrory began.

"The three kids," Cullen replied.

"Bev, Bubba—"

"Yeah," Cullen interrupted.

McCrory took the cash from Cullen and Cullen took the

pistol. "Well look. This fuckin' murder business . . . is a tough son of a bitch," said McCrory.

"Right," said Cullen.

Moments later, as he stepped from a phone booth, Cullen was arrested and accused of plotting a mass murder scheme. It was August 20, 1978. It had been two years to the day since he was arrested at the airport and charged with capital murder in the mansion shootings.

An investigator from the DA's office, Rodney Hinson, read him his rights, and a wrecker was summoned to impound the Cadillac. Handcuffed and silent, Cullen was taken to jail, where he surrendered his possessions, including $1,122 in bills and fifteen cents in change.

"Guess where I am," Cullen said to Karen Master in a telephone call.

"Where?" replied his blonde mistress.

"In jail."

"Cullen!" she cried. "What on earth for?"

"I really don't know."

On his instructions, Karen changed lines and dialed attorney Cecil Munn, who thought it unlikely authorities would hold Cullen without telling him why. Returning to Cullen, she pressed him about the charge.

"I don't know but I think it's solicitation of capital murder."

Unknown to all but Cullen's attorneys in Fort Worth, Racehorse Haynes did not leap at the offer to accept Cullen's latest defense. When he finally acquiesced, he did so for a fee approaching *$2 million*. That included commitments for his firm to assist in several civil cases pending against Cullen. Moreover, Haynes refused to leave Houston until a substantial down payment was raised.

Meanwhile, Kay Davis was livid about her uncle's arrest. "It's a frame-up . . . a goddamn frame-up," she said. "Cullen's more susceptible to a framing than a Rembrandt."

According to news leaks, Cullen's "hit list" contained up to fifteen names. Besides Eidson, there were mansion eyewitnesses Bubba Gavrel and Beverly Bass; Bubba's father, Gus; and Judge Tom Cave, who denied Cullen bond in the mansion shootings. There were also Cullen's brother, Bill Davis; W. T. Rufner; Priscilla, of course; and, surprisingly, her daughter Dee. Other targets were not identified at once and several reporters wondered facetiously why they were omitted. Former prosecutor Joe Shannon, now in private practice, seemed downright offended his name *wasn't* there.

"I was just a name on the list," said Priscilla, who seemed unfazed but somewhat vindicated by the episode. She scoffed at claims that Cullen was being framed and that she was involved. "I don't see how they could possibly suggest that I had anything to do with it," she sniffed.

Whether it was naiveté or wishful thinking, she was mistaken — terribly so.

Cullen's bond hearing lasted eight days and Racehorse all but proved he could cross-examine a tree nonstop for forty-eight hours. He badgered and baited David McCrory and exploited other state's witnesses for anything he could use in Cullen's defense.

The state argued that bond should be denied because of the felony charges still pending from the mansion shootings. Once again, prosecutors wedded themselves to a strategy of keeping the millionaire defendant in jail without bond. They succeeded, but they also exposed much of the state's case against Cullen.

If not awesome, Haynes' cross-examination of McCrory was artful. He set him up for a subsequent kill, prying loose embarrassing personal facts and recording inconsistencies. Haynes collected a treasure chest of times, dates, finances, names, and events, but he deferred any full-fledged attack on McCrory's credibility. "I suspect we'll be talking to Mr. McCrory again before long," he said.

It was the next state's witness, a karate expert named Pat Burleson, who provided Haynes with his most important discovery. McCrory had turned to Burleson in desperation when he believed he was becoming too deeply mired in Cullen's schemes. A reluctant Burleson led his misguided friend to the FBI.

Although nothing sinister was initially suggested, Haynes learned from Burleson that he had met separately with Priscilla and McCrory several times before Cullen's arrest. Thus did Burleson become an unwitting and unfortunate principal in the developing defense theory of a conspiratorial frame-up. Asked what the defense turned up on Burleson and Priscilla, attorney Phil Burleson replied, "Nude swimming in the mansion pool together—and whatever that leads to."

The defense failed, however, to block the tape of an August 18 meeting between McCrory and Cullen. Judge Arthur Tipps, brought out of retirement for the bond hearing, ruled admissible a recording made two days before Cullen's arrest when FBI agents first wired McCrory to confirm his story of a mass murder scheme.

After a discussion with McCrory about several proposed assassinations, Cullen said on the August 18 tape, *"Do the judge and then his wife, and that would be it."*

The death plan's target, Judge Joe Eidson, immediately withdrew from the Davis divorce and said he expected to be called as a state's witness against Cullen in a new felony trial.

He was right.

The streets of Houston glistened from overnight thundershowers as defense attorneys and prosecutors trudged into the Harris County Courthouse on a gloomy morning in early November. Cullen, alone at the counsel table, smiled wanly as they entered the darkly majestic courtroom. He had been in a Houston jail since September 20, his 45th birthday, after his latest trial was transferred from Fort Worth because of publicity. His 43rd birthday was spent in a jail in Fort Worth and his 44th behind bars in Amarillo.

With everyone assembled, the prosecutor read the murder-for-hire indictment against Cullen and the judge asked, "How do you plead?"

"Not guilty," the moody and embattled millionaire said evenly.

Part 8

Wallace "Pete" Moore, a tough, chain-smoking World War II fighter pilot, sat impatiently at the bench as still another chapter unfolded in the Davis legal saga. Moore was an informal but no-nonsense judge who owned an official black robe but seldom wore it. "It catches under the rollers of the chair," he explained.

Spotting the defendant seated alone at the counsel table, Moore quipped, "Cullen's so confident he's decided to defend himself."

The judge and Racehorse Haynes were good friends and sailing buddies, and more than one Scotch bottle died with both their fingerprints on its throat. But Moore's Houston courtroom was hardly the friendly environment the defense team had come to know in Amarillo.

Tolly Wilson, a veteran of the Amarillo wars, was now chief prosecutor. His most conspicuous assistant was Jack Strickland, a slender, curly-haired firebrand with an enviable record of five consecutive death penalty convictions in Fort Worth. At 35, Strickland's legal ability was exceeded only by his ego and he yearned for splashy, big-time criminal assignments. He got his chance when Tolly's original No. 2 resigned to take a job in Oklahoma.

Cullen wore his familiar gray business suit and blue tie and his dark, wavy hair appeared to be freshly styled. He showed no evidence of the raw treatment he was experiencing in the Harris County jail. Unlike Amarillo, he received no favors in Houston; when Haynes sought to change that, the lawyer was rebuffed by Sheriff Jack Heard. Cullen was confined to one of five spartan cells reserved for so-called infamous prisoners. Two former occupants were defendants in a nationally publicized homosexual mass murder case.

Karen, meanwhile, took a thousand-dollar-a-month apartment near the Galleria, a prestigious suburban shopping complex, and visited Cullen whenever possible. Upset with reporters who called her Cullen's mistress, she was now officially his fiancée. That came about after a phone call in which she declared, "The sorry son of a bitch is going to announce our marriage *or else*."

Tolly Wilson introduced the jury to the case by describing the marriage of Cullen and Priscilla, their friendships with David and Judy McCrory, and the divorce suit in the Fort Worth court of Judge Joe Eidson. He did not mention the events of August 2, 1976, because Judge Moore ruled out testimony regarding either the murders or the Amarillo trial. The prosecutor related how Cullen and McCrory met at Coco's Restaurant to discuss the alleged mass murder scheme.

"Shortly after his meeting," Tolly said, "the defendant, Thomas Cullen Davis, was arrested and subsequently charged with the crime for which he is on trial today: the solicitation, the conspiracy, the attempt to murder Judge Joe Eidson."

Armed with a storehouse of tape recordings, videotapes, and photographs, the DA's men opened their case with McCrory's initial FBI contact, Special Agent Ron Jannings. On cross-examination, Racehorse pounced on Jannings' sketchy notes of his first meeting with McCrory and plundered the agent's memory lapses for scraps of misinformation and doubts.

Haynes was less than successful with another FBI agent, Jerry Hubbell, and fared even worse with Judge Eidson, who recounted his role as a counterfeit victim. "Frankly, I was pretty shaken up by the situation," Eidson said.

After a third FBI agent established the authenticity of the tape recordings and videotapes, the state called its major witness, David McCrory, who recounted Cullen's suggestions for the removal of Beverly Bass. "Well, I am going to go ahead and have her killed," he quoted Cullen as saying, "and you are going to help me. You are going to hire somebody to have it done, and if you turn me around on it this time, I'll kill you and your whole damn family, and you know I have the power and the money to have it done."

While McCrory testified, the state unveiled its blockbuster, a sound-and-film composite of the August 20 meeting at Coco's. Haynes argued that it was a "hybrid, manufactured device," but Moore ruled it admissible. The synchronized version was by all rights the most damaging item in the state's arsenal of weapons. In a key passage, McCrory told Cullen, "I got Judge Eidson dead for you."

"Good," Cullen replied.

Concluding his questioning of McCrory, prosecutor Tolly Wilson wondered what Cullen thought of Dee Davis, Priscilla's daughter by her first marriage.

"He wanted her killed," McCrory testified.

Wilson asked what Cullen said about her.

". . . he hated the bitch."

Then Racehorse Haynes went to work, stinging McCrory like a hostile bee. But despite nearly four days of cross-examination, Haynes scored heavily in only one area. There were suspicious time gaps between McCrory's known meetings with Pat Burleson and the FBI in the days leading to Cullen's arrest. It proved nothing, but it gave the appearance that McCrory might be hiding something.

In sinister and somber tones, Haynes injected the name of Priscilla Davis.

"I didn't talk to Pat about Priscilla Davis," McCrory thundered at the height of one exchange. "I don't like Priscilla Davis." But the seeds of conspiracy, so cleverly planted in August, were now producing fruit to feed a starving defense theory.

And though Judge Moore was growing increasingly intolerant of Haynes' questions, the crafty defense attorney struck gold near the end. With McCrory obviously agitated and angry, Haynes asked him if he ever told Cullen that Priscilla tried to frame him in the mansion shootings.

"I might have," said McCrory flippantly. "I told him so many stories and lies, there's no way I can remember all of them." Thus did Cullen's chief accuser, with Haynes' help, brand himself a liar.

The state rested after Thanksgiving and, while the prosecution's case was strong, Strickland was troubled. McCrory's memory lapses were a negative factor and attempts to tie Cullen to key evidence by using fluorescent powder had backfired. Authorities put tracing powder on the fake photograph of Judge Eidson's "corpse," but no powder was found on Cullen's hands after he was arrested. Inexplicably, he was allowed to wash them when he was fingerprinted.

Despite his misgivings, Strickland had an explanation for McCrory's faulty memory. "I think it may have been brain damage from the constant harangue by Mr. Haynes. Even the jurors looked catatonic."

Racehorse provided jurors the defense theory in his opening statement. "Things are not what they may seem," he claimed. "When put into context, there was no specific intent by Mr. Davis to offend the law in any way. Instead, Thomas Cullen Davis was a victim of a conspiracy by and between Charles David McCrory, Pat Burleson, and others."

As his first witness, he called one of the "others"—Priscilla Lee Davis, still Cullen's estranged wife. Priscilla admitted going to Pat Burleson's karate studio on August 16, the day McCrory approached Burleson about contacting the FBI. She met with Burleson at the mansion on August 17, on August 18, and again on August 20, but she insisted she was totally unaware of Burleson's involvement with McCrory. She wanted to discuss security for her upcoming divorce trial. Rescued by prosecutors and by Judge Moore, Priscilla was not confronted with the lurid accusations about her lifestyle that testimony in Amarillo had revealed. She departed Houston with her reputation considerably less tarnished than a year earlier.

On the witness stand, Priscilla heard the tapes of Cullen and McCrory discussing a phantom "hit man's" preference to kill her instead of the judge. Away from the jury, she told Jack Strickland what she wanted to do to her estranged husband. "I'm going to walk in there and blow Cullen's head off," she declared.

"For God's sake, Priscilla, don't talk like that," Strickland protested. "Don't say that, even jokingly."

Although she adored the young prosecutor, there was something she neglected to tell him one morning. She had tucked her silver-plated .32 pistol in her briefcase and took it with her to the witness stand.

Pat Burleson, thinner and clean shaven, was summoned by Haynes as a so-called hostile witness. He was also a ticking time bomb, and Judge Moore warned him to control his temper or there would be a mistrial. Burleson repeated his testimony from the bond hearing in Fort Worth. He said he met separately with Priscilla and McCrory and told Priscilla nothing about McCrory's problems with Cullen.

When reporters asked Haynes why he called Burleson and

Priscilla as defense witnesses, he said, "I want the jurors to see the alleged co-conspirators." Then he set about shading in the edges of his conspiracy theory with a curious cast produced by the defense's investigative team. With mixed results, the jury was exposed to ten such individuals. They included the irrepressible W. T. Rufner, who surfaced in Houston wearing his Christmas stocking T-shirt and smelling of strong drink. But he sobered up long enough to foil defense efforts to induce the kind of damaging testimony he had provided in Amarillo.

The only witness to emerge unscathed was a platinum-blonde receptionist in a building where David McCrory worked. She said she saw McCrory meet Burleson and someone who resembled Priscilla about a month before Cullen's arrest. It proved nothing, but it fed the conspiratorial flames for Haynes. The trio denied such a meeting, but the state had no other counterattack. Strickland, recalling a surprise witness in Amarillo, said, "I think what we saw today was Uewayne Polk in drag."

The most curious person on Haynes' witness list was a self-proclaimed golf professional named Harold Gene Sexton. According to Sexton, he and McCrory met in midsummer 1978 at a Sambo's Restaurant on East Lancaster in Fort Worth. He said McCrory encouraged him to telephone Cullen, representing himself to be a police officer.

Sexton's testimony, if unchallenged, cut to the heart of the defense theory that Cullen was framed. But Tolly Wilson knew something that could blow Sexton's story to shreds. He would spring the trap the next morning.

Part 9

"Cullen's coming!"

Toward the end of testimony by Karen Master, it suddenly hit Jack Strickland that Cullen would take the stand in his own behalf. The young prosecutor all but shouted his conclusion to Tolly Wilson.

Once again, Karen was a dynamite defense witness. In Amarillo, she had provided Cullen an alibi that did not require him to take the stand. In Houston, her testimony laid the groundwork for Cullen actually to testify. Karen said David McCrory once told her that Priscilla and Bubba Gavrel had put "a contract out on Cullen's life." That foreshadowed Cullen's complex explanation for his renewed relationship with McCrory.

She also set the stage for Cullen to explain the $25,000 payoff to McCrory. According to Karen, Cullen once spoke with McCrory by phone, left the house for short while, and returned with an envelope full of money. The implication was that he obtained the cash from McCrory. Cullen would now contend he was merely *giving it back* on August 20.

Even more crucial to the defense theory was testimony regarding a telephone call she said Cullen received on August 10, ten days before his arrest.

"And when the caller identified himself or herself, what identification was given?" Haynes inquired.

"He said he was with the FBI — FBI Agent Acree."

Not only was there such a person as FBI Agent Acree, but he had confirmed in earlier testimony that he investigated an anonymous extortion threat after Cullen's acquittal in Amarillo. Acree said the typewritten threat was checked for fingerprints and a tracing device was placed on Karen's phone, but the culprit was never identified.

As Strickland had sensed, Cullen indeed would be coming forward and the defendant would now use the name of Agent Acree to explain somehow why he was discussing mass murder and hired killers in a Fort Worth parking lot.

Cullen celebrated Christmas in jail, sharing the traditional turkey with fellow inmates. Two days later, he strode to the witness stand wearing a blue-gray suit, white shirt, and dark blue tie. He looked as if he were about to conduct a board meeting at Kendavis Industries.

Like a pair of championship figure skaters, Racehorse and "the citizen accused" glided smoothly through the preliminaries. According to Cullen, David McCrory appeared one day uninvited and asking for a job. He also promised to provide information about Priscilla that would be useful in Cullen's divorce case. Cullen put him to work at a Davis subsidiary, Jet Air.

"And what was McCrory's salary to be?" Haynes inquired.

"Well, he asked me if the job would pay $50,000 a year, and I told him if there were any $50,000-a-year jobs laying around, I would apply for them myself." Jack Strickland almost gagged. Then he scribbled a note to another prosecutor: "Rare glimpse into the wit and humor of a multimillionaire industrialist."

As expected, Cullen maintained the cash that changed hands in the parking lot at Coco's on August 20 was McCrory's. According to Cullen, McCrory claimed he won it in Las Vegas and asked Cullen to keep it so his ex-wife and the IRS would not find out. Similarly, the .22 Ruger and the silencer were gifts from McCrory. Cullen did not ask for them.

Haynes moved on to the August 10 phone call Karen had described. Cullen testified the caller identified himself as "Agent Acree" and said, "We think that you're the victim of an extortion plot by David McCrory." The caller sought Cullen's help. "We want you to play along; that's the only way we're going to catch him, for you to play along and follow his suggestions."

According to Cullen, "Agent Acree" supplied h:m a phone number and instructed, "Keep our conversation confidential and I'll be back in touch with you." Therefore, Cullen thought he was cooperating with federal authorities when he discussed killing people with David McCrory.

With Haynes as a guide, Cullen's checklist of complicated and sometimes bizarre explanations continued. Odd though it may have seemed, Cullen would contend the following:

— There was no picture of Judge Eidson's body in the envelope David McCrory handed him in the car on August 20. He said the envelope actually contained tape recorder cassettes McCrory used to fake a conversation with Cullen. The recording was for the hired killers who McCrory supposedly knew. That's why Cullen would agree with McCrory to "get rid of the motherfuckers." He didn't want such tapes to find their way to Priscilla. Without tracing powder on Cullen's hands, the state could not disprove Cullen's assertions.

— McCrory wanted the tapes as assurance to the hired killers that Cullen was serious about wooing them away from

Priscilla. Cullen thought the episode might somehow be useful in his divorce case, perhaps to expose Priscilla's motivations. The first "recordings," the ones McCrory had in the envelope on August 20, were unconvincing, so McCrory asked for another. Cullen cooperated with what he thought were McCrory's taped charades on August 18 and again on August 20. That would explain why Cullen talked openly about the targets on his "hit list."

—Cullen refused to finance McCrory's schemes, so McCrory offered his *own* money to continue the operation. Therefore, the money they talked about on the tapes was not Cullen's "blood money" after all.

—And the most chilling portion of the state's August 20 tape was *not* incriminating. "I got Judge Eidson dead for you," McCrory had said. And Cullen had responded, "Good." Cullen was *just going along with the conversation*," following "Agent Acree's" instructions.

"I had no reason for wanting him dead," Cullen said of Judge Eidson.

The defendant rocked back and forth in his chair, his legs and arms crossed and his head cocked as though he were listening to a distant symphony. He was ready to furnish the most critical details of his testimony to reinforce the defense theory of a conspiracy involving McCrory, Priscilla, and Pat Burleson.

"Having heard Mr. Acree talk in court," Haynes asked, "can you testify with certainty that the person you talked to in August as being from the FBI was the same Mr. Jim Acree that you talked to in December 1977?"

It was not the same person, said Cullen.

Haynes then asked Cullen if he recalled the telephone number of Pat Burleson's karate studio, which had surfaced in earlier testimony.

"That's right."

"And was that phone number the same phone number or not that was given you in August as being the phone number of the FBI?"

It was.

Prosecutors considered Cullen's story contrived and

ridiculous, but they could only seize on one miscue.

Cullen said he tried to make two phone calls from the pay phone where he was arrested. One was to his security man and the other was to the number given for "Agent Acree." The first number was busy and there was no answer at the second, according to his testimony. At the time, it cost twenty cents to make a local call.

Since he completed neither call, he would have gotten his twenty cents back. Yet, when he was arrested, he had only fifteen cents in his pocket. For some reason, he was not telling the truth about his calls from the pay booth and prosecutors would expose the contradiction in final arguments. They wanted the jury to believe that Cullen was lying about the self-serving attempt to call "Acree" and to wonder who Cullen contacted within minutes of acquiring a pistol and silencer. At the time, investigators were convinced the gun was obtained to dispose of McCrory himself and Cullen had phoned the contract killer.

Racehorse and Cullen were walking a tightrope. Cullen testified on one hand that he believed he was cooperating with the FBI to expose McCrory's extortion plot. At the same time, he was scheming with McCrory to hire away Priscilla's hit men. He had an explanation for most if not all of the state's physical evidence, but nowhere were his "mini-cassettes" to be found. It was, at best, a paradox.

With Cullen's first courtroom testimony behind them, his lawyers faced a new and potentially devastating dilemma. A newspaper intended to report the next morning that a fire had shut down the Sambo's restaurant where golf pro Harold Sexton claimed he met David McCrory. Prosecutors were poised to destroy Sexton and perhaps Cullen with him. But the embattled Haynes recalled Sexton the next day before the state could detonate its bomb.

By the most fortuitous of circumstances, there were *two* Sambo's restaurants, one in Fort Worth and the other several miles away in Arlington. The two Sambo's were on the same road, though it changed names between the two cities. Haynes struggled to show Sexton was confused about the two restaurants. To a Houston jury, that might be understandable; to someone who grew up in Fort Worth, it would seem ludicrous.

Confronted on cross-examination by Tolly Wilson, Sexton denied knowing in advance of his latest testimony that the Fort Worth Sambo's burned. The state sought a reporter to testify the Sambo's story was already in print when Sexton was recalled. None would do so voluntarily. Finally, Tolly threw up his hands in exasperation and ended his inquiry.

Had the prosecutor known, he could have subpoenaed a reporter from the second row of the courtroom and rebutted Sexton's testimony instantly. Sexton and the reporter had discussed the fire less than an hour earlier.

From out of the Houston mist and fog they came, like movie extras gathering to watch the stars perform the Big Scene. The Davis family arrived en masse for final arguments, greeted by the press and TV cameras. Richard Haynes' wife Naomi took a seat behind Cullen in the rows reserved for the friends and family of the defendant and his lawyers.

Across the courtroom, on the front row nearest the jury box, sat Judge Joe Eidson, smoking and chatting with Mrs. Tolly Wilson. Jack Strickland's girlfriend arrived early and sat next to a secretary in the DA's office. It could have been an Amarillo rerun.

Judge Pete Moore landed his monster in mid-January but it took him two months longer than he forecast. "It's the worst ordeal I've ever gone through," he grumbled.

It had not been a cakewalk for the judge's sailing companion either. Haynes had grown testier and testier during the trial. At least twice, opposing attorneys seemed prepared to settle their disputes on the courthouse lawn. And, more than anything, Haynes was concerned with the rulings of Judge Moore, who would not be bullied or bamboozled. The jury heard little about the sex and drugs Haynes exploited so successfully in Amarillo and Moore prevented questioning about any sexual misconduct between karate instructor Pat Burleson and Priscilla. The judge's impatience with Haynes' tactics was apparent in his rebukes from the bench.

Fourteen months had passed since Racehorse stood before the jury in Amarillo and appealed for the life of Cullen Davis. He was unimpressed with his own argument there and he longed for such a moment again. That moment had come.

His head pounding from the flu, Racehorse rose on his ant-eater boots and began. For two hours, the words rolled out, long ones and short ones but most often the word "Why?"

Why were Agent Jannings' notes so incomplete? Why had he omitted so much? Why did the FBI let David McCrory call the shots? Why was Pat Burleson at Priscilla's house before Cullen's arrest? Haynes asked a hundred questions and answered only a few. Pausing finally to brush the tears from his eyes, Haynes ended with is trademark farewell "Godspeed" to the jury.

Although Racehorse was as impressive as ever, he did not overshadow Jack Strickland, who matched eloquence with biting sarcasm. The prosecutor labeled Cullen's convoluted testimony the most contrived, foolish, and flagrantly ridiculous story ever perpetrated on the ears of twelve innocent jurors. "Don't you know," he said, "that it must have galled the industrialist millionaire to have to get up there and tell you that foolish story, to make himself out to be such a fool in order to walk away from this mess?"

By virtue of his wealth and power, Cullen could do anything he damned well pleased, Strickland argued. "That's the sort of arrogance and power that I would submit to you was demonstrated by this man's actions. But Cullen never expected to be caught. . . . And he expected for whatever reason that if he was caught, he could beat it."

The juror most smitten with Racehorse Haynes, Helen Farmer, voted against him. David McCrory did not appeal to her, but she was deeply disturbed that Cullen had not sought out "Agent Acree" after his arrest. If he had been following Acree's instructions, would he not have turned to him for vindication? She scribbled on her juror's ballot: *Guilty*.

So did seven of her colleagues in the first vote that Wednesday morning. Of those who voted otherwise, one thought the state did not prove its case *beyond a reasonable doubt*. Another failed to see what Cullen could gain by killing Judge Eidson. And another simply believed Cullen's testimony.

Through fourteen votes, no one budged. At 4:05 P.M. the

following Monday, it was over. The jury was hopelessly dead-locked eight to four in favor of guilt, and Judge Pete Moore ordered a mistrial. Considering the state's evidence, it was a monumental triumph for the defense.

Long after the courtroom emptied, Racehorse Haynes sat in silent solitude, puffing his pipe. A reporter approached him and offered congratulations. He did not respond at once. Finally, he spoke. "They didn't get us, did they?"

Part 10

On a sun-swept morning in the early spring of 1979, Cullen and Priscilla met for the final time as man and wife. The occasion was the culmination of a divorce trial no less bizarre than the criminal proceedings of Amarillo and Houston. "I'm sorry, frankly, that you've had unhappiness in your lives and in your marriage," said Judge Clyde Ashworth. "If there was some way I could do it, I'd like to turn back your lives to the fall of 1968."

Dissolving the tempestuous and tragic union, Ashworth awarded Priscilla $3,475,000. She and Cullen split her attorneys' fees of $1,250,000. She got her car and her horse. Cullen got the mansion and all his company stock. Neither side seemed overjoyed, but neither appealed Ashworth's ruling. That may have been the biggest suprise of all.

Ashworth was the third judge to hear the case. When Joe Eidson removed himself because of his place on the hit list, a folksy retired judge named John Barron was appointed. It was a turbulent, abbreviated tenure. When Barron considered permitting Cullen's attorneys to remove documents from the trial record, Jack Strickland and the DA's office precipitated a stormy showdown in Barron's chambers. Strickland was interested in Cullen's financial dealings just prior to his August 1978 arrest. And he was even more curious about a 1975 sales slip for a revolver similar to what prosecutors contended was the mansion murder weapon.

Barron was furious with Strickland's intrusion, calling the young assistant DA "a wet-eared, fool prosecutor." He threatened to remove himself from the case and declare a mistrial. Barron eventually did withdraw, but not because of Strickland. He learned that the *Fort Worth Star-Telegram* was about to disclose that he and Cullen met twice in his hotel room to discuss a settlement in the divorce case.

The judge insisted he did nothing improper, but few concurred. "I'm just going to quit. I'm tired of getting my ass kicked around," he said by telephone from his hometown Bryan.

When Priscilla heard of the meetings and the mistrial, she said, "Ole Cullen has fucked up again. Talk about a dummy! He doesn't have anyone to blame but himself. He's forever an Aggie."

After three years of silence, Cullen reluctantly gave a sworn account of his activities on August 2, 1976. The occasion was a deposition in Bubba Gavrel's damage suit against him. Cullen said he dined alone at a popular short-order restaurant named Kip's. Unaccompanied, he said, he attended a movie called *The Bad News Bears*, leaving for Karen Master's home about 11:30 P.M.

Cullen and Karen were married May 24, 1979. The wedding was chronicled in an eight-column, front-page article in the *Star-Telegram*. It occurred at a friend's home at 12:50 A.M., less than an hour after the expiration of the mandated thirty-day waiting period for Cullen and Priscilla's divorce judgment. Noticeably absent from the festivities was Ray Hudson, Karen's father. "I told them I was disgusted with the way they used and discarded people," he said.

District Judge Gordon Gray convened his court on July 30 for the retrial of the murder-for-hire case against Cullen. Coincidentally, it was Priscilla's 38th birthday. To the profound dismay of district attorney Tim Curry, Gray refused the state's request to move the trial to another city and another judge. Gray was a possible candidate for Tim Curry's job. "From the state's standpoint," said Curry, "Fort Worth, Texas, is the very last place you want to try it."

A tireless red-haired firebrand named Joy Smith headed a citizens' protest against the continued prosecution of Cullen Davis and claimed to have collected 76,000 signatures to support that view. Strangers approached Cullen in public places, extending sympathy. "I know you've been railroaded and it's a goddamn shame," said one.

At times, it appeared Cullen wanted more than moral support. "You still got the women fawning over you," said a reporter.

"Yeah," Cullen agreed. "I don't have to say anything, just stand here and lick my eyebrows."

His female supporters were out in number during the trial. They were called Cullen's groupies. The stereotype was Barbie, a chunky, cheerful housewife who rarely entered the courtroom without pickles, pastries, or other such gifts for Cullen and his lawyers. She never missed a day, but she resisted unfavorable testimony about Cullen by sticking her fingers in her ears. She and the other groupies rarely squandered an opportunity to be photographed with Cullen, to touch him, or to talk with him. If Priscilla appeared in the courthouse hallway, it sounded like lunchtime at a turkey farm.

The groupies drew a judicial warning for their verbal abuse of David McCrory, who was back on the stand again. In Houston, Racehorse Haynes seized on McCrory's memory lapses. Now McCrory remembered *too much*. As Jack Strickland explored the proposed murder of Beverly Bass, McCrory interrupted to quote Cullen as telling him at Coco's: "I've gotten by with it once. . . ."

Strickland turned ashen, but that was only a shade lighter than Haynes, who demanded a mistrial. Gray overruled the motion. McCrory stuck by his new story that Cullen wanted Beverly Bass killed because she was the only state witness the Amarillo jury believed.

There were other surprises. According to McCrory, the plan to kill Priscilla was to dig a hole on Cullen's property across the street from the mansion and station a hired assassin there with guns and grenades. "Oh Lord, not grenades!" thought Strickland, shooting McCrory an incredulous look. "Please, God, anything but grenades!"

Haynes was not amused with the new revelations, either. "The next thing you know McCrory will be testifying that Cullen killed Kennedy and kidnapped the Lindbergh baby," he complained. McCrory countered by dropping Haynes' pipe stem into a partially filled coffee cup when he left the stand.

Prosecutors felt McCrory's testimony was more helpful than harmful and he was again the catalyst through which they introduced the tape recordings of August 18 and the devastating videotape of August 20. However, they were not spared a strange interlude in which McCrory denied to Haynes that he ever bragged that he could kill a rat by screaming at it.

Cullen was delighted with the rat-screaming story. "I was afraid that McCrory was going to scream at Haynes," he grinned, "and Strickland was going to fall over dead."

Strickland was not amused. "I'll take my chances with those assholes," he told reporters. "Line up all the attorneys and Cullen and let McCrory scream his fucking head off."

After spending his last three birthdays in jail, Cullen was now free on bond for his 46th. A small group joined him at a restaurant for dinner, but the gathering broke up prematurely, much to Cullen's displeasure. The trip to the mansion was deadly silent, and he marched in without saying a word. He was greeted by a young lady with a sign taped to her rear: "I want to be at the bottom of your list." The lights illuminating the conversation pit were turned on, revealing a crowd of people and decorations simulating a jail cell.

It was a classic surprise party. Two sexy ladies arrived with a singing telegram, but it was Sheriff Lon Evans who stole the show. He brought Cullen his old jail whites and sandals and a hacksaw. He also presented Cullen a "key to the jail," which, even in Texas, had to be a first.

The leadoff defense witness again was Priscilla, but her testimony was far short of sensational. Gray bluntly told Haynes, "I am not going to let you assassinate her character." It was another sign that Gray's patience with Haynes was thin. "If we keep up with this," Gray said after McCrory's cross-examination, "the judicial system is going to hell."

Priscilla confirmed under oath her connection with Pat Burleson, a vital link for the defense conspiracy theory. And a receptionist at a Davis subsidiary repeated that she witnessed a midsummer meeting of McCrory, Burleson, and someone who looked like Priscilla.

As expected, Cullen deviated little from his Houston testimony. Taking the stand on a gloriously crisp October morning, he told of his marital discord, the prenuptial agreement, the potential value of McCrory in the divorce trial, and the phone call from "Agent Acree."

Cullen's defenders doubted he would stumble over the essence of his story, but Strickland might ridicule him into a tactical error. To lower the odds of such an ambush, Cullen was warned repeatedly what to expect and how to react. "You know," said defense attorney Mike Gibson, "Cullen has never wavered from his own confidence in his innocence, in his ability to withstand the adversity of three trials and the time in jail. That shows an inner strength. He's tough."

Cullen faced a withering cross-examination by Strickland. The prosecutor's questioning turned brutal, tinged with sarcasm, mock surprise, and open incredulity when he replayed the tapes of August 18 and August 20 for Cullen. "How does the word 'Good' fit into the context of a picture of a dead judge, a silencer, and $25,000?" Strickland demanded.

After a flurry of objections and nonresponsive answers, Cullen agreed that it "might sound incriminating." Nevertheless, he stuck by his story of making a "sham" tape for McCrory and following the instructions of "Agent Acree" so McCrory's "extortion plot" could be exposed. Cullen's attorneys lost no time in describing their client's performance as virtuoso, but there were indications that Cullen was displeased with them for not restraining Strickland's fierce attacks. Unknown to the defense, Strickland was inspired by a letter from the father of mansion slaying victim Andrea Wilborn.

"For chrissakes, what now?" whispered John Bankston, who was assisting Strickland in the prosecution. The pair looked at a man named Roger Shuy adjusting his horn-rimmed glasses as he took his seat in the witness chair. They soon discovered that Shuy, a professor of linguistics at Georgetown University in Washington, D.C., would provide "expert" testimony for a new defense interpretation of the tapes.

Shuy treated the jury to such phrases as "shared reference," "internal cohesion," "conversational strategy," and "agenda organizers." Over state objections that the tapes spoke for themselves, Shuy concluded that McCrory dominated the conversations. "Mr. Davis is passive," he said, impressing the jury with his erudition.

Strickland's cross-examination spilled over into three days and was, under the circumstances, spottily brilliant — as when Shuy suggested a reference to killing Priscilla was an insignificant "subtopic." "You understand Mr. Davis is not charged with being a good or bad conversationalist, don't you?" said Strickland, his voice heavy with sarcasm.

Karen Master, now testifying as Mrs. Cullen Davis, repeated her Houston testimony while embellishing it with some new self-serving details that she had neglected to share with the grand jury.

The defense dug up another weird witness or two, including a thrice-convicted felon whose lawyer represented Uewayne Polk in Amarillo. But it was the state that shot itself in the foot this time. A new prosecution witness said he was with David McCrory in Oklahoma City when Cullen claimed McCrory was with him in Fort Worth making the missing recordings. Either the witness or Cullen was lying. If the jurors believed the new witness, Cullen's fragile story was down the drain. In a dramatic eleventh-hour twist, the defense found Oklahoma motel records that showed McCrory and his friend checked in a day later than the friend testified. The reversal did not confirm Cullen's story about the disputed meeting, but it rescued him from an incriminating lie.

Despite the setback, Strickland looked forward to a showdown with Racehorse in the final arguments. Their rematch unfolded before another packed courtroom, and this time Haynes had Professor Roger Shuy's testimony to give the defense an added twist. He now argued the state's tapes actually corroborated Cullen's contention that he was a patsy manipulated by McCrory.

Strickland defended McCrory. His star witness might be a greedy, opportunistic floater, he admitted. "But I'll go so far as to tell you this: no matter what your verdict is in this case. . . . were it not for David McCrory, that man" — Strickland suddenly pointed to a spectator in the front row — "would not be alive in this courtroom today." Judge Joe Eidson's face flushed neatly on cue, but his eyes remained locked on Strickland's pointing finger.

For more than two days, jurors reviewed the case in secret without voting, leading lawyers and spectators mistakenly to believe there might be another deadlock. But when the first ballot was taken, it was unanimous.

At the defense table, Steve Sumner put his arm around Cullen, aware that he was trembling and his body was like stone. The citizen accused looked terrified. Racehorse buried his head in his hands. "Our ship just sunk," he said. The defense attorneys did not want a verdict. They had hoped from the beginning they somehow could obtain another hung jury. They believed an acquittal on the murder-for-hire charges was unlikely and perhaps impossible.

What none of them knew was that the jury figuratively "found" the phantom cassettes Cullen claimed McCrory showed him on August 20. The panel concluded it was mini-cassettes in McCrory's envelope that caused an odd clicking noise in the state's recordings. One creative juror tried to reproduce a clicking sound using Judge Eidson's counterfeit photo and his identification cards. They made no noise. But plastic on plastic did. Therefore, the unexplained clicking *must* have been the mini-cassettes. Thus, it followed that Cullen was telling the truth.

Judge Gray seemed transfixed when he stared at the jury form. "I'm not believing this," he thought. Dispensing with the formal address to the courtroom, he blurted: "*The jury's found Thomas Cullen Davis not guilty!*" Confirming the verdict, he turned and stepped down from the bench. "Fuck," he said.

Pandemonium swept the audience as groupies scaled the railing to grope at Cullen and his lawyers. Both Cullen and Racehorse shed genuine tears that morning, possibly a first. At the prosecutor's table, Jack Strickland said bitterly, "If this is what the people of Tarrant County want, then fuck 'em. They can have it."

Amid the chaos outside, bailiffs herded the jury back into its private quarters with instructions to open the door for "no one but us." "Us" turned out to be Cullen and Karen, who thanked them for their verdict and invited them to a victory party at a nearby bar.

Tim Curry informed Jack Strickland of his decision to drop the remaining charges against Cullen in the mansion shootings. "If I had to do the good part, I can do the bad part," said Strickland, volunteering to sign the forms. He then took them to Judge Tom Cave, in whose court Cullen's legal saga began what seemed like an eternity ago.

"I'm sorry as hell to have to ask you to be the one to do this," Strickland told the judge.

"It's all right," sighed Cave. "It comes with the territory." After signing the papers, the judge pushed them across his desk. Then he dismissed the Cullen Davis affair with an obscene salute characterized by an extended middle finger.

Part 11

"Final justice! . . . Final justice! . . . Final justice!"

The chant rose to the ceiling at Duffy's saloon, a short distance from the Tarrant County Courthouse. The groupies who so ardently supported Cullen during his murder-for-hire trial were delirious now that he was acquitted. He sipped champagne and smiled.

While Priscilla labeled the verdict another "multimillion-dollar snow job," Cullen and Karen were once again celebrities. Society columnists spotted them at fancy parties and a normally reticent Cullen surfaced on local talk shows with surprising regularity.

Unfortunately, Priscilla could not avoid the spotlight either. On Thanksgiving Day, she nearly blew away Jack Strickland and his girlfriend when her pistol discharged accidentally. She was unloading it en route to the airport for a holiday with Strickland's family. The bullet fractured Priscilla's hand and splattered blood on the other woman's dress. It also may have wounded Strickland's political future.

The near-disaster aroused suspicion of a romantic link between the young prosecutor and Priscilla and even speculation about some vague conspiracy. Strickland said anyone who believed such suggestions could go to hell. "Whatever's been said of Priscilla Davis, she ain't never been accused of killing a kid," he fumed. "And I've never invited anyone to dinner who's been accused of killing a kid."

Meanwhile, David McCrory telephoned Judge Gray from a secret hideout and inquired about the disputed $25,000 that figured so ominously in the murder-for-hire trial. He had testified it was Cullen's, but Cullen insisted it was his. The jury believed Cullen, so McCrory was wondering . . .

Gray thought he scared McCrory off when he indicated McCrory might be perilously close to perjury. "I told him it seemed inconsistent to come in here and say Cullen Davis gave it to him to kill somebody and then try to claim it," Gray chuckled.

On a bitterly cold winter night, Judge Gray entertained a small group of friends at a dinner party. Oak logs crackled in the stone fireplace and shadows danced on the wall of his semi-darkened den. Unsurprisingly, he blamed district attorney Tim Curry for the state's failure to convict Cullen in three trials.

"To deny Cullen bond, Curry had to expose his whole case," Gray said. "Even at that, if I got three eyewitnesses, I'm going to win. And Curry could have convicted him in Houston if they hadn't had the bond hearing first. Without that hearing, Haynes would not have known what the state's case was, and prosecutors would have gotten him. The murder solicitation case should never have reached my courtroom."

A guest, defending Curry, reminded Gray of the public outrage when Cullen initially went free on bond in the mansion shootings. "One thing Tim says is that the system itself is to blame for the failure to convict Cullen," the guest observed. "He said the system is not designed to deal with a defendant of such enormous wealth."

Gray disagreed. "I've heard a lot of people say the system failed, but I've said and I still say the system only fails if you convict an innocent man. The system is designed to do just what happened in the Davis case. Maybe good, maybe bad, but that's the system." Refilling his glass, Gray moved to a new target. "If we continue to put up with Racehorse Haynes, the judicial system is going to hell. He could ruin the whole thing. He not only abuses the system, he makes a farce of it."

Postmortems were nothing new to the Cullen Davis trials. "What ifs" abounded in any discussion. If the state had not contested bail in the mansion shootings, would Racehorse Haynes have been summoned? Cullen hired Racehorse only after Judge Cave ordered Cullen jailed. Then the question becomes: where would the defense have been without Haynes? What if Haynes had not learned of the link between Priscilla and Pat Burleson at the second bond hearing? What if Cullen had not been allowed to wash his hands when he was arrested in the murder-for-hire case?

And maybe the biggest "what if" of all: Cullen's money. "If I had been poor, one or two things would have happened," Cullen himself said after the Amarillo verdict. "At least I would have been granted bond. And I would have ended up in the penitentiary in no time flat."

What if Priscilla had not damaged the state's case with her duplicity about sex and drugs at the mansion? Joe Shannon suspected she was protecting her interest in the divorce suit at the same time that she was the state's key eyewitness in a murder trial. "You just can't try two lawsuits at once," he complained. What if Judge Dowlen had blocked the defense from pursuing sex-and-drug scenarios as Pete Moore and Gordon Gray did? Many thought the Amarillo jury convicted Priscilla as surely as it acquitted Cullen.

And there was one other "what if" that had nothing to do with parlor postmortems. It had everything to do with Jack Wilborn's state of mind after his daughter was gunned down in the mansion basement. Wilborn plotted the ultimate revenge for several days, ignoring a series of warning phone calls. Police contacted him and told him he was under surveillance. Friends begged him to do nothing "rash." Bill Davis, despite his brotherly disenchantment with Cullen, sent word: "Don't do anything drastic. The law will take care of it."

Ultimately, Wilborn made his own decision. "I finally realized that if I did something similar to what Cullen did, even though he may have deserved it, that it would have just brought a lot of pain to a lot of people."

Kay Davis said once that Cullen never did the expected. On May 4, 1980, he proved his niece correct once again. With Karen at his side, Cullen walked up the aisle of the First Baptist Church in the Fort Worth suburb of Euless and publicly professed his faith in Christ. His conversion followed a visit to the mansion by television evangelist James Robison, who said of Cullen, "We prayed that God would take over his life."

Karen and Cullen abandoned their high-profile social life and opened the mansion to religious gatherings. Cullen donated his art collection of gold, ivory, and jade to Robison's ministry and then parted with his biggest treasure of all, the mansion itself. The sale price of the house and surrounding acreage reportedly was $30 million.

Before Cullen and his new wife moved out, the mansion spawned a final mystery. Robison and he concurred that the art objects, reportedly valued at $1 million, were of secular origin and Robison deemed them worthless "in the eyes of the Lord." They hammered the objects into bits and threw them into Lake Worth. Much later, divers recovered Cullen's broken collection from the lake bottom. Experts described the objects as "Taiwan Jade" and suggested their value was greatly exaggerated. That raised a provocative question or two on the Fort Worth cocktail circuit, none of which was ever answered satisfactorily. Did someone originally rip off Cullen when he bought the "art"? Or was Cullen's Christian charity not as grand as supposed? Or, ultimately, was the Internal Revenue Service the intended foil?

In any case, Cullen and Karen settled into a more modest dwelling and remained active churchgoers as the tenth anniversary of the mansion shootings approached. While freed from the criminal charges that he had fought for more than three years, Cullen's life was not without challenges. He still faced civil suits stemming from the mansion shootings. And, with the collapse of oil prices, Cullen and his brother Ken were fighting desperately to save their financial empire from banks and other creditors.

Bubba Gavrel's personal injury suit originally asked for $3 million in damages, but now his claims had ripened to $15 million. His lawyer said he would be crippled for life. Plaintiffs in the other suits included Priscilla, the Stan Farr estate, and, of course, Jack Wilborn, father of the slain 12-year-old Andrea.

In the spring of 1986, Cullen quietly settled out of court with Gavrel. "As far as we're concerned," said Bubba's father

Gus, "it's over with. I think Cullen tried to do the right thing by Bubba. Now it's something we'd like to forget." Bubba and Beverly Bass announced plans to marry in the fall.

Other figures in the Davis case were unimpressed with Cullen's accommodating gestures toward the Gavrels. "It didn't tell me anything I didn't already know," said Priscilla, now a grandmother in Dallas. "My suit never was about money."

Jack Strickland was no less cynical. "I think Cullen just admitted in civil court what he refused to admit in criminal court," said Strickland, who left the DA's office after prosecuting the Davis case. "And as he has done so many times over the years, he's just bought his way out of a jam. He's let his money do the talking."

A judge ordered court records in the Gavrel suit sealed, but published accounts put Bubba's payoff at close to $1 million. Attorneys said such settlements are often less expensive and risky than jury trials and should not be open to interpretation.

That same year, Cullen encountered plaintiff Jack Wilborn not in court but at the Word of Faith Church in a Dallas suburb. According to Wilborn and his wife Betty, Cullen approached them at the end of a Sunday evening service and asked forgiveness "for what I did." Cullen did not specifically mention Andrea's name, but, to the dead girl's father, the inference was clear. Wilborn, his wife, and Cullen embraced. They all wept. Another churchgoer witnessed the emotional meeting but did not hear Cullen's remark. She did recall that Wilborn turned to her and said, "Cullen has just asked us to forgive him." She said she and the others present "assumed he wouldn't ask forgiveness for anything but murdering Andrea."

Not so, said Cullen through attorney Steve Sumner. Cullen confirmed the visit to Wilborn's church but insisted *he* was forgiving Wilborn for past transgressions such as the 1960s raid on the Green Oaks Inn. That sounded ludicrous, but probably no more so than his testimony in the murder-for-hire case.

By 1986, Sumner had risen from rookie investigator to chief counsel for Cullen and he tried his damnedest to be supportive of Cullen's stance in the Wilborn exchange. He told an

AP reporter: "If in fact your article is implying or suggesting there was an admission, or even the slightest inference of an admission of a crime by Cullen Davis, that is ridiculous."

Jack Strickland scoffed at Cullen's version. "That's kind of like John Wilkes Booth sending a condolence letter to Mrs. Lincoln. It doesn't do one thing to put back the pieces of the various lives he ruined. It doesn't do one thing to restore what I thought was a miscarriage of justice. All it really does, I suspect, is make Cullen feel better."

Stan Farr's sister, Lynda Arnold, interpreted the church encounter as a confession. She recalled Cullen's lusty courtroom supporters and said, "I hope there's some people out there who now feel like bimbos."

District attorney Tim Curry said the exchange between Cullen and Wilborn had no legal significance in criminal court. Even if the Stan Farr murder case was resurrected, the state's "Speedy Trial Act" precluded prosecution a decade later. Said Curry: "Cullen could stand up on the pulpit and admit the whole thing and there wouldn't be a damn thing we could do about it."

An Epilogue

Fort Worth, Texas, 1988

Had she lived, Andrea Wilborn, at 24, might now be a college graduate, a wife, and maybe a mother. At 44, Stan Farr could be reunited with his two children, now teenagers. Priscilla's bullet wounds have healed and she mixes a busy social life in Dallas with the self-imposed responsibility of raising her live-in granddaughter. At 46, she still contemplates writing a book about her experiences.

Unchallenged as the state's foremost criminal attorney, Haynes still makes headlines even though he's slowing down and mellowing out. Racehorse no longer fights Cullen's battles; it is doubtful that Cullen could afford him.

Tim Curry is still district attorney, despite Gordon Gray's prediction in 1979 that Curry would be ousted by the voters if Cullen was not convicted. Tom Cave, in whose court Cullen's criminal proceedings began and ended, no longer has a court. He resigned after a 1987 sex solicitation scandal.

The month of August continued its hauntingly significant link to

Cullen's life. He married his first wife in August 1962 and divorced her in August 1968. His firstborn came in August. His father died in August, and he married Priscilla in August. The mansion shootings were in August 1976, and he was arrested in the murder-for-hire scheme in August 1978. This past August, on the steps of the Tarrant County Courthouse, Stan Farr's relatives announced plans to pursue their civil damage suit against Cullen. Until then, it appeared he had put most of his legal troubles behind him.

August is the most difficult month of all for Jack Wilborn. "I've been thinking a lot about Andrea," he said on a recent anniversary of the shootings. "I always do at this time of year."

With the presumption of innocence preserved by two jury acquittals and two mistrials, Cullen struggles to save the last traces of his family fortune. Creditors forced his company into bankruptcy and the once benevolent banks seized control of Kendavis Industries from him and his brother Ken. Cullen later filed for personal bankruptcy, and Karen sold her furs and jewelry, at least those she didn't donate to the church.

The mansion where Cullen lived with his second and third wives, and where Stan and Andrea died, is unoccupied but still making headlines. "Like oil heir T. Cullen Davis' once massive fortune, his dream house is in shambles," reported the Dallas Times Herald *this summer. "It has fallen prey to thieves, vandals and neglect." Souvenir hunters have pried bronze tiles from the massive double doors. The plate-glass windows have been smashed and the hardwood floors are scarred and strewn with litter and beer bottles. The walls are spray-painted with obscenities and the six lavish bathrooms are overflowing with trash.*

Developers hoped to build a sprawling community of homes, condominiums, and shops on the property, with the mansion serving as a plush clubhouse for residents. Those dreams have been destroyed by a crumbling Texas economy.

Priscilla visited the old homesite one day and was aghast. The trees were dead and the shrubbery was choked by weeds. "The bush!" she exclaimed. "The bush!" She spoke of the shrubs behind which she hid a dozen years ago and the bush that sheltered her from the man in black. "The bush is gone," she said.

So, too, are the criminal battles, which forged legal reputations and challenged courtroom strategies.

The bitterness remains. Priscilla and Jack Wilborn consolidated their civil suits and together met Cullen in a spectacular $16.5 million trial in 1987. Witnesses revived the horror stories of August 1976 and once *again identified Cullen Davis as the man in black at the mansion that night. A jury deadlocked again, but this time only one vote stood between Cullen and culpability. The resulting mistrial was a resounding victory for Cullen and attorney Steve Sumner.*

Moments after the judge declared a mistrial, foreman Kenneth Pool emerged from the jury's secret chambers and marched angrily from the courtroom. Tears cascaded down his cheeks.

"Cullen," he said later, "got by with murder."

4

AND DELIVER US
FROM EVIL

An Essay

Part 1

Texans rape, pillage, plunder, philander, and kill with a flair. A dubious and curious distinction, but a distinction nonetheless. That's not to suggest we do it expertly or even well, just somehow differently.

There is a mystique about Texas lawlessness, probably dating back to frontier days. We had real cowboys and cutthroats, Indian raiders, and Mexican bandits. Texas itself was settled by any number of people escaping from something or somebody. Butch Cassidy and the Sundance Kid weren't Texans, but, along with their desperado cronies, they hung out here.

Blame it on Hollywood, but there remains a fascination with Texas-flavored treachery. That may sound crass or flippant, but despite our history of violence, we dare not take ourselves too seriously. After nearly three decades of chronicling the murders and mischief of the Texas rich and not-so-rich, I can only conclude that whatever the appeal, it's very real and it's not going away anytime soon.

This is not to say that Texas has some kind of lock on world-class skullduggery. Florida, New York, and California come readily to mind as worthy contenders. But consider this: who would pay to see *The Iowa Chainsaw Massacre*? We are all sick to death of J. R., Sue Ellen, and their TV show *Dallas*, but would a hundred million people watch *Des Moines* or *Salt Lake* or, God forbid, *Cleveland*?

Of course not.

Does anybody have a police force to rival the Texas Rangers? How about a district attorney like Henry Wade, who prosecuted Jack Ruby? Or a criminal trial attorney as crafty and colorful as the late Percy Foreman? Or even his protégé Richard "Racehorse" Haynes?

Where else but Texas would you find a gumshoe like El Paso's J. J. Armes, who had no hands, or a crack private eye like Houston's Clyde Wilson, who had but one eye? J. J. got more ink but Clyde got more results and is indeed "the Eye of Texas."

How about a Depression-era bandit couple like Bonnie and Clyde? Or a modern-day serial killer like Henry Lee Lucas, the demented drifter who claimed to have slain hundreds but later decided, "I only killed me Mum."

Find me a blood-curdling horror story and I just might find you a Texas connection. Charlie Manson's sidekick, Tex Watson, was from the tiny Texas town of Copeville, and Richard Speck, who massacred the Chicago nurses, was from Dallas.

Show me a judge like Roy Bean, the Law West of the Pecos, or anyone more outrageous than Bille Sol Estes, my all-time favorite con man. "You can shear a sheep every year, but you can't skin him but once," proclaimed Estes, a West Texas wheeler-dealer who made millions in phony fertilizer tanks. How many city slickers from New York or Chicago ever made a fortune selling phantom cow manure?

Think about it.

Billie Sol's buddies included Lyndon Johnson, the late president, and Crooked John, a quasi–bounty hunter who once did his dead-level best to kill me during a high-speed chase on a mountain road overlooking El Paso. I was chasing Billie Sol for a story and Crooked John was chasing me.

Ol' Crook never got around to apologizing, but he sent me a couple of big black opals and a silver-plated telephone cover with his name and number inscribed on it. I returned the gems, which wounded him gravely, but we became friends anyway.

And where else but Texas would a politician marry Miss America, get himself convicted of bribery, leave the state legislature in disgrace, return home, run for county judge, and *win*? Ask former House Speaker Gus Mutscher, who now presides over Washington County by day and holds court nightly in the best little saloon in his hometown—owns the joint, in fact.

Judge Gus was a key figure in the Sharpstown Scandal of the seventies, a rotten little affair that came to be known as Watergate West. Like Watergate, Sharpstown began as hardly more than high-level chicanery, a modest bank-stock scandal laced with political intrigue and corruption. In time, Sharpstown took a monstrous toll in political careers and substantially altered the course of Texas history.

The scandal's namesake and villain was Houston financier Frank Sharp, who was granted immunity from prosecution in exchange for his testimony. That was like freeing a shark to catch a minnow. Only one person ever went to jail, former insurance commissioner John Osorio, and he probably was the most honorable one of the whole bunch.

Texans play politics and poker for keeps. An East Texas lawmaker staged his own shooting for publicity and a Texas Supreme Court judge fled the country after a perjury conviction. They caught that judicial rascal in the Caribbean, hauled him back to Texas in a billionaire's borrowed airplane, and tossed him in jail.

And poker? Just a few years ago, a Saturday night session in an Odessa apartment ended in a blazing gun battle. Police found cards and shell casings scattered on the floor, but few other clues. Not a single player survived.

Could any place but Texas glorify a bordello? Better still, *would* any place but Texas glorify a bordello, especially one called the Chicken Ranch? Well, we did. Larry L. King christened it *The Best Little Whorehouse in Texas* and took it to Broadway and then to Hollywood and made millions—which raises another question. Can you visualize a Broadway musical called *The Best Little Whorehouse in Rhode Island*?

New Mexico? Oregon? Nebraska?

Nope.

Part 2

*Dallas, Texas (AP) — Hardly had the echoes of gunfire
faded in Dealey Plaza when the storm began.*

*A city of hate, they cried, in a state too big, too rich,
too proud, too violent, and surely peopled by lunatics, ex-
tremists, bigots, rednecks, and coarse oil millionaires.*

*"There's something rotten in the state of Texas," said the
periodical* Nation. *"It is, of course, entirely true that President Kennedy could have been assassinated anywhere: but
he wasn't. The terror was not loosed upon us all from Tul-
sa or Albuquerque or Shreveport: it happened in Dallas."*

Lee Harvey Oswald wasn't a Texan, but they tried to make
him one. Writing once about the Kennedy slaying, I wondered why the country wanted to hold Dallas responsible. No
one blamed Memphis for the murder of Martin Luther King
or Los Angeles for the slaying of Robert F. Kennedy. But
you get the picture. For some reason, Texas was different.
Given the mood of the times, it wasn't surprising that someone wanted to kill Oswald, but it was embarrassing that Jack
Ruby did so in the basement of the Dallas police headquarters.

In 1981, a Dallas misfit named John Hinckley wounded
President Reagan and three others in an assassination attempt
in Washington. I flew immediately to Lubbock in West Texas
to track Hinckley's activities during his interlude as a student
at Texas Tech. For seven years, he popped in and out of town,
sporadically attending classes at the university. But he left
a meager legacy, mostly as a forgettable face in a campus
crowd of thousands, and I so reported. "He ate lots of hamburgers, watched lots of television, and read lots of Hitler."

Imagine my surprise a day or so later when *Newsweek* magazine disclosed this: "Hinckley's slide into darkness seemed to
pick up speed once he entered Texas Tech . . . in the fall of
1973. Academically, Texas Tech's reputation is modest, but
its 23,000 students take pride in their parties." I totally missed
the slide into darkness, and I was shocked that I had overlooked the relevance of the students' attitude about parties.

The *Wall Street Journal* didn't tell us much about Hinckley,
but revealed that Tech was "a prosaic state-run university on

the dusty flatlands of the Texas Panhandle." Until that moment, I was unaware Lubbock was no longer on what Texans call the South Plains but was suddenly up there in the Panhandle, probably masquerading as Amarillo. So you can guess my chagrin when I next realized how badly I had been scooped by the *Washington Post*, which reported: "A penchant for guns hardly strikes anyone as ominous in free-wheeling Lubbock, where some university students carry guns to class and the pistol-packing frontier Texas tradition runs deep and long."

Need we wonder why non-Texans look at us so strangely? I spotted no heavy artillery, but maybe I was just lucky to get off the campus alive.

Although I never knew Lee Harvey Oswald, I was one of seven journalists who served as pallbearers at his funeral in Fort Worth. Later, I came to know and admire his widow Marina and to know and tolerate his mother Marguerite. Marina told me once she agreed with a psychologist who theorized that her sexual rejection of Oswald was the final straw that drove him to the sixth floor of the Texas School Book Depository. Years later, after she changed her mind, Marina told me she didn't recall such a statement. But she didn't deny making it.

Marguerite, on the other hand, was a total paradox, who was fond of calling Texas reporters to wail about real or imagined journalistic transgressions. She routinely ended her tirades by slamming down the phone after a burst of angry profanities. But I admired her moxie and was truly saddened by her death. I always marveled that she could proclaim her son innocent of the Kennedy killing, yet label herself a "mother of history" because of the tragedy in Dallas.

Marguerite was not a native Texan, but she was peculiar enough to pass for one.

Lee Harvey Oswald was the best-known Texas sniper, but no less terrifying was a burly ex-Marine named Charles Whitman. On August 1, 1966, Whitman murdered his wife and his mother, dragged an arsenal atop the University of Texas tower in Austin, and opened fire on the serene campus below.

The ninety-minute siege spread to nearby city streets and the toll reached fifteen dead and thirty-one injured before police and a bookstore employee stormed Whitman's perch. They killed him with pistol and shotgun blasts.

Part 3

Texas crime has given new meaning to the word "Candy" — as in Candy Mossler, Candy Montgomery, Candy Barr, and the Candy Man.

Investigators maintained Ms. Mossler killed her millionaire husband with the aid of her nephew, who happened also to be her lover. Authorities also contended that Candy Montgomery, with at least a hint of malice, hacked up her boyfriend's wife with an ax. Juries acquitted them both.

Candy Barr was a baby-faced stripper who had the misfortune to get caught with a trace of marijuana in her possession. She was assessed fifteen years in prison and actually served three of them.

Houston's Candy Man, to collect an insurance policy, murdered his young son with poisoned Halloween candy and was eventually executed. Texas justice may be uneven and often shameful, but it's not *all bad*.

The late Thomas Thompson, a splendid storyteller from Fort Worth, immortalized John and Joan Hill in the Houston-based bestseller *Blood and Money*. Hill was a wealthy plastic surgeon who allegedly killed his socialite wife by injecting poison in her pastries. He, in turn, was killed by a hired gunman. The hit man purportedly was bankrolled by Joan's vengeful father, Ashe Robinson. Neither Hill nor Robinson was ever convicted.

Ditto Cullen Davis of Fort Worth. I would like to think author Gary Cartwright and I shed a little light on the Davis murder case in his book *Blood Will Tell* and mine, *Texas vs. Davis*. We always thought Cullen was the "man in black," but Racehorse Haynes kept convincing juries otherwise.

In fact, Haynes got so good at his job that prosecutors considered him a bigger menace to society than some of the folks he defended. Haynes could occasionally be outlandish but was always stylish, and he remains the most gifted and relentlessly dedicated criminal attorney I've ever met. I asked him once who he would hire if he was in trouble. Haynes said he would hire himself—if he could get himself interested in the case and afford the fee.

Not everyone was as enthusiastic over Haynes' talents. While researching my book on the Davis case, I was summoned through a third party one day to meet covertly with Cullen's brother Bill. The younger Davis urged me to use my influence to persuade Cullen's former mistress, Karen Master, to move out of the mansion. He was convinced Cullen would eventually kill her, most likely because she did not sign a prenuptial agreement before they married. He also handed me a copy of a television film in which Racehorse Haynes outlined for Dan Rather the extremes he might go to in order to win a case. Bill Davis insisted the interview demonstrated that Haynes was every bit as dangerous as Cullen and should be exposed before he corrupted the nation's young legal minds. Bill also informed me that our conversation was "off the record."

Although I considered this a great vignette, I honored his demand and wrote nothing in my book about the meeting. Years later, Bill and I crossed paths at a party, and he was sharply critical that *Texas* vs. *Davis* contained nothing about our conversation.

"You told me it was off the record," I reminded him.

"You stupid son of a bitch," he laughed. "When did you writers start getting ethical?"

One final observation before leaving the Davis affair, the case in which I was most intimately involved: while the Davis women genuinely loathed one another, I found each to be appealing in a different way and I rather liked them all.

Sandra and Karen, wives No. 1 and 3, were real beauties. Both were bright and interesting, and I was constantly amazed that Sandra remained crazy over Cullen long after their divorce. Karen's charm sometimes suffered from a shortage of sincerity, but she was the greatest witness ever to enter a Texas courtroom and take the stand for her man. Tammy Wynette would have wept with joy.

At Cullen's Amarillo victory party, the one with the judge,

jurors, and courtroom bailiffs in attendance, Karen cornered me about midnight and asked if I believed her testimony.

"Of course not," I said, a little tipsy.

"Do you think I would continue to live with a man who I thought killed a 12-year-old girl?"

Grinning a mite foolishly, I told her, "Karen, I don't think you have a choice."

She stalked off in a snit, but we continued to be good friends until she got religious or read my book, whichever came first.

The Davis women never fared too well in print, which was a bum rap of sorts. Priscilla, wife No. 2, danced to the beat of a different drummer, but she was never short on spunk or long on pretension and above all she was a survivor. In probably his least gracious moment, Racehorse attacked her unmercifully after the Amarillo verdict, somehow forgetting that she'd been seriously wounded and her daughter and her boyfriend murdered by a gunman the State of Texas maintained was his very own client.

She should have slugged him. Hell, *I* should have slugged him.

After divorcing Cullen and moving to Dallas, Priscilla was asked if she might someday remarry. She thought not. "I'm kinda like the Statue of Liberty," she shrugged. "Nobody wants to pay the upkeep but everybody wants to say they've been there."

Finally, there was Cullen's niece Kay, a dynamite blonde who preferred animals to people and reminded me of Sue Ellen Ewing—except sexier, meaner, tougher, and more cunning. I liked her immensely.

I told Kay one night I'd feel less threatened if Cullen wanted to kill me than if she wanted to kill me. She just laughed and flashed me a look that suggested I might be a tad smarter than she first suspected.

Part 4

Fort Worth (AP) — It was a gaudy mix of burglars, bootleggers, and billionaires, rogues and royalty, whores and hit men. Rednecks and roughnecks and college kids on the prowl.

It was cold beer and hot dice and warm summer nights dancing under the stars at Lake Worth.

It was murder and mayhem, cops and robbers, rhythm and blues and the big band sounds of Billy May and Paul Whiteman.

It was the Rocket, the Skyliner, the Black Cat, the Show-boat, the Barrel, the Casino, the 3939, the Four Deuces, the Coconut Grove, the Bad Liquor, Massey's, and the lure of a young baby-faced stripper named Candy Barr.

It was the Jacksboro Highway, or Texas 199, a neon ribbon of revelry called Thunder Road that flowed north-west out of Fort Worth toward Azle, Jacksboro, Wichita Falls, and Amarillo.

In its heyday, a ten-mile stretch of that highway was a sizzling symbol of the state's rough-and-tumble heritage and a playground for the brave, bold, adventuresome, and foolhardy.

The lights flickered and dimmed years ago. And now the party's about over.

Farewell, Thunder.

Ah yes, Thunder Road, Fort Worth's own killing fields. No one ever confused it with the French Quarter or the Vegas Strip, but for a generation or two of rowdy Texans, it was a lot of both — and more. Some of our most dedicated thugs lived and died or disappeared on Thunder Road. But by the late eighties, the Jacksboro Highway of yesteryear had become a toothless lion and a bit of an eyesore and was about to be plowed under for a new eight-lane freeway.

Carolyn Miller grew up along the highway and defends it to this day: "They weren't all killers. They just loved to fight."

At roughly 2:30 one morning, a Jacksboro Highway club owner who demands anonymity left the Scoreboard Lounge after attending a wedding party for a friend. In the parking lot, two punks stuck a knife at his throat, took his money and his ring, roughed him up, and left him lying on the ground.

"We ought to kill you," said one.

"You damn sure should," he gasped.

The assailants laughed and left.

Later, after paying $250 to a stoolie, the club owner tracked down one of the muggers outside a beer joint. Luring him into his darkened car, he extracted an eyeball and a substantial number of teeth and shot off both of the guy's kneecaps. Then he dumped him in front of a hospital and drove away. Noticeably impressed by the Jacksboro justice, the second mugger fled to Canada and has not been heard from since.

Fort Worth hoods and street characters, some more lovable than others, were aptly named. There was Jerry the Burglar, whose sweaters reportedly carried the monogram "JTB." And there was Winegourd Willie, a bookie with a face right out of Dick Tracy but a heart of 24-carat gold. Winegourd died of old age, but a gangster nicknamed "Chock" did not. An underworld crony wired his car to a remote control bomb and just before Chock turned left, he was history.

Like Winegourd Willie and Chock, Texans go for nicknames. Dallas alone had its Dapper Bandit, the Friendly Rapist, and a cat burglar called the King of Diamonds. And then there was Animal McFadden, who gave the word "animal" a bad name. He raped, killed, and kidnapped before an army of cops caught and caged him in East Texas.

While many of our scalawags and scuzzies got away with assorted murder and mayhem, Lenell Geter and Kenneth Miller were two Texans who did not. Unfortunately, neither was guilty.

Geter, a black engineer, was convicted of robbery in Dallas and jailed before the news media took up his cause. Despite grumblings in the Dallas DA's office, Geter won his freedom and the case made a dandy movie.

The saga of Texas fugitive Kenneth Miller was the most unusual story I ever wrote for The Associated Press. It was a classic case of mistaken identity and it proved once again that truth is decidedly stranger than fiction.

The Miller saga was fascinating because of its bizarre twists and it was inspirational because of its women. Each was courageous in her own special way. Against terrific odds, Janelle Kirby, Jenny Dennis, and Deborah Hankins refused to let William Ted Wilhoit ruin their lives and they emerged as a sisterhood of survival. Lee Mulholland risked arrest and her reputation to help Kenneth Miller escape, and Dianna Oppermann put her very life on the line to join Miller in flight.

It's Hollywood even down to its mystifying conclusion. And remember the name Wilhoit. He could rape and rob at will, then complain bitterly when investigators swore in his presence. We will hear from him again, and not just in the movies.

Part 5

Lotus Land's Big Cigars discovered years ago that Texas crimes often played well on the Hollywood screen. Two that come to mind were *The Sugarland Express* and *The Town That Dreaded Sundown*, but one of the best ever was 1988's *The Thin Blue Line*, an innovative documentary directed by Errol Morris. The film makes an unusual but still persuasive argument that the wrong man was convicted and condemned to die for the 1976 slaying of a Dallas police officer.

Rare indeed is a literary season that escapes without a Texas crime story. Among the best were *Evidence of Love*, the Candy Montgomery drama co-authored by Jim Atkinson and John Bloom, and Gary Cartwright's *Dirty Dealing*, the saga of the star-crossed Chagra family of El Paso and the first assassination ever of a federal judge. In *The Santa Claus Bank Robbery*, A. C. Greene vividly recounted a Christmas Eve misadventure in the small town of Cisco. Steve Salerno wrote about the Vickie Daniel murder case in *Deadly Blessing*, and Carlton Stowers' award-winning *Careless Whispers* provided a graphic account of the Lake Waco rape-murders. Three books were written about the Cullen Davis case, and a fourth is in the works.

The slaying of Houston lawyer James Campbell and his wife provided more than enough material for two books, *Daddy's Girl* by Clifford Irving and *Cold Kill* by Jack Olsen. The case went unsolved for nearly three years until Clyde Wilson, the Eye of Texas, sent a sexy young operative named Kim Paris to seduce a confession out of the killer, David West. West claimed he killed at the request of his onetime girlfriend,

Cynthia Campbell Ray. She was the plump, psychotic daughter of the slain couple who would contend she was terrorized by her father's incestuous advances. I'm not making this up. Such things really do happen in Texas.

Texans aren't necessarily obsessed with crime, but a case could be made for sex and football. And all three figured in the mysterious death of Billy Mack Fleming, a small-town high school football coach who fell for the school secretary. So did the assistant principal, who was accused of killing Billy Mack. A jury acquitted him.

And speaking of football icons, what about the Dallas Cowboys? They may be America's Team, but back home, some of our star-spangled heroes strayed out of bounds. Drugs and morals charges disgraced more than one player, and a former lineman even robbed his own mother. Still, the Cowboys produced more all-pros than all-prison.

If Texas had a Hall of Shame for vermin and villains, it would include:

—The leader of a Fort Worth motorcycle gang who ordered a baby killed by injecting battery acid into its veins. He was enraged at the child's father for supplying him with bad dope.

—The nurse in Kerrville who was accused of murdering nearly a dozen infants in her care by injecting them with a muscle relaxer to create the appearance of Sudden Infant Death Syndrome. She was convicted in one such case.

—The angry immigrant who turned a north Dallas club called Ianni's into a bloodbath after a young woman spurned his invitation to dance.

—The husband who concealed a bomb in his wife's luggage before she and her child boarded an American Airlines flight from Austin to Dallas. His insurance scam was exposed and the plane spared when the bomb misfired.

—A University of Texas student named James Cross, who raped and strangled two coeds, hid their bodies in his closet, and entertained his girlfriend that evening in the same apartment. Assessed a life sentence in 1965, he won a new trial twenty years later. A jury convicted him again.

And, if there was a roll call for bizarre Texas crime, it surely would include:

— The Fort Worth housewife who grew weary of her husband's kinky sex habits and shot him nine times in what Racehorse Haynes claimed was self-defense. She never went to jail.

— The so-called Friendship Murders in Odessa. A businessman used hypnosis and chloroform to kill one acquaintance and purportedly poisoned two others with cyanide. A jury gave him life in prison after a prosecutor claimed he controlled his friends through "shared paranoia" and enjoyed watching them die.

— The Legion of Doom, an up-scale group of student vigilantes who used dead cats, car bombs, and other forms of intimidation to shape up the riffraff at Fort Worth's Paschal High. Their misguided crusade got them in a heap of trouble, but they all escaped jail.

Let's give the trophy for Most Bizarre to the case in which a man tape-recorded his own murder. It happened in 1982 in the Rio Grande Valley town of La Feria.

A man named Billy Staton concealed a mini-recorder under his shirt before visiting his young daughter at the home of his former wife and her new husband. Staton, 26, wanted proof of their animosity toward his visitation rights. Instead, the recorder picked up the sounds of him being bludgeoned to death by the couple and an accomplice. The trio then killed Staton's 26-year-old fiancée, who was waiting outside in his car. Police found the recorder three weeks later when they pulled Staton's body from a drainage ditch.

Based largely on the recording, which prosecutors described as "23 minutes of murder," Paul and Sherry Wolf, both 21, and their companion were convicted and sentenced to life in prison.

Part 6

Not only is there a remarkable diversity of Texas crime — it frequently occurs with a kicker.

When a member of the Dealey newspaper family was kidnapped in Dallas, police caught the villains, Henry Wade prosecuted them, and a jury convicted them. At Wade's urging, jurors then condemned them to five thousand years in prison.

I guess a life sentence just wasn't harsh enough.

A Fort Worth judge named Tom Cave presided honorably and often nobly over much of the Cullen Davis case, then caught a dose of the middle-age crazies. He fell in love with a prostitute, which was a bit dicey. Because she had been a defendant in his court, that ill-fated romance led to a sordid "sex for leniency" trial and eventually to his resignation from the bench.

A shame. I liked him. Still do, in fact.

I traveled to Galveston once to write about a troubled millionaire named Shearn Moody, Jr., later immortalized by *Texas Monthly* as "The Sleaziest Man in Texas." Though reported to be a shade on the gay side, Moody was not much worse than your average spoiled rich kid, at least until he started stealing money from the charitable foundation that bore his family name. Private eye Clyde Wilson caught him, but it took years to convict him. Even so, justice was not served at once. The judge dropped dead before Moody could be sentenced.

The megabuck Hunt brothers of Dallas beat a federal wiretapping charge years ago but were nailed in 1988 by a bunch of Peruvians who accused them of cornering the silver market. Cost 'em millions in civil damages, but it beat going to jail.

In the San Antonio barrios, they sang underground ballads about Fred Gomez Carrasco, a flashy thug who may have killed a score of his competitors in the brown heroin trade out of Mexico. He eluded police for months, but they nabbed him one Saturday night at the Tejas Motel. When they finally got him to the state slammer in Huntsville, he proceeded to organize the longest prison siege in U.S. history. An army of officers put an end to the bloody revolt, and a Texas Ranger's bullet put an end to Carrasco's life.

If there ever was a story with a kicker, it was one the AP called "The Texas Tragedy."

The saga of Donnie Wallace began in the 1950s when he was Lufkin High School's star running back and Sue Ann

Rucker was a pretty cheerleader. It was young love too serious for her parents' liking, so she dutifully broke it off and headed for Southern Methodist University. Donnie got a football scholarship at Tyler Junior College, where he met and married a homecoming queen.

Twenty years later, Donnie was a millionaire contractor in the posh bedroom community of Kingwood near Houston. With Sue Ann divorced and his own marriage on the rocks, they rekindled their old love affair. One evening, he left Sue Ann at his apartment and drove to his former home to pick up his two sons for dinner. Within minutes, he lay dead on the hallway floor. One son told the police he killed his father after Donnie threatened the other son with a knife.

Donnie's parents and sisters refused to believe that account. But there was no evidence to prove otherwise.

"Donnie and I had something very special," Sue Ann told me. "He felt like we were put on this earth for each other, that it was only a matter of time before we got together. We *were* special. I know it sounds silly but we really were. It's hard to sit here and think somebody's dead because he loved you."

Love and marriage were a dangerous mix in the life of Price Daniel, Jr., too. It was about his death that I once wrote:

> *LIBERTY, Texas (AP)—Until that rainy night in January, few had ever heard of Vickie Daniel.*
>
> *At 33, she was short and shapely, very blonde and very private, and most remembered her as the bright attractive waitress at the local Dairy Queen.*
>
> *At 39, Price Daniel, Jr., was also very private, but prominently so, a man of wealth and power whose name was synonymous with Texas politics.*
>
> *Vickie's anonymity and Price's life ended shortly before nightfall on January 19. She killed him with a single bullet fired from a bolt action .22 rifle.*

The son of a former Texas governor and U.S. senator, and himself a onetime Speaker of the Texas House of Representatives, young Daniel was destroying his legacy from within.

Testimony indicated he abused drugs, alcohol, and Vickie.

He was buried on a dreary, overcast day beneath three great oaks along "Governor's Road." Later, after the rich and influential mourners left, I stood at a fence and surveyed the dozens of expensive floral sprays surrounding the grave. As I turned to leave, I noticed a single piece of litter, a discarded soft drink cup. From the Dairy Queen.

During her subsequent murder trial, Vickie told me she wasn't much amused by the irony of the Dairy Queen cup I mentioned in my story. But we became friendly, if not friends, and I was not unhappy to see her avoid prison. There was never any question she killed young Price, but a judge found no malice or premeditation and acquitted her.

Politics and turmoil have always been kissing cousins in Texas. Remember Speaker Billy Clayton and Brilab? Attorney General Jim Mattox and the Mobil Oil mess? Both were acquitted, but nonetheless besmirched.

And what about the real biggie, Box 13?

The late Coke Stevenson accused Lyndon Johnson of stealing the 1948 U.S. Senate election with a South Texas ballot box stuffed with votes from the grave. LBJ rode his 87-vote victory into national political prominence and eventually the White House.

Back in Texas, we always called him "Landslide Lyndon."

At the heart of the Box 13 furor was George Parr, the "Duke of Duval." Parr ruled Duval County like a dictator while Republicans routinely convicted him and Democrats routinely pardoned him. Finally faced with prison during the 1970s, the aging political boss got in his car, drove to a remote corner of his ranch, and killed himself.

As Hollywood likes to remind us, bloodshed is no stranger to Texas ranches. A Texas model for police brutality stemmed not from metropolitan indifference but from rural confusion on the famous Four Sixes Ranch near the Panhandle town of Borger.

Several of Borger's finest chased a fugitive onto the ranch late one night and in the darkness proceeded to gun down not the fugitive but the ranch foreman. They even handcuffed the mortally wounded rancher and jerked him around a bit before he died. Racehorse Haynes got involved in that caper, which cost the City of Borger a bundle.

Like Texas justice, Racehorse is not all bad.

Extraordinary things really do occur on Texas ranches. We've got modern-day cattle rustlers and more than a little drug-dealing. Denton rancher Rex Cauble was linked to a ring of marijuana smugglers called the Cowboy Mafia and became one of the few Texas millionaires ever to wind up in prison.

But it was a rancher near Kerrville who took the prize for nefarious originality. Until caught and convicted in 1986, he and his son were kidnapping drifters and forcing them into slavery, which reduced their labor costs considerably in those tough economic times. It got nasty after a rebellious slave was tortured to death with a cattle prod and his body set afire.

Even Racehorse Haynes couldn't rescue the renegade ranchers from jail. But he tried.

Part 7

On a Saturday night in 1988, a crowd of twenty men gathered at a remote ranch in the South Texas brush country for an evening of drinking and illegal cockfighting. Their amusement included the abduction and gang rape of a 19-year-old housewife from the nearby community of San Diego. It could be argued that traces of Texas macho compelled the defendants to claim the victim, a mother of two, wanted to be kidnapped, assaulted, and abused on a carhood and elsewhere. Jurors didn't buy that. The first person prosecuted was convicted and assessed a twenty-year prison term.

Still, that nightmare will be with us for a while.

The most notorious sex crime in Texas history occurred near Houston in the early seventies. Elmer Wayne Henley, only 17 at the time of his arrest, was convicted of killing six youths in a mind-boggling string of twenty-six homosexual slayings. Henley told police he and a companion, David Owen Brooks, procured teenage boys for a man named Dean Corll to sodomize and kill. He confessed he raped, tortured, and shot some of the victims himself and helped Corll strangle others.

In the strangest of twists, police arrested Henley in August 1973 after he killed Corll in Corll's suburban Pasadena home. Then he led officers to a boat house and showed them where to dig. More bodies were found at Lake Sam Rayburn and on the beach at High Island. Henley and Brooks both were convicted but escaped Old Sparky, the electric chair in Huntsville. Their crimes took place after the U.S. Supreme Court struck down the original Texas death penalty statutes and before a new law could be written.

A pity. Any punishment less than death in Texas usually means parole in less than twenty years.

Police and prosecutors from five Texas cities met secretly in Lubbock in 1980 to discuss a series of West Texas rapes. "Incredible," they concluded. A single ski-mask rapist was attacking young single women along an 800-mile route that included Lubbock, Amarillo, Wichita Falls, Abilene, and Fort Worth.

What's more, he showered and groomed his victims to destroy the medical evidence of his perverse assaults. "It kind of raised the hair on the back of your neck as you listened to this," Bill Morgan of the Lubbock Police Department told me later. "I was skeptical as hell about a single rapist when I went in. But I wasn't when I came out."

The group agreed the rapist would soon be apprehended. He was maybe a little too smart, too brazen, too kinky, too driven. "We'll get him because he can't stop what he's doing," an Amarillo detective said.

But something was wrong with that theory. The vicious nighttime assaults ended as suddenly as they began. Still, the police case book labeled "The Traveling Rapist" remained open for years.

And the state's most mobile rapist apparently was never caught.

Even more mysterious was the 1975 case of Midland attorney Richard Prigmore. I spent a week in West Texas looking into his violent and unexplained death and left more puzzled than when I arrived.

A successful attorney, Prigmore, 40, lived a double life apart from friends, associates, wife, and family. Until he walked into a trap in nearby Odessa, Prigmore was unknown to FBI agents and certainly not a suspect in their half-million-dollar burglary investigation. Linked through a credit card to stolen jewelry and art treasures, Prigmore posted $20,000 bond soon after his arrest and disappeared into the night. The next day, a utility worker traveling a lonely country road near Shallowater found his mangled body in a ditch. He had been run over by a train.

He died as he lived: a total enigma.

Years later, I dropped by the FBI office in Midland and asked an agent I knew what he'd eventually learned about Prigmore. "Nothing," he said.

In the early eighties, I learned through a minor investigative coup that a doctor from Athens in East Texas had been a frequent source of drugs for a slew of high-profile Texans. His name was Marcus Welby Young—believe me, I'm *not* making any of this up—and his clientele included Willie Nelson, a couple of obscure Dallas Cowboys, and even Priscilla Davis, who was estranged from Cullen at the time.

Young, a celebrity groupie, had pleaded guilty to a drug offense and was sent off to the federal pen at Big Spring to join Billie Sol and a few other white-collar crooks and con men. I telephoned the prison on the chance that a remorseful Marcus Welby Young might talk with me.

"He's not here now," I was told.

"Where might he be?" I wondered.

"He's downtown."

"Downtown?"

"At his office."

"*His office?*"

"Yes. At the Chamber of Commerce."

"You're kiddin' me?"

"No. He's at the chamber working on a special project."

"And what is that?"

"A concert."

"A concert?"

"Yes. A Willie Nelson benefit concert."

Nowhere but Texas.

Part 8

Yes, nowhere but Texas.

They shook down the Indians for the island of Manhattan and they peddled swampland in Florida for real estate, but nobody can rival our own Billie Sol Estes.

The second or third time Billie Sol got out of jail, he blamed his troubles on compulsiveness and told me he was cleaning up his act for keeps. "I'm just one drink away from being a drunk and just one deal away from being back in prison," he said. "I'm a compulsive person. I'm a compulsive drinker and, if I smoked, I'd be a compulsive smoker. Anything I've done, it's been compulsive."

In the next breath, he outlined a gloriously improbable scheme for growing grapes in the West Texas desert to corner the wine market.

Stay tuned.

Billie Sol was the best of our wheeler-dealers, but not the only one. There were slant-hole drillers in the East Texas oil patch, charlatan bankers preying on the small towns of West Texas, and fast-buck condo promoters along the interstate in North Texas.

Then there was our own Clinton Manges to the south. Though he was never convicted of anything significant, they called Ol' Clinton a liar and a fraud and accused him of all manner of sinister deeds. He responded by describing one such detractor as "the most pious, sanctimonious, rat-faced little weasel I ever saw in my life."

Name-calling aside, he battled big oil, big banks, big law firms, and a grand jury system he claimed was corrupt, brutal, and vindictive. With the help of his buddies in Austin, the Desert Fox of Duval County won more than he lost.

Bless his heart.

Texans love to gamble, and it's never seemed to matter much that it might be illegal. Beneath our Bible-belt veneer we have patronized places like the Inn of the Golden West, where for years the seventh floor was a semiprivate haven for the oil rich around Odessa and their games of chance.

Until the state attorney general shut it down.

The Monte Carlo of casino-style gambling was once the coastal city of Galveston, and no one profited more than insurance and hotel tycoon W. L. Moody, Jr. That was odd because W. L. was a bit on the pious side. Whatever his view on local vice lords Sam and Rose Maceo, Moody did nothing to interfere with the cash flow into his five island hotels. "I'm not in the casino business," he sniffed, "and they are not in the hotel business."

Indeed, nowhere but Texas.

When a Fort Worth cop ran over a deer with his patrol car, fellow officers butchered and barbecued it for their annual picnic. A local tabloid named the *Press* learned the deer was a child's pet. Always alert to the exotic angle, the newspaper composed an immortal headline: "POLICE EAT KIDS' PET."

The Texas Rangers gave us an awesome legacy of violence and brutality, and the police in Dallas and Houston have struggled to live up to it.

In San Antonio, a cop even killed a cop. A cop shot a cop in Dallas, too, but not on purpose.

I would never suggest it's a one-way street out there. Teenagers in Midlothian executed a young narcotics agent who masqueraded as a student, and a vagrant in Dallas gunned down Patrolman John Chase under the most chilling of circumstances.

"Kill him, kill him," a bystander was heard to say as Chase futilely pleaded for his life.

Part 9

They called him the Devil's apostle, a heretic, a liar, an infidel, an atheist, and, in the words of the late H. L. Mencken, a "past master of invective."

And some of those were his friends.

"I confess to a sneaking respect for Satan, for he is preeminently a success in his chosen profession," William Cow-

per Brann, the Waco iconoclast, said more than a century ago. "He sat into the game with a cash capital of one snake. . . . Now he's got half the globe grabbed and an option on the other half."

Brann was cursed, threatened, horse-whipped, kidnapped, almost lynched, and finally shot in the back and killed by an irate Baptist.

—From an AP story on 19th-century Texas journalist William Brann.

Texans can't claim a franchise on killers for Christ, but we met our quota. One of the great fire-and-brimstone crusaders of all time, J. Frank Norris, shot a dissenter once — killed him dead, in fact. And was acquitted. Norris also burned down his Fort Worth church a couple of times and they never got him for that either.

My own favorite zealot was tent preacher David Terrell. Gone for a while but surely not forgotten, the beloved Brother Terrell showed up near Brownwood in the early seventies. At his heels was a poor but dedicated and generally harmless flock that settled in the woods and hills of the region. Before building a church at tiny Bangs, his followers gathered frequently beneath a huge canvas tent to watch Brother Terrell holler and heal and raise holy hell.

Curious, I drove out to Bangs one Saturday night with Jerry Flemmons of the *Fort Worth Star-Telegram*. It was a marvelous show. I wrote later how Brother Terrell healed a tent full of "female disorders" and collected everything from a gold tooth to a goldfish. Ordering all heads bowed and eyes closed for the farewell prayer, he slipped out the back way, loaded his bounty into a Mercedes, and sped off into the night.

Not long afterward, he returned to the pulpit to condemn journalists in general and Jerry and me in particular. He put a terrible curse on us both that night. I thought it was all kind of a hoot until my golf game went to hell.

The feds finally got Brother Terrell for income tax evasion, which left me wondering how they went about taxing that goldfish. Brother Terrell's out of jail now, and a bigger martyr than ever.

But that prosecutor in the case of the Reverend Walker Railey is right. It *was* a bad year for preachers. Not only for Jimmy Swaggart or Jim Bakker, but for our own shepherds in Texas as well. A Dallas minister was charged with a series of rapes, another lost his pulpit because of illicit romance, and Walker Railey remained deplumed and in disrepute. And they weren't the only ones.

Rapist William Ted Wilhoit, villain of the Kenneth Miller story, was in prison, his ministerial calling on hold. Even Cullen, a lay preacher of sorts, still embraced his religion but lost all his money.

Oh, Lord, tempt us not, forgive us our Texas transgressions and, for heaven's sake, deliver us from evil.